Soul Sisters

JEREMY P. TARCHER/PUTNAM
A MEMBER OF
PENGUIN PUTNAM INC.
NEW YORK

Soul Sisters

THE FIVE DIVINE QUALITIES OF A WOMAN'S SOUL

PYTHIA PEAY

Most Tarcher/Putnam books are available at special quantity discounts for bulk purchase for sales promotions, premiums, fund-raising, and educational needs. Special books or book excerpts also can be created to fit specific needs. For details, write Putnam Special Markets, 375 Hudson Street, New York, NY 10014.

JEREMY P. TARCHER/PUTNAM
a member of
Penguin Putnam Inc.
375 Hudson Street
New York, NY 10014
www.penguinputnam.com

Library of Congress Cataloging-in-Publication Data

Peay, Pythia.
Soul sisters : the five divine qualities of a woman's soul / Pythia Peay.
p.   cm.
ISBN 1-58542-162-6
1. Women—Religious life.   2. Femininity of God.   3. Women and religion.
4. Goddess religion.   I. Title.
BL625.7.P43   2002   2001057462
291.4'082—dc21

Printed in the United States of America
1   3   5   7   9   10   8   6   4   2

This book is printed on acid-free paper. ♾

BOOK DESIGN BY DEBORAH KERNER/DANCING BEARS DESIGN

To My Mother,
Maria Sheila League:
for life,
for imagination,
for books,
and for her magical Latin spirit.

Acknowledgments

THE INSPIRATION FOR THIS BOOK EMERGES DIRECTLY FROM THE MANY rich and varied friendships with women I have enjoyed over the years. Each in her own way is a treasure—large-hearted, interesting, loving, soulful, funny, devoted, creative, and brave. Their gifts of the spirit have given me heart for the journey. Because of them, I have rarely felt alone. Because of them, the challenges of life are easier to shoulder and less difficult to understand. Because of them, the spiritual path we have walked together has been a shared miracle of faith. And because of them, I have always, always been able to laugh—even, on many occasions, to still giggle like the girls we once were. My friends, in short, are all true soul sisters. For those who have had the courage and generosity to lend their life experiences to this book, my deepest thanks. And for those women whom I have had the occasion of meeting for the first time for the purpose of writing this book, I extend my great appreciation for trusting in me enough to share your stories with the world.

I would like to give a special thank you to Taj Glantz for always being there, always having faith, and for being a light and a guide along the inner pathways of the soul. Pir Vilayat Inayat Khan and the Sufi Order, as well, for initiating me into the timeless practice of meditation and for upholding the ideal of spiritual universality. To my circle of Sufi friends with whom I once shared precious weekly women's meditation classes: Murshida Vera, Kristen, Zeb-un-nissa, Amida, Tatiana, Reza, Julie, and Chalice, among others—thank you all for unbreakable bonds of the spirit that endure over time. To Zuleikha, for sharing the wine of spiritual friendship over the years. And to Nona Boren, my Jungian analyst and wise woman guide, thank you for your patience and for helping to midwife my creative voice.

A warm and loving thanks to Lis Akhtarzandi for her awesome capacity for wise friendship, the rare gift of unconditional acceptance—and laughter! Susan Roberts, for the companionable pleasures of endless hours of conversation on all manner of topics, and for her deep heart. To Sylvia Seret, for her enduring support, and for sharing with me the day-in/day-out tasks of motherhood and spicing those tasks with the magic of dreamwork and astrology. To Elise Wiarda, for her sweet nature, healing energy, and spiritual devotion. To Harriett Crosby, for infecting me with the contagious passion of her selfless service to the planet. And likewise to Dodie Brady, Corinne McLaughlin, and Diane Perlman for their commitment to making the world a better place. To Tatiana Von Diergardt, for our sisterhood in human rights work. To Nancy Kadian, for sharing the Sufi path and for years of tea and conversation. To Dana Gerhardt, for inspiring me anew about the mysteries of the moon, and for being my partner in the astrological journey of MoonCircles. To Janet Myerson, for her loyal character and friendship over the years, and to Janet, Karen, and Arlene for teaching me how to dance. I would like to thank dear friends and warm-hearted Ann Cochran and Shannon Savage for being gal pals in the risky adventure of mothering teen boys, and for taking phone calls in the middle of the night. To my first circle of girlhood friends: Virginia, Cheryl, Debbie, Janet, and Cindy. To Angela Hanson, for being an angel. To some old and dear friends: Ayesha Rognlie and Sharda Brody, for teaching me wisdom when I was young; to my college roommate Cindy Butler, for a connection undimmed by time and distance; and to Santa, for her magical imagination. To Kristen Flance, for being a support through many phases of my life, and for her sensitive spirit. To Martha Tompkins, for her grit and bravado. To my fellow writers, Barbara Graham, for her dauntless nature and wry humor; and Debra Goldberg, for her expert dream interpretation and intellectual companionship. I am indebted to Anne Simpkinson and Chuck Simpkinson of *Common Boundary* magazine for giving me dream assignments in the field of my heart's desire and for allowing me to bear witness to the dynamic and unfolding field of alternative spirituality and psychology. Thank you to Anne, too, for her friendship and for nurturing me as a writer, and to two other great women friends and editors, Joan Connell of *Religion News Service* and Stephanie von Hirschberg at *New Woman*. I would like to acknowledge the support and expertise of Susan Rodberg, my "computer healer," who patiently put up with my panicked phone calls for help, and also Torii Lilly, friend to me and my two dogs. Thanks also to astrologer-activist

Caroline Casey and Buddhist teacher Tara Brach, for raising the energy in my hometown and for being soul-sister neighbors. And thank you to my neighborhood companions: Pauline, Anna, Nancy, and Lolly.

This book, of course, would never have come into existence without two very important men in my life: my publisher, Joel Fotinos, and my editor, Mitch Horowitz. Thank you both from my heart for your extraordinary vision in the field of publishing, for your enthusiasm, and for making the work of writing books such a stimulating adventure—with surprises around every corner! A big thank you to my soul sister and agent, Nancy Ellis, for standing by me through the good and the bad weather of a writer's life—you three are a great team!

Last, I would like to thank my family: to Terry Peay, for being a good friend, a great dad, and the best ex-husband a woman could ask for; and to his wife, Anne Peay, for being a friend to me and an encouraging stepmother to my sons—thank you both for the family we share. To my sister, Colleen Carroll, who walks a parallel path as an artist, mother, and meditator, and who knows me well, and to Jules and Lily. To my writer friend and the brother who makes me laugh, John Carroll, and his family, and to Steven Carroll, a brother who has always been there for his sister. To my sons' sweet paternal grandmother, Gladys, and to my mother and her sister, my aunt Fiona, for being living examples of soul sisters and for being two gutsy women brave enough to always think and act outside the box of convention. And finally, thank you to my three gorgeous, gifted sons who are the reason itself for living and writing, and who inspire me always and forever with the incredible miracle of their unbelievable beings: Kabir, Amir, and Abe. May the sacred feminine within each of you be deepened through this book.

Contents

Someday there will be girls and women whose name will no longer mean the mere opposite of the male, but something in itself, something that makes one think not of any complement and limit, but only of life and reality: the female human being.

RAINER MARIE RILKE,
Letters to a Young Poet

Introduction

LIKE THE CARVED FACETS OF A JEWEL, THE FACES OF FEMININITY ARE many, varied, and beautiful. Indeed, the gift of the women's liberation movement has been to show that the talents of women do not just shine in marriage and child-raising, but in all spheres of life, from politics and sports to art, science, religion, journalism, medicine, and business. Thus, in the last decades of the twentieth century, women's wide-ranging creativity has flourished as never before. This historic watershed has opened up endless vistas of possibility for women, allowing them an unprecedented opportunity to experience the precious freedoms so long enjoyed by men.

> *From the time we are born, there is a wildish urge within us that desires our souls lead our lives, for the ego can only understand just so much.*
>
> CLARISSA PINKOLA ESTÉS,
> *Women Who Run
> with the Wolves*

At the same time that they have made such remarkable strides, however, women have found themselves subjected to all the stresses, fears, doubts, and losses that have marked the human condition since the beginning of time. As all the world's spiritual traditions have taught, success in the outer world is rarely lasting, but is as fleeting as a cloud racing across the sky. Material wealth gained through years of hard work can be lost in a moment; the professional achievement of a lifetime can turn to failure in a day. Just like one close friend I know who worked for years to put together a very substantial business deal, only to watch it fall apart over the course of several hours, women, like men, are often forced by circumstances to confront the deeper side of life: What is the meaning of life? What really matters? Who am I? Why was I born? What happens after death?

It is at just such a critical juncture that religion offers itself as a natural source of solace and inspiration. Like a spiritual fountain, it showers the sparkling droplets of faith on souls parched by the hard dryness of everyday life. But for those women who have felt oppressed by the patriarchal perspectives of mainstream religious traditions that, over the centuries, have restricted them from positions of power or authority, religion can be an uncomfortable place to turn.

This leaves many women in a very cold and unprotected place—especially in the overcrowded, technological, and harshly competitive marketplace of today's world. For myself, the idea of existing without the support of a spiritual worldview would be like trying to live without the sustenance of food or the protection of clothes. I simply could not imagine it. At the same time, the question of belonging to an organized religion has never been an easy one to resolve. Like many other women I know, I have wrestled painfully with the issue of how to fashion some kind of external religious structure. Both as a girl growing up in the Catholic Church and as a student in a spiritual organization headed by a man, I have had to reflect deeply on how religious traditions have diminished my role as a woman. For many women, as for myself, the problem is sometimes resolved by an imaginative sorting through of what is worth keeping in a religious tradition and what may be discarded.

But this is where the real story of women's spirituality in the twenty-first century begins. All across the country, all around the world, women are picking up the discarded threads of patriarchal religions and reweaving new myths, rituals, and traditions for themselves. Like a beautiful quilt made from discarded fabric, the new religious form that they are shaping is at once old and new. Though many of the prayers, practices, images, texts, and meditations are ancient in derivation, the reassembled picture is radically different. For one thing, the focus has shifted away from an exclusively male god to a cosmos that includes a goddess, too. God can now be addressed as "She" as well as "He." Imagine, if you will, the ceil-

In Sumer, She was Inanna; in Egypt, She was Isis; in Canaan, Her name was Asherah. In Syria, she was known as Astarte; in Greece, Demeter; and in Cyprus, Aphrodite. Whatever Her supplicants called Her, they all recognized Her as the Creatrix of life, nurturer of young, protector of children, and the source of milk, herds, vegetables, and grain.

LEONARD SHLAIN, *The Alphabet
Versus the Goddess:
The Conflict Between
Word and Image*

The Eternal Feminine draws us on.

GOETHE, *Faust,*
"Heaven," LAST LINE

ing of the Sistine Chapel with the central image repainted along these lines: a reclining, powerful, wise woman with long, white hair extends her arm across the heavens, stretching forth the forefinger of her hand to touch the extended hand of a young, beautiful maiden—sparking, through their touch, Creation into being. Now you have an inkling of the transformation occurring at the heart of modern-day religion and spirituality.

Indeed, there is a new iconography in the making that celebrates the feminine image of God as She once flourished in temples and caves throughout the pre-atriarchal ancient world. This iconography is based on the image of the goddess figure in all her radiant forms—the slender-waisted Minoan Snake Goddess, the wide-hipped, heavy-armed Maltese Mother Goddess, the Greek maiden Kore, the breast-studded Mother of Animals at Ephesus, and so on. And though there is disagreement among archaeologists and scholars regarding the historic role played by the Great Goddess in ancient times, what matters most is that the image of the divine feminine has emerged as a myth for our time. The re-emergence of statues, texts, and traditions of the Great Goddess from around the world satisfies a deep soul need in many contemporary women. Just to imagine God as a woman is powerful medicine, curing an ancient wound. As the tall, beautiful, black woman in Ntozake Shange's now-famous play *For Colored Girls Who Have Considered Suicide When the Rainbow Is Enuf* proclaimed: "I found God in myself and I loved her fiercely."

If religion is about what is of intrinsic, lasting worth—what is divine, sacred, and holy—then the return of the goddess is really about the return of respect for woman-in-herself, rather than as an appendage or helpmate to man. Woman, according to this worldview, is no longer peripheral; she is central to civilization. Says feminist theologian Carol Christ, "Female power is strong and creative . . . the divine principle, the saving and sustaining power, is in herself."[1] And if religion is about morals and ethics, then the return of the goddess is also about the return of a different set of values that has as much significance for men as for women. Instead of placing supreme value on the independent and self-sufficient individual, the divine feminine encourages interdependence, interconnectedness, and mutuality. Instead

Inanna, Astarte, Ishtar and Isis,
We reach down the years of women
To Your love and wisdom.

COSI FABIAN, "PRAYER OF DEDICATION," FROM *Her Words: An Anthology of Poetry About the Great Goddess,* EDITED BY BURLEIGH MUTIN

The earth is at the same time
Mother,
She is mother of all that is natural,
Mother of all that is human.

HILDEGARD VON BINGEN, TRANS. BY GABRIELE UHLEIN, FROM *Her Words: An Anthology of Poetry About the Great Goddess,* EDITED BY BURLEIGH MUTIN of dominating and controlling nature, the divine feminine represents reverence for nature's web of life. Instead of dismissing feelings and emotions, the divine feminine interprets them as a source of wisdom. Instead of ignoring the physical needs of the body, the divine feminine regards the body as sacred. This different set of values has been summed up by psychologist Carol Gilligan as an "ethic of care." As Carol Christ asks, "What if we asked ourselves every night: How does what I did today nurture life?"[2] It is not that the feminine way of spirituality is better than the masculine way, but that masculine values absent the balancing effect of the feminine, and vice versa, becomes extreme and therefore negative and destructive. Fairy tale after fairy tale, for example, tells of how kingdoms suffer when the queen dies and the king is left to rule alone.

Some may wonder what meaning this spiritual shift in focus has for today's woman—a woman who may not even know or care about the goddess movement. For one thing, it may help her to place the struggles of her life within a larger, more meaningful framework. To know that, after centuries of being silenced, she is giving voice to a new woman's story, at once old and new, may help her to make sense of those times when she is lost or confused. The revolution brought about by both political and spiritual feminism, for example, has meant that women today have to think twice about everything. With every step they take, whether embarking on a career, exploring a faith tradition, or starting a family, they must be doubly conscious. While daring to undertake new adventures once denied them, they must put their feminine instincts aside and act like a man in order to get ahead and ensure equal treatment—wondering, all along, whether they have sacrificed a part of themselves in order to fulfill a goal that in the end may have no lasting meaning. Drawn to the domestic sphere of family, they must constantly beware of being eclipsed by the needs of family and husband; or, on the other hand, they must watch that the demands of their own work does not eclipse family altogether. Should they decide to explore a religious tradition dear to their hearts and rich with meaning, they must struggle to find their way along a path dominated by masculine imagery and power structures. Whatever it is that women undertake, they are on a teeter-totter, constantly balancing competing instincts and needs. This extends even to the way a woman dresses—is she too feminine and flirty-looking, or should she dress to make a more serious and authoritative impression, like a man?

For Wisdom is more moving than any motion: she passeth and goeth through all things by reason of her pureness.

WISDOM OF SOLOMON 21–7, FROM
The Divine Feminine: Exploring the Feminine Face of God Around the World, ANDREW HARVEY AND ANNE BARING

Male and female created he them.

GENESIS 1:27

Often, in fact, I have wished to step outside the boundaries of my gender. I have wished to write and think and act like a human being, not like a woman. The desire to be wholly free and liberated this way, I think, is at the very heart of feminism. Yet at the same time, the kind of liberation I and many other women are seeking may not be possible until the social and historical context of our existence has been fully confronted and explored. The life I live as a woman is inevitably influenced by the centuries of oppression women have endured in the past. Though my life today is but a pale shadow of that oppression, the ridicule and marginalization suffered by my foremothers continues to reverberate in subtle and not-so-subtle ways, while the conditions of many women in this country and in third-world countries remind me that violence against women continues to be a real and present danger. Too, I cannot ignore that I have been born into the body of a woman; my physical reality, such as pregnancy and childbearing—even the way people see me in the street—has powerfully shaped much of my life experience.

Still, women's long march out of oppression is well on its way. Though the ideals we are striving to attain and the reality we still must live often clash dramatically, exciting new stories are emerging. These stories of women in formation will one day form a treasury of plotlines and resources for future generations of women to build upon. As the feminist historian Gerda Lerner has written, human beings have always used history as a way to find their direction forward into the future, choosing whether to depart from the past or repeat it. Yet while men have had the benefit of recorded history to build upon, she points out, women have not. "Lacking knowledge of their own history," she writes, "women thinkers did not have the self-knowledge from which to project a desired future." Without knowledge of their past, she continues, women could not test their ideas against those of their equals. Therefore, women were forced to argue with the "great man" in their heads instead of being encouraged by their foremothers.[3]

This book follows in the evolving lineage of women's storytelling. It takes its place alongside the growing number of books about the goddess and feminine spirituality, about women's inner spiritual lives, about women in the arts and the workplace, and about women's friendships. It is filled with stories combining all

The spirit of the valley never dies.
It is called the subtle and profound female.
The gate of the subtle and profound female
Is the root of Heaven and Earth.
It is continuous, and seems to be always existing.
Use it and you will never wear it out.

LAO-TZU,
The Way of Lao-tzu

We cannot learn how women develop spiritually from men. The responsibility for describing this process is ours, as women.

SHERRY RUTH ANDERSON
AND PATRICIA HOPKINS,
The Feminine Face of God

these topics—mixing together stories of women from the past, stories from my own life, and stories of my friends and their friends. Thus, it is not only a book about the bonds between women, but also a narrative about how, through the events of their everyday lives, women are recombining, reimagining, and revisioning all the assorted elements of their lives into a rich and complex new mythology. Ordinary and extraordinary, these accounts are a lexicon to which other women can turn for inspiration. No longer should women have to remain isolated from one another, silenced from the feminine collective wellspring of creativity and intelligence. Instead, they should have a heritage of "soul sisters" and soul-sister stories to turn to, past and present, for help in living their lives. "When we seize the chance to tell our story," writes Christine Downing, "we seem to know that its beauty and power comes from its being our story, a never-before-told story. We are released from the illusion that there is one right version of the story. . . . We take it for granted that there are many different patterns, each with its own pains, its own gifts."[4]

> *Had there been a man behind each brilliant woman, there would have been women of achievement in history equal to the numbers of men in achievement.*
>
> GERDA LERNER, *The Creation of Feminist Consciousness: From the Middle Ages to Eighteen-seventy*

> *In the old myths, weaving was women's speech, women's language, women's story.*
>
> CAROLYN G. HEILBRUN, *Hamlet's Mother and Other Women*

To show how women are adding new dimensions to old ways of thinking, I have chosen to organize this book according to the qualities of courage, faith, beauty, love, magic, friendship, and peace. According to Pir Vilayat Inayat Khan, a Sufi meditation teacher with whom I studied for many years, the divine qualities are themselves a kind of spiritual path. They are the medium through which the divine manifests in our lives; in them, we see the shaping influence of the hand of God molding and creating us. As Pir Vilayat writes, the obstacles and roadblocks we face are "the creative catalyst through which spiritual evolution occurs."[5] This is similar to the messages implicit within fairy tales and myths that show heroes and heroines engaging with life's challenges, emerging not only victorious, but also transformed in some way. In the difficult are the friendly forces, says Rilke, the "hands that work on us." Thus through the terrible problems we each must endure throughout life, something unforeseen transpires: Facing fear, for example, we become strong and courageous. Facing doubt and despair, we develop the faith of saints. Overwhelmed by the ugliness and horrors of the world, we discover beauty. Through the confusing maze of relationships, we become initiated into the mystery of love. In a world dominated by reason and logic, we learn to evoke magic. In a world of overwhelming alienation, we develop the quality of friendship. And in a world still suffering the wounds of war, we work toward peace.

While the chapters in this book draw upon the wisdom of male thinkers and teachers, they are primarily about the way women today have courage, exemplify faith, create beauty, show love, make magic, understand friendship, and uphold the ideal of peace. There are, of course, many other qualities, but those are other stories for other times. Indeed, in the same way the Persian story-teller Sheherezade spun fables that enraptured a vindictive and bitter king, transforming him into a kind and caring husband, women's "soul-sister" stories can play a role in changing a depressed and lonely society into a more peaceful and loving culture. They do this by showing how the depth and authenticity characterizing women's friendships are a form of creative sistering that help each woman weave soul into the fabric of her life. These modern-day connections are reflections of the ancient bond that once existed between priestesses as they tended the temple; between Mary and Martha, sisters of Lazarus, as they endured the passion of Christ; between the Native American wise woman and her friends and daughters; or Demeter, whose grief over the loss of her daughter, Persephone, was relieved by the raunchy humor of the old woman Baubo. For whether joining together to help a neighbor die, drawing around a close friend suffering from her lover's suicide with prayers, or simply hiking and talking about men, children, business, or politics, most girlfriends feel sustained by one another in a wordless, implicit understanding of what it means to be a woman.

Looking back over my life, I realize now how precious are those enduring bonds of authentic sisterhood that have been forged over the years. This familial kinship, however, extends not just to my girlfriends, but also to the invisible companionship provided by the "soul sisters" of those women saints and mystics who have illuminated the world's religious traditions—those women whom, over the years, I have looked to as examples, and prayed to for comfort. For what is a "soul sister" if not another woman who, whether today or a thousand years ago, has done her best to serve her fellow human beings in kindness and compassion, to solve those problems life hands her in as graceful a way as possible, and to love God as best she knows how?

How many women today find a script, a narrative, a story to live by?

CAROLYN G. HEILBRUN,
*Hamlet's Mother and
Other Women*

Mystical practice and discipline enabled women to proceed to another level of re-definition—in their visions, dreams and writings they asserted the female component of the Divine.

GERDA LERNER, *The Creation
of Feminist Consciousness:
From the Middle Ages
to Eighteen-seventy*

Like the intertwining snakes of the double helix on the ancient healing symbol of the caduceus, the synthesis of both the inner- and outer-life journeys forms the narrative thread of *Soul Sisters: The Five Divine Qualities of a Woman's Soul.* It contains a gathering of traditional perspectives from some of the world's religious traditions and shows ways in which these qualities can be used to enhance and strengthen the inner lives of women today. However, just as ancient jewels are excavated, polished, and recast in new settings, some of these practices have been reconfigured by me in a way that addresses the needs and problems of contemporary women. The new feminist mysticism is not only about transcendent spirituality—it centers instead on the small, daily rituals of cooking, housecleaning, nurturing friendships, caring for pets, planting flowers in springtime, shoveling snow in wintertime, having babies, burying loved ones, making money, watching bodies change over time, and discussing dreams, astrology, and relationships. This feminine mysticism links women together in a potent form of "earth magic" drawn from the wisdom of the world's faiths.

The heart of this project is best expressed in a vision I had nearly ten years ago while travelling through Sedona, Arizona, with several women friends. In it, I saw all the women goddesses, saints, and mystics that had existed throughout time encircling the earth—Greek goddesses, Christian mystics, Buddhist saints, and Sufi holy women all joining hands in a ringing, singing necklace of love and support for our fragile planet. The spirit of that vision, I hope, will be the inspirational source illuminating this book.

CHAPTER ONE

The Feminine Face of Courage

LIKE EVERYONE'S CHILDHOOD, MY YOUTH WAS FILLED WITH A THOUSAND stories of a thousand frights. My mind, as Calvin wrote, was "a permanent factory of fears." At night, I shivered in my bed, convinced that a ghost was haunting the bedroom of the hundred-year-old farmhouse in which I grew up. Like a movie screen that caught the projections of my worst fantasies, my bedroom window transformed at night into an entrance for robbers or scary spirits. Traumatized by school exercises preparing us for nuclear war, I became certain that "the bomb" would obliterate us all. Then there were the fears that, like a thick gauze, pervaded my family, brought on by the rages of an alcoholic father who in sudden anger would fly at me or my siblings.

> Queen Boadicea still towers above her reckless horses. . . . In her case the hand that once rocked the cradle now drives the chariot and shakes the spear. . . . Her conduct is no longer unnatural but triumphant. Her glory may be expected to endure.
>
> ANTONIA FRASER,
> *The Warrior Queen*

Still, each time I felt fear, I felt something else, too: Especially when I was very young, I would sometimes "sing myself strong," the sound of my voice rising in my throat like a victory, breaking free of the taloned grip of fear. Or, alone in the fields or in the woods, I would dance, the confident survivor of life's trials. One of my abiding sources of courage was a nightly practice I had of looking deep into the night sky. There, the infinite mystery I confronted made whatever struggle I was facing here on earth seem infinitesimal in comparison.

But there was courage to be found where I lived as well—my circle of six girl-friends never failed to leave me feeling strongly supported. I still recall the slumber-party game we used to play: With one of us lying down in the center of the circle, pretending to be dead, the others would gently place one or two fingers underneath. Together, we would lift the body; as it rose up, seemingly by spirit, we'd shriek in horrified laughter. A childish game—but a perfect metaphor for the gentle, invisible way that girlfriends support one anther.

At the same time, while I was growing up, the many small feats of courage with which I faced certain everyday situations strengthened that soul quality within me. It became a dance—a rhythmic interweaving between two gods, two life-presences that between them created something durable and precious. One incident I've never forgotten occurred when I was about twelve or thirteen. My father, who was quite a horseman, had insisted on breeding and raising a horse for each one of his four children. As the oldest, I was the first to watch as my horse was born, then trained by my father for me to ride. Though his name was Sombra, Spanish for shadow, he was golden-colored, proud, and very high-spirited. Still, my dad insisted that I accompany him to catch Sombra out in the field, saddle him up, then take him for a ride. For years, I endured this ritual, always nervous and fearful that I would be kicked, fall from the saddle, or lose control. Then one day as I was dismounting, my arms became tangled in the reins and I stumbled backward, inadvertently pulling my horse down with me. But instead of falling on top of me—which would have been the most natural way for a horse to fall—Sombra twisted away to the side, protecting me from his weight and landing hard on his knees. Everyone came running, exclaiming over how my horse had saved me (later, in fact, some local farmers noted how unusual it was for a horse to fall to its knees this way). Getting up from the ground, I was trembling from head to foot—but then and there, my dad made me get right back in the saddle. That day, I mastered a certain kind of courage—the courage to act despite wrenching physical fear, and the courage to trust a creature of the natural world. The lesson, clichéd though it may be, stuck with me that if I fell out of the saddle, I had to get back up in it right away.

Everyone's life is filled with these ordinary, garden-variety parables of courage. If we are responsive to them, they are the ways in which the hand of life shapes that quality within our character. They become reserves of strength that we can draw upon in adult life. Even my father's alcoholism became a kind of family tragedy that taught me a lot about human nature and the limits of courage. As an adult, I claimed that fiery inheritance, using it to walk my own spiritual path outside mainstream religion, to live communally, to marry and have three sons by natural childbirth—then eventually to divorce, endeavor to co-parent with my sons' father, and embark on life as a single woman and a writer. Like a white-water rafter, courage was my muscle, my oar, and the lightninglike energy that bore me through life's riskier passages. It was courage that prodded me down the spiritual path where one never knew what lay around the next corner, and courage that took me down to the deepest layers of my unconscious psyche. It was courage that gave me strength to parent three high-spirited and willful boys through their teens. It was courage that allowed me to think that, with no degree or professional training, I could dare to write—to pick up the phone and "cold-call" editors, to interview prominent thinkers, and to

Risk! Risk anything! Care no more for the opinions of others, for those voices. Do the hardest thing on earth for you. Act for yourself. Face the truth.

KATHERINE MANSFIELD

He who has done his best for his own time has lived for all times.

JOHANN VON SCHILLER,
Wallenstein's Camp

believe in the power of my own creative imagination. Though often frightened, I have been happiest living out on the edge, where life isn't only a matter of safety and security, but also an adventure to be lived forward. Still, I never drew courage from myself alone, like some mountain climber braving solitary peaks. Instead, I have been supported every step of the way by an ever-widening circle of friends who, some thirty years later, form the nucleus of my life. The fact that they are always there for me, no matter what, has made me feel like the cherished member of a secret club of "Mother Couragers."

Looking back on my life from the perspective of half a century, it seems to me that courage is the source of all other qualities—the queen of attributes, the "Mother Courage" of fairy tales. Poet Maya Angelou has said that courage is "the most important of all virtues, because without courage, you cannot practice any of the other virtues consistently." Indeed, there is something about the quality of courage that is closely connected to the life force underlying existence. In fairy tales and myths, it is a magic substance that transforms hapless fools into triumphant victors. The courage to brave risks, it seems, makes heroes and heroines of the most ordinary among us. It takes enormous courage, for instance, to have faith in a world riven with meaninglessness or to find hope in the midst of despair. It takes courage to speak a truth that may engender scorn, result in the loss of one's career—or even the loss of life itself. It takes courage to see beauty amid ugliness in a cynical world, and to radiate peace in situations of great uncertainty and anxiety. In other words, it takes courage to overcome the narrow limitations of our selves, and to seek to become large souled enough to manifest in the here and now the glorious, transpersonal attributes of the Divine.

So profound, so essential to life, so creative a matrix is the quality of courage that the Christian theologian Paul Tillich devoted an entire book to exploring it's metaphysical dimensions. In his classic treatise *The Courage to Be*, he wrote that courage "is self-affirmation 'in spite of,' that is in spite of that which tends to prevent the self from affirming itself." The courage to affirm oneself, Tillich explained, could not be philosophically understood without taking into account the existential fear implicit in life itself— the fear and anxiety posed by the ever-present threat of "nonbeing." This fear is threefold: the anxiety of fate and death; the anxiety of guilt and condemnation; and the anxiety of emptiness and loss of meaning. When an individual faces a life-threatening illness, for instance, or a soldier risks his life for his country, that person acts with courage "in spite of" the possibility of physical annihilation. When a person has betrayed their own better nature, yet still gets up the next morning and tries again to fulfill their higher destiny, that person acts with courage "in spite of" the anxiety of moral despair over the gap between what they are and what they ought to be. And when a person experiences the emptiness of existence, yet still affirms meaning in life, that person acts with courage "in spite of" the loss of a spiritual center. Thus, for Tillich, courage does not remove anxiety. Instead, courage "is the readiness to take upon oneself negatives, anticipated by fear, for the sake of a fuller positivity."

(And it was shown to her) how serious and dangerous it is curiously to examine the things which are beyond one's understanding, and to believe in new things . . . and even to invent new and unusual things, for demons have a way of introducing themselves into suchlike curiosities.

ADMONITION ADDRESSED TO
JOAN OF ARC, FROM
Saint Joan of Arc,
VITA SACKVILLE-WEST

DRAW COURAGE FROM THE STARS

Courage not only comes from actions we take in spite of our fears, but also arises from a mysterious source that lies outside and beyond the narrow framework of our ordinary lives. We can draw power from this wellspring by gazing at the night sky, drawing energy from the illuminated face of the universe that gazes back at us like the face of a majestic being. If you are feeling afraid and uncertain, go outside and sit beneath the stars. Contemplate the distant reaches of outer space that surround our

*tiny sapphire globe of a planet. Take strength from the energy that rains down like
light from the stars. Draw courage into your heart from the vast soul of the cosmos.
Be emboldened by the knowledge that life is much larger, grander, and more noble
than you could ever imagine. If heroes and heroines are bigger than life, it is because
they are aware of the grand scale of the drama of existence. Staring into the night
sky, receive into yourself the courage that comes from being in touch with the wild,
beautiful miracle of life. See the story of your life written large in the stars above.*

Those who possess the "courage to be," writes Tillich, are gifted with vitality
and dynamic strength—that is, "life power." Courageously embracing life "in spite
of" its constant threats and disappointments, in other words, imbues one's spirit
with vitality and energy. This definition of courage is interesting, because throughout most of recorded history, courage has been narrowly interpreted in a physical
sense. It has been thought to be the defining virtue of
warriors and conquerers, athletes and explorers. Consider, for instance, conquerers such as Alexander the
Great or Napoléon Bonaparte, warriors such as the Japanese samurai or the cowboys of the American West, and
explorers such as Christopher Columbus or Lewis and
Clark. The death-defying activities of war, aggression,
conquest, and physical feats of daring have been for centuries the time-honored playing fields of courage.

Though not as often as men, women, too, have
risked death as warriors, and have been pioneers and
political revolutionaries. Women have literally fought,
writes Antonia Fraser in *The Warrior Queens*, "as a normal part of the army in far more epochs and far more
civilizations than is generally appreciated." Too, the rise
of feminism as a political movement by such intrepid
pioneers as Susan B. Anthony and Elizabeth Cady Stan-
ton has given women their own lineage of heroic role models, myths, and stories to
inspire them in their daily lives. Who, for instance, is not moved by the fact that
these two women suffragists have now taken their place among America's founding fathers in Statuary Hall at the Capitol in Washington, D.C.? More recently, as
the November 2001 issue of *Sports Illustrated* attested, the women who worked as
nurses, firefighters, paramedics, and rescue workers in the aftermath of the terrorist attacks on the World Trade Center were a moving testament to the extreme limits of physical courage that are as possible for women as they are for men.

*If one advances confidently in the direction
of his dreams, and endeavors to live the life
which he has imagined, he will meet with a
success unexpected in common hours.*

HENRY DAVID THOREAU

*They helped every one his neighbor; and
every one said to his brother, Be of good
courage.*

ISAIAH 41:6

But as historian Gerda Lerner has written in *The Creation of Patriarchy*, feminist thinkers have not sought to do away with the singular patriarchal lens through which history has been seen and recorded. Rather, they have opened up another way of seeing. This new "doubled vision," she writes, has added "the female vision to the male and that process is transforming . . . It is only when both eyes see together that we accomplish the full range of vision." Indeed, as women are revisioning politics, the family, and religion in the wake of feminism, so too are they expanding the definition of qualities and virtues such as courage.

In addition to outright boldness in the face of overwhelming odds, for example, women have complemented traditional masculine forms of death-defying acts of bravery with their own brand of courage that embraces life even as it is threatened. Embodied in the life-affirming image of the Great Goddess, the feminine face of courage says yes to the miracle of existence in the face of destruction, failure, and personal despair. This form of courage finds expression in the assertive acts of ordinary life: the young mother who gets up and fixes her child breakfast the day after losing her husband; the woman who cares for her friend through an illness; and the grandmother who raises a grandchild in the absence of her own son or daughter. This kind of optimistic life spirit may seem deceptively unassuming; without it, however, it is unlikely that society could hold its center. It is the way of women, as well as many men, to be intensely attached, to care deeply, and to nurture steadfastly: to have the courage, in other words, not to give up on life even when life has seemed to give up on us. It is the kind of courage that comes to mind when I hear stories of inner-city mothers raising their children amid poverty, violence, and futurelessness. It is the same simple courage, in fact, that arose to complement the physical courage of the firefighters and policemen who lost their lives in the line of duty September 11—the bare-bones bravery exemplified by those men and women who, the day after, had to get up and go on living. This awe-inspiring courage for life is what Eleanor Roosevelt referred to when she wrote in her autobiography, "Life was meant to be lived, and curiosity must be kept alive. One must never, for whatever reason, turn his back on life."

Indeed, for men as well as women, courage these days has become an even

Let courage be thy sword and patience be thy shield, my soldier.

HAZRAT INAYAT KHAN

I want to take life by the horns as if it were a young bull, but I won't stab it in the flank nor pass a sword through its throat nor thrust myself over the horns, not that, but I will dance with it, dance with the awkward bull. Dance.

DEENA METZGER, FROM
*Tree & the Woman Who Slept
with Men to Take the
War Out of Them*

more complex task, perhaps, than in ancient times. Living as we do in a world shadowed by the threat of terrorism, environmental destruction, and nuclear attack, it requires a lot of bravery just to get out of bed in the morning and shoulder the responsibilities of the day, or to simply find the energy to live in a world where nothing is for certain. But this is where women have something else to offer as well. For in addition to the courage to nurture and sustain the gift of life, they also possess in great measure the ability to give encouragement to those around them, what feminist psychologist Judith Jordan describes as "supporting courage in others."[1] While in the past courage has been extolled as a trait found in the solitary individual, Jordan writes that courage redefined from a feminist perspective can also be understood as "courage in connection," or the strength that individuals derive from their relationships with each other. Ask any woman, for example, what her closest friends do for her, and she will most often reply that they provide her with a vital source of support and encouragement that often not even a husband or lover can give. In almost every interview I conducted for this book, this form of encouragement was so precious that nearly every woman said she couldn't imagine living without it.

Be strong and of a good courage; be not afraid, neither be thou dismayed: for the Lord thy God is with thee whithersoever thou goest.

JOSHUA 1:9

Religion in its humility restores man to his only dignity, the courage to live by grace.

GEORGE SANTAYANA,
Dialogues in Limbo

Jane Holmes Dixon, Suffragan Bishop of the Episcopal Diocese of Washington and the second woman to be elevated to the office of Bishop in the Episcopal Church, movingly described the support she received from her close friend, radio personality Diane Rehm. During a talk they both presented at a women's Sacred Circles conference held at the National Cathedral in Washington, D.C., Dixon described Rehm's gift of courage to her in the difficult journey she undertook to become a member of the male-dominated Episcopal clergy. "One of the things I find in my own life . . . is that shame is an emotion many women know better than men," said Dixon, "and how easy it is for me to drop back into those patterns of thinking 'what did I do wrong.' When I am facing a situation or a person who is very likely to cause me to feel that way, I tell Diane. And she always says to me, 'You can do it. You've done it before. Don't let them get you down, because you're okay. And a lot of days I start the day with that in my heart."

In other words, thousands of women have whispered, shouted, or whooped to each other, "You go, girl!" For, like Dixon and Rehm, women everywhere are inspiring one another to be brave—whether in their ongoing quest to achieve equal power; in their creative endeavors; in their efforts to advance humanitarian causes; or in the extraordinary strength that they bring to the ordinary tasks of raising children and sustaining a family. The modern heroine is the definition of the true hero, who, according to mythologist Joseph Campbell, is "the champion . . . of things becoming," and "the champion of creative life." The stories of my women friends and the obstacles they have overcome have made them in my eyes as courageous as chivalrous knights of old or as fearless as military generals. They tilt at dragons, overcome great odds, and are just plain remarkable in their talent to keep on going. The following stories of courageous women from history, mythology, and from the lives of my own close friends and contemporary women tell their own tale of the feminine face of courage. They offer symbols, messages, and examples from which to weave the pattern of your own banner of courage—be it physical, emotional, political, creative, or spiritual. I hope that they inspire you to be the heroine of your own life—the "knight-ess" of your own quest.

> *I have three treasures. Guard and keep them:*
> *The first is deep love,*
> *The second is frugality,*
> *And the third is not to dare to be ahead of the*
> *world.*
> *Because of deep love, one is courageous.*
> *Because of frugality, one is generous.*
> *Because of not daring to be ahead of the*
> *world, one becomes the leader of the world.*
>
> LAO-TZU,
> *The Way of Lao-tzu*

WARRIOR QUEENS FROM HISTORY

Because so few were recorded in the annals of history, images of women as fierce fighters and crusaders stand out as doubly bold and meaningful. A modern woman may not actually find herself in a position of having to "take up the sword," but she may have to make a presentation before an all-male board of directors, plead a case in court, run for political office, or confront an abusive partner. She can draw courage from a lineage of women who either risked their lives on the battlefields alongside men or were spirited enough to overcome the narrow prejudices of their day and speak the truth. Here are several women heroines to inspire you to fight the good fight—whatever battle you may be facing.

SOJOURNER TRUTH

"Where did your Christ come from? Where did your Christ come from? . . . From God and a woman! Man had nothing to do with Him . . . If the first woman God ever made was strong enough to turn the world upside down all alone, these women together ought to be able to turn it back, and get it right side up again!" So spoke the black woman preacher who stood up in the back of the audience and insisted on being heard at the historic Women's Rights Conference in 1851 in Akron, Ohio.

Born Isabella Baumfree, a slave, she adopted the name Sojourner Truth at the age of forty-six and spent the next forty years as a fiery public speaker in the crusade against segregation and slavery—and on behalf of women's rights. Even into her eighties, she challenged segregation by boarding streetcars and sitting in the white section—thus ensuring a dramatic public expulsion by the conductor. A thousand people attended her funeral, where she was immortalized by feminist Lucy Stone as "a terrible force, moving friend and foe alike." (From The Creation of Feminist Consciousness *by* Gerda Lerner, *and* What Every American Should Know About Women's History *by* Christine Lunardini*)*

> *Sometimes life pushes us, and there is usually wisdom in it that we only see later.*
>
> DIANE GILMAN, FROM
> *Lighting A Candle,*
> *Quotations on the Spiritual Life*

MARY HARRIS "MOTHER" JONES

Born in Ireland in 1830, Mother Jones, as she later became known, spent the first forty years of her life as a conventional daughter, wife, and mother. Through her husband, an ironworker with whom she had four children, she became introduced to the union cause. After an epidemic of yellow fever wiped out her entire family, she became an active union organizer, encouraging laborers to stand up for their rights. The following account from her autobiography describes her efforts to organize the Coaldale miners to join the union:

"I went to a nearby mining town . . . and asked the women if they would help me get the Coaldale men out. . . . I told them to leave their men at home to take care of the family. I asked them to put on their kitchen clothes and bring mops and brooms with them and a couple of tin pans. We marched over the mountains . . . beating on the tin pans as if they were cymbals. At three o'clock in the morning we met the Crack Thirteen of the militia patrolling the roads of Coaldale. . . . I said, "Colonel, the working men of America will not halt. . . . The working man is going ahead!" [The Colonel then threatens to charge her with bayonets.] "We are not enemies," said I. "We are just a band of working women whose brothers and husbands are in a battle for bread. . . . We are here on the mountain road for our children's sake, for our nation's sake . . ." They kept us there till daybreak and when they saw the army of women in kitchen aprons, with dishpans and mops, they laughed and let us pass. An army of strong mining women makes a wonderfully spectacular picture." (From The Autobiography of Mother Jones*)*

QUEEN JINGA OF ANGOLA

In the seventeenth century, a bold woman named Queen Jinga fought long battles against the invading Portugese. Here is how a man, the Dutch Captain Fuller, commander of her personal bodyguard, admiringly described her: "In man's apparel . . . hanging about her the skins of beasts, before and behind, with a Sword about her neck, an axe at her girdle, and a Bow and Arrows in her hand, leaping according to the custom, now here, now there, as nimble as the most active among her attendants, all the while striking her Engema, that is two Iron Bells, which serve her instead of Drums. . . ." Queen Jinga was also reputed to have had more than sixty young men as husbands. (Adapted from The Warrior Queens *by Antonia Fraser)*

Queen Maeve

The ancient Celtic saga, the Tain, begins with a husband and wife's quarrel over a bull. In bed at night, Queen Maeve is forced to admit to her husband Ailill that her prize bull has defected to the King's herd because he refuses to be led by a woman. Taunted by her husband's claims that he is more royal King and brave warrior than she, recounts Antonia Fraser in The Warrior Queens, *Queen Maeve launches a military campaign to secure for herself the legendary Brown Bull of Ulster—thus vanquishing her husband's claims to superiority. In her quest, Maeve must battle the legendary Cuchulainn, champion of the Brown Bull. Queen Maeve is to the Tain, writes Fraser, what the Greek goddesses are to the Iliad, "the physique and appetites of a woman, the magic powers of a goddess."*

Cuchulainn's fellow warrior Cethern vividly conveys the heroic power of the Celtic goddess-warrior Queen Maeve: "A tall, fair, long-faced woman with soft features came at me. . . . She had a head of yellow hair and two gold birds on her shoulders. She wore a purple cloak folded about her, with five hands' breadth of gold on her back. She carried a light, stinging, sharp-edged lance in her hand, and she held an iron sword with a woman's grip over her head—a massive figure. It was she who came at me first." (From The Warrior Queens *by Antonia Fraser)*

Courageous Women from History

Courage could be said to be like an inner pilot light—when it is lit, we feel powered from within by the soul's flame to accomplish our ideals. When this inner pilot light is extinguished, we may feel literally "dis-couraged" or lacking in the physical enthusiasm necessary to carry us across the hurdles we may be facing. In my own life, there have been many times when I have felt as if this inner pilot light has burned low. One way I have been able to rekindle it is through my imagination. Storytelling, for instance, is a time-honored method of inspiring courage. How, for instance, did our ancestors cope with the terror they felt, alone in a violent and unpredictable landscape in which death was but a heartbeat away? They built a fire beneath the stars, gathered round in a circle, and told stories of heroes who had survived similar hardships. Most of these stories, of course, were "male tales." Only in the last decades, with the long-overdue establishment of women's history, have women finally had restored to them a foundation of stories from which to draw strength. Like men, they can now stand supported on the shoulders of women who have gone before them, and can know that their own stories are links in a lineage stretching forward into the future.

MOVIE HEROINES

When it comes to inspiration, there is nothing like a movie—a modern-day myth— to give strength and enthusiasm. Three recent movies present female role models of extraordinary courage for the faint of heart. Rent them when you are feeling anxious and uncertain, yet want to feel—and be—brave: Laura Croft, Tomb Raider *for occult adventure;* Crouching Tiger, Hidden Dragon *for warriorlike integrity and grace under pressure; and* The Contender *for sheer gutsiness to be a woman of power and politics.*

As a writer who has often struggled to make financial ends meet, the story of Isak Dinesen has always given me courage to keep working at my craft despite the lack of outer reward. It is difficult enough to shape sentences and paragraphs out of abstract wisps of thoughts, but harder still when the rent is coming due and the tires on the car are dangerously worn. During those pressing financial times, I often would think of Dinesen living on her coffee plantation in South Africa. Stricken with syphilis from her first husband, her lover Denys Finch Hatton away on big-game hunts, and her life on her beloved farm threatened by falling coffee prices, Dinesen took up the habit of writing . At night, surrounded by the vast silence of the African landscape, she would sit at her dining room table "to write stories, fairy tales and romances, that would take my mind a long way off, to other countries and times."[2] With only her servant Farah to keep her company, she wrote, "figures, voices and colors from far away or from nowhere began to swarm around my paraffin lamp."[3] Like the

That is at bottom the only courage that is demanded of us: to have courage for the most strange, the most singular, and the most inexplicable that we may encounter. That mankind has in this sense been cowardly, has done life endless harm; the whole so-called "spirit-world," death, all those things that are so closely akin to us, have by daily parrying been so crowded out of life that the senses with which we could have grasped them are atrophied. To say nothing of God.

RAINER MARIA RILKE,
Letters to a Young Poet

legendary Sheherezade who saved her life through her tales, Dinesen's writing was itself an act of courage that not only saved her from despair, but ultimately enchanted a worldwide audience.

In fact, it was one of Dinesen's own mottoes that initially inspired me to take up writing. As she tells the story in her wonderful essay, "On Mottoes of My Life," she had returned to her homeland, Denmark, after the failure of her coffee plantation in Kenya. Humiliated by her poverty, devastated by the sudden death of her lover, and dependent upon her family, she writes that her books began to "demand to be written." Yet first, says Dinesen, her new enterprise, like every other one she had undertaken in her life, required a motto. She found one in a newspaper account of a French boat that had gone down off Iceland with her flag flying: the boat's name was *Pourquoi Pas?* meaning "Why Not?" Adopting this free-spirited phrase as her new standard, Dinesen wrote all her books under the sign of this "joyful and exacting spirit," that, she writes, turned the pathetic wail of "why?" into a "call of wild hope." Immediately upon reading this, I assumed the same motto for myself, as to the listening ears of my soul it rang out like a call to adventure challenging me to take up an exciting new quest. The very exuberance of the phrase, the excitement it stirred whenever I repeated "Why Not?" freed me from any heavy restrictions of what a writer "should be" or what a woman like me "should not" or "could not" do. Thus liberated to follow the voice of my own muse, I set out on the journey to become a writer; whenever I have felt disspirited about my writing, I recall this motto and the path of adventure opens up once again. I still do not know where my writing will eventually lead me, but the motto "Why Not?" gives me the courage to continue to face the unknown.

Centuries before Dinesen wrote herself out of hardship and into fame and success, the fourteenth-century author Christine de Pizan (1365–c.1430) also faced poverty as a single woman. Like a knight who took up the sword to defend himself, Pizan picked up her pen and began to write—an act that led her to become the first known woman to earn a living as a writer. Born in Venice, Pizan moved with her family to Paris, where she was educated at the Court of Charles V. At age fifteen, she was happily married to a man who encouraged her literary development. But by the age of twenty-five, Pizan found herself widowed with three chil-

In order to govern it is not necessary to be a man, but to have courage.

GIOVANNI BOCCACCIO,
Concerning Famous Women

Yes, as my swift days near their goal,
'Tis all that I implore:
In life and death a chainless soul,
With courage to endure.

EMILY BRONTË,
The Old Stoic

dren for whom to provide. Faced with a stack of debts and no income, she began copying and illustrating books. A remarkably ambitious woman who involved herself in the politics of her time, Pizan soon became famous as a poet, writer, and historian and was commissioned to write a biography of Charles V.

Following her early success, Pizan then embarked upon an even more daunting mission: to challenge the widespread mockery of women as intellectually weak-minded and inferior to men. She did this through the book for which she became most widely known, charmingly but deceptively titled *The Book of the City of Ladies.* In it, Pizan engages in a dialogue with three "lady spirits": Reason, Rectitude, and Justice. Why is it, she asks them, that women have been denied the virtue of "high understanding and great learning," by men who "maintain that the mind of women can learn only a little"?[4] In response to her inquiry, the three ladies cite from history a long list of women's accomplishments, ranging from the brilliant poet Sappho to Nicostrata who invented the Latin alphabet. Pizan's bold treatise became one of the first compendiums of women's history; at the same time, it was a decidedly unapologetic and smartly reasoned argument on behalf of women's intelligence and moral worth. Pizan's spirited defense of women to the male authorities of her time triggered a long-lasting debate on the status of women, known as the *querelle des femmes.* Indeed, some may be startled to learn that for some 400 years, a debate raged throughout England and Europe on whether or not women were fully human, could exercise reason, or could control their emotions. Like a Gloria Steinem or a Simone de Beauvoir centuries ahead of her time, Pizan's personal experience transformed her into a passionate advocate of women's emancipation through education. Warning women of the dangers of dependence, she encouraged them to become strong, resourceful, and to develop "the heart of a man."[5] Whether writers or stockbrokers, artists or athletes, women today can rightfully lay claim to Pizan as a woman's heroine in her own right.

Pizan's story overturns old myths of women as helpless princesses in need and men as their gallant saviors. History in fact is richly laced with the stories of women like Pizan who not only achieved great things for themselves, but took a stand and championed the rights of others as well. From Britain's Queen Boadicea to France's Joan of Arc, women as much as men have acted as courageous knights,

We can never know what strengths and revelations might be on the other side of our fears until we face them and feel them all the way through. True positive thinking is the mental stance of surrender, simply trusting the process. We learn to accept what is.

JACQUELYN SMALL,
Awakening in Time

One man with courage makes a majority.

ANDREW JACKSON

rescuing victims from oppression and injustice. For sheer brilliance of bravery in this category, the story of the Grimke sisters would fill the sails of any woman lacking the courage to write, speak out, or do whatever else it is she might dare to imagine.

Born to a South Carolina plantation family, Sarah and her younger sister Angelina were raised in an environment of wealth and high social standing. They were also firsthand witnesses to the cruelty of slavery and, as women, were denied the rights enjoyed by men—the right to vote, to hold public office, or even to have a voice in church affairs. In 1837, these two respectable sisters shocked the patriarchal establishment of their time by lecturing to mixed-sex audiences on the subject of abolitionism. Then, on February 21, 1838, Angelina Grimke went a step further and addressed the Legislature of the State of Massachusetts. Until that day, no woman had ever spoken publicly to a legislative body. The courage it took for her to do this is apparent in her description of that event: "I never was so near fainting under the tremendous pressure of feeling. My heart almost died within me. The novelty of the scene, the weight of responsibility, the ceaseless exercise of mind thro' which I had passed for more than a week—all together sunk me to the earth. I well nigh despaired."[6]

*Setting out on the voyage to Ithaca
you must pray that the way be long,
full of adventures and experiences.*

CONSTANTINE PETER
CAVAFY, *Ithaca*

*If you are very valiant, it is a god, I think,
who gave you this gift.*

HOMER, *The Iliad,* BK. I

Slightly built, dressed in a gray Quaker dress, her deep blue eyes framed by dark curls, Angelina challenged the standing room–only audience before her. "I stand before you as a repentent slaveholder. I stand before you as a moral being and as a moral being I feel that I owe it to the suffering slave and to the deluded master, to my country and to the world, to do all that I can to overturn a system of complicated crimes, built upon the broken hearts and prostrate bodies of my countrymen in chains and cemented by the blood, sweat and tears of my sisters in bonds."[7] Angelina Grimke's soaring words that day stirred the souls of her listeners; her reputation as an orator continued to draw such large crowds that some feared the galleries might collapse. Yet so despised as traitors did the Grimke sisters become in the South that they became exiled from their land of birth and were never allowed to return. Though they continued to lecture to overflowing audiences in the North and played a pivotal role in the antislavery movement with the pamphlets they published, the outpouring of criticism spurred by their public visibility eventually led them to champion the cause of women's rights. Much like Pizan some 400 years earlier, the two sisters became compelled to fight throughout their lives for their rights as "moral, intelligent, and responsible women,"[8] who were the equals of men.

Despite the wrenchingly difficult struggles they each faced, Isak Dinesen, Christine de Pizan, and the Grimke sisters all lived long, fruitful, and adventurous lives. The fate of the young Noor-un-nisa Inayat Khan, however—a woman whose courage in the name of liberty is a tale to be told and retold—ended on a tragic note. I first heard her story when, at the age of nineteen, I became initiated as a Sufi by the meditation teacher Pir Vilayat Inayat Khan, who was her brother. Pir Vilayat and his sister, Noor-un-nisa, grew up in Paris, France, among four children born to the famed Indian Sufi mystic Hazrat Inayat Khan and his American wife. I still remember my awe at hearing Pir Vilayat—a wise-looking, white-haired meditation teacher—describe the fearless eagerness with which both he and his sister joined in the fight against the Nazis' cruel reign of terror.

While Pir joined the Navy, his sister Noor, as she was called, volunteered as a radio telegrapher. Exquisitely beautiful, with large brown eyes, jet-black hair, and velvet skin, Noor possessed the luminous radiance of a natural mystic. Truly the eldest daughter of her father, a skilled Indian musician, Noor played the harp and wrote children's fairy tales. Her work during the war, however, led her down a radically different path from what her life seemed to promise. Recruited by the BSC (British Security Coordination), Noor, working under the code name "Madeleine," became a secret agent transmitting messages between the British War Office and the French Resistance. Soon after she began her dangerous mission, however, many of the leaders of the secret network she belonged to were arrested—leaving her the sole transmitter. Placing herself in the gravest danger, she continued to transmit, even refusing the offer made by her London superiors to send a plane for her. After several months, Noor was betrayed to the gestapo, arrested, and imprisoned. During her capture, she displayed great fierceness, "clawing the air" like a tigress, "trembling with rage," her eyes flashing as she let loose a stream of insults—kicking, pulling the hair, and even biting the wrist of her captor so hard that she drew blood.[9] Taken to the Nazi headquarters in Paris on the Avenue Foch and interrogated at length, Noor refused to give up any information to her captors. Twice, she attempted to escape—the first time scrambling through a bathroom window and crawling along a dangerously high ledge. In all his career at the Avenue Foch, her interrogator, Ernest, had never "encountered a prisoner who made so much diffi-

> *I refer those actions which work out the good of the agent to courage, and those which work out the good of others to nobility. Therefore temperance, sobriety, and presence of mind in danger, etc., are species of courage; but modesty, clemency, etc., are species of nobility.*
>
> BENEDICT BARUCH SPINOZA,
> *Ethics*, PT. I

culty." At the same time, he was "impressed by her steadfastness and her self-control . . ."[10] Another prisoner being held at the same time, British captain John Starr recalls that the guards "all had an admiration for Madeleine—and so had I."[11] Starr also related that, though Noor appeared self-possessed during the day, at night she could be heard sobbing, often until the early hours of the morning.

Now therefore keep thy sorrow to thyself, and bear with a good courage that which hath befallen thee.

The Apocrypha,
11 Esdras 10:15

Courage is resistance to fear, mastery of fear—not absence of fear.

Mark Twain,
Puddn'head Wilson

In interviews after the war, Noor's principle guard, Ernest, learned with surprise of her Indian heritage—if Noor had made known her titles as an Indian, or had not been so ferocious, he said, her story might have ended differently. But because of her refusal to claim special privilege and her attempts to escape, Noor was eventually taken to the prison in Karlsruhe, Germany, where she was kept in isolation for ten months. From there, she was transferred to the Dachau concentration camp. As Pir Vilayat recounts the final chapter of the story of his sister in his book *Awakening: A Sufi Experience*, Noor was kicked repeatedly by her Nazi guard "as she lay on a cement floor in chains, suffering agony from enormous hematomas all over her body. She was in agony throughout the night, exposed on the cement floor, without shelter. The next day, she was whipped and hit to the point that she was, as a witness said, a bloody mess. Then she was made to kneel and was shot in the head from behind. But she didn't cry. Her last words were "*Vive la liberte.*" Apparently, there was still some motion in her body when she was thrown into the oven that is still in Dachau."

For those who heard the story directly from Pir Vilayat, it was impossible not to be profoundly changed. The loss of such a beautiful soul as Noor was such a tragedy that to hear it cut a sword mark on the heart. Yet at the same time Noor's example inspired many Sufi students to take up human-rights work, balancing their inner lives with outer work in the world, righting the wrongs of injustice. And whenever Pir Vilayat would lead a meditation, calling upon his students to become a "knight of light and awakening"—dedicated to relieving the overwhelming despair of the human condition and to becoming a part of the "rescue operation" to the suffering—I took that vow in the name of Noor, a true woman and knight of courage.

THE COURAGE OF DEEP LOVE

Forged through trials by fire, these four remarkable women from history show how heroes are created through the courageous way they respond to the seemingly impossible challenges with which life presents them. Pir Vilayat, for instance, frequently tells the story of the Indian woman who, in keeping with Hindu tradition, faced death on the funeral pyre after her husband's demise. Frightened, the widow sought help from a woman guru who had a pet cobra. If she could pet the cobra, the guru said, she would be spared her fate. But if the cobra sensed her fear, she would fail the test and it would bite her. As frightened as she was of the cobra, the young widow was more frightened still of dying—so putting aside her fears, she petted the cobra. Because of her courage, it did not bite her. The moral of this story, writes Pir Vilayat, in *Awakening*, "is not only that the young widow was spared being sacrificed on the funeral pyre, but that through the crucible of this extreme circumstance she became a living testament to the power of human courage."

> *No coward soul is mine,*
> *No trembler in the world's storm-troubled*
>   *sphere:*
> *I see Heaven's glories shine,*
> *And faith shines equal, arming me from fear.*
>
> EMILY BRONTË,
> *Last Lines*

Like the woman in the parable, my close friend Lis Akhtarzandi was also once a young widow. Though she did not face death on a funeral pyre, she did face an almost insurmountable set of circumstances as potentially deadly as any cobra. Though Lis and I walk different life paths, her incredible passage from a suddenly widowed mother lacking in work skills to the successful vice president of a marketing company has always awed me. More important, her example has given me courage to be brave in ways I might never have imagined if not for our friendship. Whenever I have felt overwhelmed by my life—dragged down by a house to clean, meals to cook, rebellious kids, and a stack of work to do—I have only to think of Lis to get a soul-lift.

Born in England, Lis is a green-eyed, vivacious blonde who radiates vitality and warmth. Her story begins when, as a young girl of eighteen living in London, she met and fell in love with Bijan, a handsome Iranian man who was studying abroad to become a doctor. When Bijan decided to move to Washington, D.C., to continue his studies, she followed. As he worked toward his Ph.D. and M.D. degrees, Lis worked at various odd jobs, created a community of friends, and had two beautiful daughters, Samantha and Emily. In 1977, Bijan graduated and took his first job setting up blood banks for the Middle East. It was a decision that entailed a move for the family back to his homeland of Iran; at the time Lis was thirty-three and her daughters were five and nine years old. Though their first year in Tehran was exciting and happy, recalls Lis, there "was a very strange political climate beneath the surface. There was a lot of sheer extravagance, and a great disparity between the haves and have-nots." Bijan's grandfather had been in charge of the military for Reza Shah, the Shah of Iran's father, and her husband's family remained strongly tied to the military. Still, there was a lot of family merriment, and Lis loved being "surrounded by a lot of love and gregarious, fun people—it was wonderful."

After an idyllic summer spent abroad in Europe with her children and husband, they returned to Tehran in September of 1978. Soon after, in an ominous sign of what was to come, a terrible massacre occurred. "All these people came running to the blood bank where Bijan worked, with buckets and bags and whatever they could find," Lis recounts. Gradually, the political climate of unrest and revolution began to escalate, and soon, many of their friends started to leave. By Christmas, Iran was in the throes of an open revolution. Strict curfews were imposed, and everyone had to be inside by 4:00 or 5:00 P.M. As frightened as they all were at the time, says Lis, the curfew and political unrest drew them closer together as a family. As her husband had always led such a busy life, either studying all night or working on weekends, she says, they rarely had had time together. Now, she says, "we would climb into bed together each evening with a paraffin lamp and take turns reading and entertaining each other. It was wonderful to look back on, as we became very, very close."

> *For without belittling the courage with which men have died, we should not forget those acts of courage with which men . . . have* lived *. . . A man does what he must— in spite of personal consequences, in spite of obstacles and dangers and pressures—and that is the basis of all human morality.*
>
> JOHN F. KENNEDY,
> *Profiles in Courage*

But by the end of February 1979, Lis and her husband had begun to discuss leaving the country. Members of his family were being taken from their homes and put in jail; some had been executed. They devised an elaborate tracking system to monitor one another's safety. In the midst of this "total, total chaos," Lis recalls, her husband called one evening to say that he was on his way home. But he never made it. As she recounts in a voice heavy with sadness, "He had a heart attack about a mile from the house. When I got to the hospital, he was in a coma, and I was told that his chances for surviving were very slim." His coma lasted for a month; as she travelled back and forth to the hospital in the midst of a raging revolution, Lis says, she was careful to cover her head with a scarf and to avoid drawing attention to herself. When her husband finally died, Lis says she felt as if "there was a pit inside myself that had no bottom. It was a physical ache; I was so incredibly sad and empty." With their lives in turmoil and terrible things happening to her extended family, she says, there was little support available to her, as "Bijan was only one of the many tragedies that were happening at the time." Longing for the familiarity of her own cultural rituals, even the funeral failed to bring her comfort. Instead of being placed in a coffin, her husband's body was wrapped in a shroud and, according to Muslim custom, hoisted above the shoulders of men who then carried it around the mosque seven times. "Thunder clouds filled the sky and professional mourners screamed and wailed. There were families walking around trying to find loved ones they had lost in the revolution, examining photos of the dead pinned on the walls in hopes of identifying them— the cemetery was total hysteria and suffering."

*Two o'clock in the morning courage: I mean
unprepared courage.*

NAPOLEON BONAPARTE,
FROM *Las Cases,
Memorial de Ste. Helene*

After the funeral, Lis was forced to confront her new fate. She knew she had to leave the country—but, as an Iranian citizen, she recognized that this would require great skill and diplomacy on her part. Within a month, she was able to get her two daughters out of Iran and back to England to live with her parents. Four months later, Lis left Iran with two suitcases and barely anything of her past. "At that point I swore that I would never get attached to any physical possessions as long as I lived. To be free and clear and have only what was important, which were the children, was my goal," she says.

On her return to England, she found her parents equally devastated by the circumstances she had endured. Her father, a former chief of police accustomed to being in control, had gone into a deep depression during her ordeal; her girls, too, were also suffering from the death of their beloved father. After six months "getting body and soul" back together for herself and her family, Lis returned to the states to begin her life anew. Describing herself as a "total Pollyanna" who had always thought that her husband would provide for her, Lis says that at the time she had "absolutely no skills. The word office scared me, and I couldn't even put paper in a typewriter. I hadn't driven for years, and hated it—I would only drive in short spurts, like a rabbit, and never deviated from my routes. I had tons of fears to deal with—I was not at all the appropriate person to be left to bring up two children on my own."

"Green, battered, and depressed," says Lis, she took the first job she interviewed for as a receptionist/secretary. "Whenever someone would walk by my desk I would just smile and pretend to type. I didn't even know how to file." But Ed and Loretta, the couple who hired her to work for their company, were patient. Eventually she began to assume more responsibilities around the office, such as balancing the accounts and paying the taxes. Gradually, says Lis, the dark cloud that had cloaked their lives began to lift. For one thing, she was beginning to gain a sense of confidence in herself on the job and, she says, started to "feel my wings." When Ed, the owner of her firm, decided to open a market research company, she reached for the opportunity it provided. "I had always had a head for numbers. So I went to them on bended knee and pleaded with them to give me a position." As the young company grew, so did Lis, saying that she "loved what she did and was totally challenged by it. Finally, I had found something that I really did well. It took me a long time to discover that I'm really good at sales." Soon she was travelling around the country giving presentations to companies like Pepsi, Johnson & Johnson, Colgate, and Procter & Gamble—eventually working her way up to become vice president of sales, as well as building the company into a success. Along the way, she parented her daughters through their teens, put them both through college, and planned lovely weddings for each of them.

We have no reason to mistrust our world, for it is not against us. Has it terrors, they are our terrors; has it abysses, those abysses belong to us; are dangers at hand, we must try to love them. . . . Perhaps everything terrible is in its deepest being something helpless that wants help from us.

RAINER MARIA RILKE,
Letters to a Young Poet

Twenty-two years after the death of her husband and her daughters' father, Samantha and Emily are both married and launched on successful careers of their own. Still with the same company, Lis just finished remodelling her retirement dream home and is enjoying a relationship with a caring new boyfriend. Looking back upon her life from this perspective, she ponders whether, if her husband had not died, she would have ever been called upon to develop her strengths the way life forced her to do. "What I discovered was that as a woman I have cultivated a strong core of knowledge about my own capabilities that has grown stronger and stronger. Now, rather than use that core of intelligence to seek more business challenges, I want to explore those areas of my life that have been pushed to the background, such as creativity and my friendships. I don't think I'm going to be thinking back, at the pearly gates, on my business career."

"Because of deep love," wrote the sage Lao-tzu, "one is courageous." Indeed, when I ask Lis what gave her the courage to go on after the death of her husband, she replies that "everything that gave me courage was for the kids. The need to nurture them beyond the place they had been in was extremely strong. It was so important that I show them an incredibly positive, can-do attitude that I almost talked myself into believing it. I needed to show them by example and by living that I thought life was still beautiful and had so many great things in it to experience—that there really was a bright sun out there and a wonderful future beyond the greyness."

THE COURAGE TO ENCOURAGE

As my friend Lis gave courage to her daughters to go on living in spite of the death of their father, so, too, has she been a source of inspiration to many of her friends who have been strengthened by her example. If she could survive such a tragedy, emerging from it a strong and successful woman, they reason, then they could find it inside themselves to overcome their own life challenges. While no one can bear our adversity for us or solve the riddle of our individual fates, we can help one another to get through the hard times. As psychologist Judith Jordan points out, the root word for courage comes from the French *"coeur,"* meaning heart. And if there is one thing women do best for one another, it is to offer heartfelt encouragement in the midst of despair.

> *They believed liberty to be the secret of happiness and courage to be the secret of liberty.*
>
> LOUIS DEMBITZ HOLLWEG,
> WHITNEY V. CALIFORNIA

Zainab Salbi is a woman whose mission in life is to give encouragement to women—especially to women who have endured the agonies of war. In 1993, she responded to the suffering of women survivors of rape and torture in Bosnia-Herzegovina and Croatia, founding what is now Women for Women International. The basis of her organization is friendship, linking women in peaceful countries together with vulnerable women in areas of life-threatening political upheaval.

The story of how Salbi founded her organization is a profile in courage. Born in Iraq, she grew up during the Iran-Iraq war, which began when she was ten years old. As she watched dead bodies arrive at neighbors' houses, death became a daily part of life. Any day, she knew, might bring her own death or the loss of all her family possessed. Finally, after the war's end, Salbi, by then twenty years old, came to the United States on vacation. As fate would have it, Iraq invaded Kuwait during her absence. Unable to return to her country because of the sanctions and imbargo, she became separated from her family. "To be away from the war was even more challenging than living through war, because my family was there and I was here—I so wanted to be with them," she recalls.

By the time the Gulf War was over, however, Salbi had decided to take advantage of the educational opportunities available to her and to remain in Washington, D.C. Not long after she had begun to make a life for herself, the war in Bosnia erupted. For Salbi, this was the first war in which her own country was not involved or that did not directly involve her or her people. "There were many wars during the eighties," she explains, "but when you are involved in fighting your own war, you don't have time to think about what other people are going through." The experiences she had had growing up amid war activated within her a sensitivity to the suffering of others. Thus as horror stories about the rape camps and massacres taking place in Bosnia began to pour in, she felt seized by the conviction that she had to do something to help. Initially, she attempted to volunteer at women's organizations or to sponsor a child—only to find that no programs yet existed for Bosnia.

"So," says Salbi, who speaks in a strong, uplifting voice, "I came up with the idea of sponsoring women myself." Newly married, she and her husband travelled to Croatia just six months after their wedding. As they visited the refugee camps, she listened to women's accounts of how they had been raped and tortured, or had had to watch in horror as their husbands were murdered or their homes burned to the ground. Responding to the needs expressed by those she interviewed, Salbi decided to create direct women-to-women links that would provide monthly installments of cash for each woman to use in whatever way she thought best. More important, sponsors from other countries would also communicate on a regular basis through letters, thus offering emotional, as well as financial, support. The only thing a woman had to do to qualify, says Salbi, was to "be in need of help."

> *With goodwill and trust in God, self-confidence, and a hopeful attitude towards life, a man can always win his battle, however difficult.*
>
> HAZRAT INAYAT KHAN

Following her return from her sojourn in Bosnia, Salbi wrote and distributed a brochure on her organization, which she originally called Women for Women in Bosnia. Word spread quickly and women from across the country began to respond. Working full time, Salbi and her staff of volunteers sent one hundred percent of the money they received in donations to the women they had "adopted." Her husband, equally committed to her cause, dropped out of his Ph.D. program in order to work full time to fund the organization. Though their first several years of marriage were marked by financial hardship, they began to receive a lot of media attention; within two years, President Clinton had honored them for their work. Seven years later, reports Salbi proudly, her organization has gone from a zero budget to a budget of $1.5 million. Their paid staff of more than twenty provides assistance to more than 3,500 women worldwide. Thanks to appearances on the Oprah Winfrey Show, Salbi's organization has expanded by more than six hundred percent in one year, and has now distributed nearly $5 million to more than 10,000 women.

During her fact-finding missions abroad on behalf of Women for Women International, Salbi has braved life-threatening situations. Yet because of her wartime experiences as a young girl growing up in Iraq, she remains unfazed by war's dangers. "I am not afraid of war anymore," she says. "I can go to war zones and hear bullets and missiles and it doesn't make me fearful. I can sleep right through them." When she went to Bosnia during the war and heard shots from snipers, for example, says Salbi, "I was very relaxed. Part of that is because I knew I was in a war situation: my attitude was that whatever happens, happens. If I'm meant to die that day, then I'm meant to die."

Salbi's fearlessness, however, is coupled with empathy for the bitter loneliness that accompanies life in a war zone. "It is very devastating," she says, looking back on her own experience growing up, "when you feel you are the only one who is going through something and that no one is there for you." For as physically destructive as war can be, says Salbi, it is the emotional isolation of war that often causes the most grief. Many women, she says, feel "bitter and abandoned by the whole world. They think that no one knows or cares about them." Thus the heartfelt encouragement they receive from their sponsors' letters

He who can live up to his ideal is the king of life; he who cannot live up to it is life's slave.

HAZRAT INAYAT KHAN

can be literally lifesaving. "To get that letter from one person saying 'I do care about you and I know what is going on and I want to help' has such an impact on their spirits that it gives me chills," says Salbi. "When I visit these women, they tell me how they cherish each letter they receive. One woman told me she saved her letters in a box, then locked the box and safeguarded it in her closet. Another put it under her pillow and read it every night. They all saved the letters they received and told me that they read them repeatedly. It's almost as if these letters were the only outside source of support they were receiving."

Salbi's work on the frontlines with women suffering the horrors of war reaffirms psychologist Judith Jordan's research into the positive dynamics of encouragement as an added dimension to the quality of courage. Although society elaborates a myth of "separate courage" that emphasizes action and will in the face of death, she writes, several new studies show that "the presence of other people, either physically or in the thoughts of a frightened person, alters the quality of courage that emerges."[12] Supporting courage in others through empathy has all too often been devalued as "women's work," and should rightfully be restored to its place as a vital function within society. Indeed, despite the enormous differences in their lives, what links these women together across the boundaries of religion and culture is the shared feminine experience. "The letter-writing highlights the common ground we share as women," says Salbi, "and leads to intimacy in communication. They feel they are in contact with someone who knows where they are coming from—even though their sponsor may not have had to suffer atrocities, they can understand how much a woman cares about her child, or how she was in pain when something happened to a family member."

From this expanded perspective, courage becomes a multifaceted experience that transforms both the individual facing a challenge and the person offering encouragement. Salbi's experience travelling throughout the world supporting uplifting the lives of women suffering the horrors of war, for instance, she says, has strengthened her in many ways. "I've learned to be grateful and patient and to thank God for everything I have—and to not take anything for granted. Everything I've seen—women who one day have a house, a car, a family, a two-month vacation and the next day they are refugees with nothing—has strengthened my spirituality and how I look at life."

> *Life shrinks or expands in proportion to one's courage.*
>
> ANAÏS NIN

**EXERCISES IN COURAGE
FOR THE FAINT OF HEART**

☼

Like the Cowardly Lion in *The Wizard of Oz*, most of us believe that courage is something we have to have before we can act on it. Trembling with anxiety, we turn away from the risk we yearn to take because we do not feel strong enough. Unless we possess the bravado of a superwoman or the guts of a brassy CEO, we think, we just don't believe we have what it takes to do brave things. But the truth is, courage is something that is earned when we go ahead and "act anyway"—even though we may be quaking inside with fear. As a writer, for instance, I have often felt shy and intimidated by editors. Many times I have sat at my desk, staring at the phone, heart beating and pulse racing, dreading making a "cold call" to an editor who has never heard of me to "pitch" a story idea. And this is what I say to myself, "Why not? Why not go ahead and try, even if they hate it and you end up sounding like a stupid person who makes no sense?" I've felt the same way interviewing people who are smart, famous, and powerful. And yes, I've often stumbled over my words, sounding muddleheaded or uninformed. When I first began to write, I was so paralyzed with fear over how an editor might criticize my writing that I dreaded putting words on paper. What I've learned in the process of becoming a writer, however, is that there is no way to get rid of fear. The only cure is to go forward and do what has to be done anyway. "You gain strength, courage, and confidence by every experience in which you really stop to look fear in the face," wrote Eleanor Roosevelt. "You are able to say to yourself, 'I lived through this horror. I can take the next thing that comes along.' You must do the thing you think you cannot do."[13]

While I have mostly developed courage by facing fear head-on and practicing the art of "acting anyway," there are a few practices that I've cultivated along the way to help prime the inner pump of courage. Take what you like from the following exercises, and feel free to design your own "courage-in-training" program.

WRITE THE EPIC OF YOUR BRAVEST DEEDS

Some of the world's greatest literature is based on the plot of how an ordinary person overcame great obstacles and performed heroic deeds against all odds. From the Viking sagas to *The Illiad* and *The Odyssey,* all the world thrills to the tale of a hero. The reason for this is simple: Life is generally filled with hardship and challenge, and requires from us a great deal of courage. As the feminist writer Carolyn Heilbrun has pointed out, women need to add the "quest plot" to the more traditional narratives of love and relationship that have defined their lives. Thus, in addition to reading inspiring stories of courageous individuals, another thing I do is to remember all those things that I've done in the past that I never thought I could do, or things I've endured that I never thought I could survive. For ultimately, we have only to look to our own lives to see that we are our own best source of courage.

I have learned over the years that when one's mind is made up, this diminishes fear, knowing what must be done does away with fear.

ROSA PARKS,
CIVIL RIGHTS HERO

If courage is the quality that you most feel you are lacking, then begin a "courage journal" and keep a running list of your most courageous deeds. No matter how inconsequential or trivial, honor them, for they are the gifts that life gave you to develop courage. The small feats of bravery you perform help to prepare you for the larger obstacles you may one day face. Remember that courageous acts are those things you have done "in spite of" a limitation or drawback. While I have never faced life-threatening risks, life has called upon me to have courage in other ways. To help inspire you, here is my own list:

1. I dropped out of college when I was nineteen and moved to California to live in a Sufi commune, in spite of having no idea where my path would lead me.

2. I parented three sons through their teens, braving wild parties, late-night visits from the local police, and endured many long nights of anxiety, in spite of my lack of confidence as a parent who knew what she was doing.

3. I wrote a proposal to a major New York publication, then talked to the editor on the phone, in spite of my heart-pounding insecurity.

4. I sat with my father as he was dying, then, in spite of our long and troubled relationship, helped him to find the courage to face his own soul and die peacefully. After that, despite my lack of financial skills, I settled his estate.

5. I wrote a book in spite of the fact that I had no idea how to write one.

6. I wrote another book, in spite of the fact that the first one was cancelled.

7. I kept on writing, in spite of the fact that the second one was cancelled.

8. I'm still writing, in spite of all the above!

INVOKE AN INVISIBLE COMPANION

Every hero needs an ally. Joan of Arc was accompanied by her angels. Socrates had his daimon. Indeed, the heroes and heroines of myths and fairy tales were never expected to accomplish their brave deeds alone or un-aided. Instead, they were granted a savvy and canny guide from the other side. One of the greatest sources of courage in my life has been the insight and wisdom I have received from the invisible world of gods and god-desses, spirit and animal guides, and angels. As fright-ened and alone as I have sometimes felt in the "real" world, my spirit-world companions have always been there to help me along the way.

To call upon the assistance of your invisible com-panion, you may want to find a secluded place where you can sit in silence. To strengthen the focus of your attunement, it helps to light a candle or incense as a way of "drawing a curtain" between yourself and the dis-tractions of the world. After you have done that, mentally draw a circle of light around the circumference of the spot where you are sitting. Further deepen the

A ship in port is safe, but that is not what ships are built for.

BENAZIR BHUTTO,
FORMER PRIME MINISTER OF
PAKISTAN AND FIRST FEMALE
HEAD OF AN ISLAMIC COUNTRY
IN MODERN HISTORY

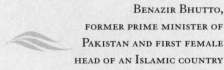

silence by repeating a favorite prayer or breathing practice. After you are centered, call into the circle before you the fear that you are currently facing. Perhaps it is the boss who intimidates you at work, or maybe it is the fear of failure you risk by undertaking a creative venture. It could be that you are afraid of financial loss or the absence of respect from loved ones and friends. It may even be the loss of the security of one's family or home. Whatever the fear, name it and face it.

> *Stay with me, God. The night is dark,*
> *The night is cold: my little spark*
> *Of courage dies. The night is long;*
> *Be with me, God, and make me strong.*
>
> "A Soldier—His Prayer,"
> ST. I FROM A POEM FOUND ON A SCRAP
> OF PAPER IN A SLIT TRENCH IN
> TUNISIA DURING THE BATTLE
> OF EL AGHEILA, PRINTED IN
> *Poems from the Desert,* BY MEMBERS
> OF THE BRITISH EIGHTH ARMY

After you have directly confronted your fear, invoke the presence of the Divine. Ask that, if your undertaking is in harmony with the will of God, you be granted an ally to assist you. With your consciousness still as a mirror, allow an image to arise from the depths. If you are embarking upon an artistic adventure, perhaps your guide will be one of the nine muses, or an artist from the past. If it is a political quest, maybe your guide will be one of the traditional heroes, such as Joan of Arc. Or your guide could be an animal that sustains you with courage, an angel, or an ancestor from your family past whose work you are carrying forward. You could also feel your guide simply as a strong, but nameless, presence by your side. After asking for your ally's blessing on your quest, give thanks for the assistance that has been provided to you.

TALISMANS AND COLORS OF COURAGE

As it is told in the Greek myth of Perseus, the jealous king who has adopted the young man sends him on a dangerous quest to obtain the snake-tressed head of the wicked Medusa. Frightened for his life—for one glance from Medusa will turn a man to stone—Perseus is heartened by the sudden appearance of the god Mercury. The fleet-footed god gives Perseus a magical pouch, then advises him to seek out three things he will need for his journey: a shield as bright as a mirror, a pair of winged sandals, and a swordlike sickle. By his wits, Perseus obtains these magical objects from the three Grey Women and successfully accomplishes his mission. With his shield as a mirror, he captures Medusa's reflection, then cuts off her head in a single blow with his magic sickle. Placing her head in Mercury's pouch, Perseus uses his sandals to fly swiftly through the air back home to his kingdom.

There is wisdom in this myth, for it tells us that courage flourishes best when it is mediated by attributes such as intelligence and skill. Courage, in other words, is an energy to be used for something, rather than an end in itself. Thus, knights held banners aloft as they rode into battle, and for centuries, individuals have carried talismans to protect them and make them brave. Indeed, the quality of courage has always been draped in rich colors and ornate symbolism. Thus, one way to further enhance courage in your own life is to choose a symbol or talisman that evokes the cause or ideal toward which you are working. You may even wish to find small replicas of these symbols and place them on your altar or somewhere where they can draw the magnetism of courage into your life. The following list of accoutrements traditionally associated with the quality of courage may help to get you started on your quest:

> *Freedom is a system based on courage.*
>
> CHARLES PEGUY, FROM *Halevy,*
> *Life of Charles Peguy*

THE SWORD—Symbol of intelligence and wisdom, the sword is a tool of mental clarity and discernment. It can be used to "cut through" fear and doubt, and to focus one's energy on the goal to be achieved.

THE CHALICE—The feminine image of courage, the chalice is symbolic of nurturing and compassion—the "deep love" recognized by the sage Lao-tzu as the secret of true courage.

THE COLOR RED—Bright red is the color of blood, fire, and flags. It heartens, quickens, and stimulates the life force. It gives strength, power, and passion. The color of action, ardour, and enthusiasm, it is the traditional color for Irish warriors. Tinged with violet, red became purple—the imperial color of nobles, generals, patricians, and emperors.

A BANNER—Flown high above knights and soldiers as they went into battle, a banner or pennant declared on whose behalf one was being courageous. If you had a banner, what would it proclaim? For whom are you courageous? For what are you courageous?

A SHIELD—When we are called upon to have courage, it requires of us that we enter into a risky situation where it is likely we could be wounded through some kind of failure or loss. A shield symbolizes the necessity of protecting oneself and defends that within us which is most vulnerable to attack.

GET PHYSICAL WITH MARS

While Mars is a male god traditionally associated with masculine pursuits such as war and conquest, astrologers know that Mars is an archetypal energy equally found in the charts of women as well. In my own chart, for instance, Mars plays a prominent role, conjunct my rising sign in Virgo and in the first house of Aries. The natural ruler of Aries in the Zodiac, Mars is the sign of initiative, risk-taking, and adventure. A true pioneer, Mars takes us to the edges of all that is known and secure. He endows physical strength, athletic ability, and in-your-face boldness. His color is red; his element fire; his quality courage; his animal the ram. He is fierce, warrior energy—something that we must all call upon at one point or another in the course of our lives.

Mars is the god to call upon when your fear looms larger than your courage and threatens to render you paralyzed. At that moment, it helps to simply picture the god himself: even a woman will need assistance from her masculine side. You may imagine Mars as I do, outfitted in a royal red tunic, ornate breastplate strapped over his broad chest, leather sandals, and a brass helmet. His sword glitters at his side, its handle resplendent with jewels. His eyes flash fire and lightning; his body is all sinew and muscle.

Oh courage . . . oh yes! If only one had that. . . . Then life might be liveable, in spite of everything.

HENRIK IBSEN,
Hedda Gabler

Because Mars represents raw power and crude energy, however, his is not an energy to call upon while in a meeting, or even while meditating. Rather, Mars is a visceral god who is best experienced when exercising: running, fast walking, hiking, or in the midst of sweaty aerobic exercise. Then, the fear that has gripped your body, the anxiety that permeates your being, is melted away in the heat of Mars's burning energy. Those athletic highs are peak "Mars moments" when a person is imbued with raw, forceful energy and warriorlike strength—necessary qualities that support the flowering of courage in your life.

Indeed, it may sound silly, but in the spirit of "if it works, do it," one of my personal favorite "courage rituals" is to dance or sing along to popular music. There is nothing like the hard, gutsy beat of rock and roll to raise my spirits and stir my juices. If I feel stuck, or blocked by forces more powerful than myself, I put on a favorite piece of music and dance away. If I don't have the house all to myself, then I get in the car, roll up the windows, and turn up the radio full blast. One of my favorites is the theme song to *Chariots of Fire.* The musical score is a perfect accompaniment to the opening movie scene of the young athletes running along the beach; in my imagination, I run, too—filled with the joy and pleasure of being alive. Another piece of music with a feisty, high-spirited beat is by the New Radicals, "You Only Get What You Give." While some of the lyrics are aimed at teens, some phrases work just as well for adults in need of an energy surge—giving us a sense that, no matter how hard life gets, we'll find the "music inside" to make it through: "But when the night is falling and you cannot find the light, if you feel your dream is dying, hold tight, you've got the music in you."

✫

MEDITATION ON NIKE ATHENA, GODDESS OF VICTORY

Victory is the crowning outcome of all our courageous efforts. Whether we have used our courage to overcome personal limitations in order to become accomplished in an art or skill, or whether we have called upon our courage to survive insurmountably difficult circumstances, victory is that one, triumphal moment when we can celebrate the successful outcome of all our strivings. Recognizing that courage was an energy that could be drawn forth from even the most reluctant hero by the promise of victory, the Greeks created a special goddess, Nike. The constant companion of Athena, Nike was at her side as she led armies into battle—but only for just causes. Beautifully imaged in the fifth century B.C. marble statue *Winged Victory of Samothrace,* Nike is a study in motion. Though headless, enormous, feathered, graceful wings extend behind her, the whole of her body is a fluid stream of upward motion, as if she were running forward to leap into the sky. One can only imagine her head tilted backward, face turned heavenward in the joy that comes from the sweet taste of victory.

For man, as for flower and beast and bird, the supreme triumph is to be most vividly, most perfectly alive.

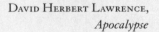

DAVID HERBERT LAWRENCE,
Apocalypse

To meditate on Nike Athena, as she is sometimes called, imagine her at your side when you are facing your most difficult moments: when you are most afraid, dispirited, or lacking in courage. You may also want to summon her spirit when you are wondering why you are even trying to accomplish the task set forth before you—in other words, when life lacks meaning and all your efforts seem futile. Then is the time to feel the subtle, upward rush of her wings, the spirit of victory whirling around you, enlivening your energy and inspiring you with the courage you need to keep on going. She is your constant companion; she walks beside those whose fate in life is to be called upon to have great courage. And with her blessing, you can achieve your aim. Indeed, those who are the victors in life know that it is not the achievement of one's goal that is sweetest in the end, but the glorious feeling of satisfaction when, in spite of everything they have had to work to overcome, a person can say to themselves, "I did it."

> *The only courage that matters is the kind that gets you from one moment to the next.*
>
> MIGNON McLAUGHLIN,
> WRITER

RECOMMENDED READING

The Awakened Warrior: Living with Courage, Compassion & Discipline, edited by Rick Fields (Tarcher/Putnam, 1994)

The Courage to Be by Paul Tillich (Yale University Press, 1980)

Finding My Voice by Diane Rehm (Knopf, 1999)

Freeing the Soul From Fear by Robert Sardello (Riverhead Books, 1999)

The Grimke Sisters from South Carolina, Pioneers for Woman's Rights and Abolition by Gerda Lerner (Schocken Books, 1973)

The Heroine's Journey: Woman's Quest for Wholeness by Maureen Murdock (Shambhala, 1990)

Isak Dinesen: The Life of a Storyteller by Judith Thurman (St. Martin's Press, 1982)

Joan of Arc: By Herself and Her Witnesses by Regine Pernoud (Scarborough House, 1994)

Noor-un-nisa Inayat Khan (Madeleine) by Jean Overton Fuller (East West Publications, 1971)

Out of Africa and Shadows on the Grass by Isak Dinesen (Vintage Books, 1985)

Personal History by Katherine Graham (Vintage, 2000)

The Places That Scare You: A Guide to Fearlessness in Difficult Times by Pema Chodron (Shambhala, 2001)

Sojourner Truth: A Life, A Symbol by Nell Irvin Painter (W.W. Norton & Co., 1997)

Uppity Women of Ancient Times by Vicki Leon (Conari Press, 1995)

The Warrior Queens by Antonia Fraser (Knopf, 1989)

What Every American Should Know About Women's History: 200 Events That Shaped Our History by Christine Lunardini, Ph.D. (Adams Media Corporation, 1997)

SUGGESTED MUSIC

Meditative Listening

> *Antarctica* by Vangelis, audio CD
> *Beethoven's Ninth Symphony,* audio CD
> "Voices"; "Echoes"; "Messages" by Vangelis, from *Voices*, audio CD

For Running or Dancing

> *Beggars and Saints* by Jai Uttal, audio CD
> "Chariots of Fire" by Vangelis, from *Themes*, audio CD
> *Journey of the Drum* by Sounds of Blackness, audio CD
> *New Beginnings* by Tracy Chapman, audio CD
> "Sweet Honey in the Rock*," Selections* 1976–88, audio CD
> *Totem* by Gabrielle Roth, audio CD
> *Xena: Warrior Princess*, audio CD
> "You Get What You Give," by New Radicals, *Maybe You've Been Brain-washed Too*

CHAPTER TWO

The Feminine Face of Faith

SINCE EARLIEST CHILDHOOD, MY LIFE HAS BEEN CRADLED BY FAITH IN AN invisible presence. Along the way, I have called this presence by many names: God, Fate, God the Mother, Nature, my Higher Self. But named or nameless, this mysterious force has always been there, inaudibly coursing through my life. As sweet and loving as this presence has oftentimes felt, it has also been a force with which to be reckoned. As a child growing up in the Catholic Church, as a young woman exploring Sufi mysticism, in midlife discovering the symbolic world of the psyche through dreams and therapy, and as a writer seeking to articulate in words the inexpressible mysteries of the Divine, I have been urged by this presence ever deeper into what I can only describe as a lifelong spiritual quest.

In the "Awakening of Faith," a commentary on the Mahayana Shradkotpada Shastra by the Indian sage Ashva Ghosha, Master Paramartha writes that as advanced Boddhisattvas practice the true Samadhi of Mind-Essence, they will acquire ten great treasures; the sixth being that "their faith in the purposive good-will of the Tathagatas and of the wisdom and compassion of Buddhahood will increase."

In the book of faith that is the story of my life, no single moment stands out as the one when I "found God." Theologian Paul Tillich has defined faith as the state of being "ultimately concerned." In this sense, I have always had faith, because I have always been fascinated by the larger questions of reality. To begin with, spirit was never separate from my life. I grew up in a hundred-year-old farmhouse that pulsed with the psychic energy of ghosts and spirits past. Partly because of my mother's own strong spiritual bent, I had no trouble believing in fairies, angels, and other "invisibles." Although I later came to feel discomfort with the Catholic Church, as a child I loved to pray to Jesus and Mary. Nature, too, was part of this early tapestry of belief: Once while walking down a country lane on a lyrically beautiful spring day, I turned my head to watch a flight of birds. Suddenly, it was as if the whole world tilted, a veil parted, and a luminous energy suffused everything with a pearl-golden light. In poetic language, you could say that the heavens opened up, and for one moment, I had stepped beyond the ordinary boundary of time and glimpsed reality as it truly is.

I was also, and still am, a vivid dreamer. As a child, I often had dreams that were "out of body" experiences. One of the most dramatic dreams I recall was of being on an ancient, black barge that was supernaturally large and crowded with people in robes. As an adult, I recognized the barge from Egyptian mythology as the boat that ferries souls to the other side. I came to interpret that dream as an initiation into my lifelong involvement in the esoteric mysteries. The seminal spiritual event of my youth, however, happened after I had dropped out of my first year in college. Disappointed by the lack of "true" knowledge for which I had been searching, I had moved back home to study spirituality on my own.

Then one night I was invited to attend a lecture at Unity Village given by a Sufi teacher named Pir Vilayat Inayat Khan. The instant he sat down and began to speak, I knew this was my teacher, and his teachings were my path. At the end of the lecture, I signed up to attend a meditation camp that was being held in Arizona. With her long blonde hair and enormous blue eyes, the woman behind the registration table looked like an angel to me. Her name was Taj, and that was our first encounter as lifelong soul sisters. Many months passed after that evening, however, and no word came regarding registration for the camp I so eagerly awaited. It was 1971—years before the spiritual movement became as organized as it is today. Feeling frightened that I might never see my newfound teacher and friend again, I fell asleep one afternoon and had the following dream: I was sitting in a room with all my friends. Suddenly, I found myself standing in a small, beautiful sanctuary with gold walls engraved with symbols. In the center of this sanctuary was a lectern; on it was an enormous, ancient book. The pages of this book were made of old parchment and were covered in a dense script. Beside the book stood a very wise, holy Indian man, dressed in black robes and with some kind of black turban on his head. Though I don't remember the words I read, I understood in the dream that this man was the author, and that the text was a book of timeless wisdom.

At just this moment in the dream, I was jerked awake by the loud ringing of the phone. When I picked it up, a woman identified herself as the director of the upcoming Sufi camp. Through a haze of sleep, I listened in amazement as she began to give me directions to the camp's location, appropriately named Paradise, Arizona. A few weeks later, I arrived by Greyhound bus at the camp, where I found my spiritual community, my spiritual teacher, my husband—and my dear soul sister, Taj. There, too, I saw pictures of Hazrat Inayat Khan, the father of Pir Vilayat, the Indian mystic who had founded the Sufi Order in the West in 1910—and the mysterious wise man in my dream. Not long after this, I moved to California, where I married and lived with my husband in a Sufi communal household. There I dedicated myself to raising my three children and doing spiritual work: studying Sufism, teaching meditation classes, and helping to run a spiritual center. Among my sweetest memories are the weekly women's meditation classes I attended, where a small circle of friends regularly meditated on women saints.

> Faith consists in believing when it is beyond the power of reason to believe. It is not enough that a thing be possible for it to be believed.
>
> VOLTAIRE

FINDING A FAITH-HOLDER

My close friend Susan likes to say that women act as "faith-holders" for one another. What she means by this is that a true soul sister can help her friend stay focused and centered on her quest to live her best life and fulfill a cherished ideal. By doing this, a woman helps to keep the faith in her friend's unlived potential, even when the rest of the world is doubting or rejecting her goals as impossible dreams. In my own life, I have been blessed with women friends who have never given up faith in me as a writer or as a mother. Says Taj, "We have to have somebody who is on our side. Sometimes it only takes one person to help us feel we're not alone."

To strengthen the quality of faith in your life, seek out a close woman friend who can hold aloft the light of faith and hope whenever you feel overcome by doubt. Just to hear a friend voice her confidence in you can help disperse the fog of confusion and help guide you back to your path. The strength of her faith in you can help you keep faith with your inner guidance.

Likewise, you may want to practice "giving the gift of faith" to your own close friends. Perhaps you have a friend who is struggling to hold her marriage together, get her doctorate, paint, or start her own business. Let her know that you are proud of her efforts—that you have no doubt she will one day succeed, and that you are there for her. As I have discovered, to have just one friend who never doubts the successful outcome of your efforts—whatever form that might take—is a priceless treasure beyond measure.

Though the first phase of my spiritual explorations were marked by certainty and devotion to one particular path, the second phase ushered in a period when I began to restlessly doubt the direction of my life. Content with my inner work, I felt that I had no real connection in the outer world except through my husband and sons. Suddenly, it was no longer enough to be a seeker after God. Instead, it became important to find out how that knowledge fit into the world in which I lived. Was it useful? Did it help to alleviate the suffering of others? And what was my role in life? It was at that time that I took up my work as a writer, gradually lessening my external involvement with the Sufi Order but always inwardly connected through my practices. Now, age fifty and looking back over the last several decades, I see how skepticism and belief worked together to help me achieve a more mature faith grounded in the everyday world.

Belief is the food of the believer; it is the sustenance of his faith. It is on belief he lives, not on food and water. Faith is the ABC of the realization of God; this faith begins by prayer.

HAZRAT INAYAT KHAN

Indeed, the golden strand of faith threading my life has been plaited together with the darker thread of doubt. For while faith in a divine intelligence has provided me with an unerring sense of guidance, acting on it has sometimes cast me adrift from more familiar moorings. And because I increasingly came to rely upon a faith that stemmed from underground forces deep within myself, rather than from an external religious authority, its promptings have often left me feeling alone in the world. There have been times over the decades of my spiritual quest, for instance, when I have longed for the secure haven of a traditional belief system. I have wanted to consolidate my jumble of prayer, therapy, meditation, writing, and occult interests into one path—be it Christian, psychic, Sufi, astrologer, or inspirational writer. Naming my explorations, I have thought, might make me feel less isolated, less odd. If only I could give my organic inner life an official-sounding label, I would find my place in the outer world. Over the years, though, as these disparate elements within me wore against one another—the way wind, ocean, and rock wear against one another—I began to see that my spiritual path was taking on its own form, as naturally beautiful as the gracefully shaped driftwood lying on the beach. I began to see that the spiritual phenomena shaping my destiny—the dreams, visions, and intellectual insights—were as profoundly real as the elemental energies that shape the earth. To recognize my spiritual path as being shaped by the natural forces of mystical experience rather than by the external codes of organized religion has been both comforting and empowering. But more than that, it has truly been the only way that I have found that I can live.

My personal journey of faith is not unlike that of many contemporary women whose spiritual quests have led them down labyrinthine paths filled with strange twists and odd turns. For many, the search has turned on the question of how to find a tradition that answered the needs of their own uniquely feminine souls. Rather than a paternal organization who authorized what they should believe and how they should behave, they sought a faith that nurtured a direct, intimate connection between themselves and the mysteries of creation. Rather than worship a far-distant presence in some transcendent heaven, they sought a knowable God present in the fields and forests, the kitchens, offices, and schoolrooms of the everyday working world. Some were able to do this within an established tradition while at the same time working to transform patriarchal views that excluded images of God as woman, and that refused women positions of authority. Others like myself chose to explore more mystical, unconventional forms of spirituality, patching together a spirit-quilt, rich in color and diverse in pattern. By improvising and improving upon what was available to them, women seekers today have become creative innovators—spiritual artists and entrepreneurs—within the field of religion. In this revolutionary process, women have both kept the faith and reconceptualized it along feminist lines.

It is important to point out that the issue is not that men's and women's souls require separate faiths. After all, as the Sufi scholar Annemarie Schimmel has written in *My Soul Is a Woman: The Feminine in Islam,* "There ought to exist no difference between man and woman in the realm of spiritual life." Rather, the task for women, as well as men, has been to bring into balance scales that have tipped too far in one direction too long. Even the male-oriented religion of Islam, Schimmel points out, recognizes that "life cannot exist without the polarity of man and woman." The Koranic verse (Sura 2:187) that says to a man "Women are a raiment for you and ye are raiment for them," Schimmel explains, means that "one is always the altar ego of the other." Likewise, commenting on the feminine face of faith, Suffragan Bishop Jane Holmes Dixon quotes from the first chapter of Genesis, "So God created man in his own image, in the image of God created he him; male and female created he them." Thus, as women speak out more about their faith and assume more leadership roles, says Dixon, they "hold up and give witness to the creation in the (female) image of God."

Why has the resurrection of the feminine image of the Divine in our time proved so important to women's faith? Feminist theologian Carol Christ answers that question when she writes that "The simplest and most profound meaning of the image of the Goddess is the legitimacy and goodness of female power, the female body, and female will."[1] Thus, the image of God as Goddess has become a potent symbol of those values that, along with women, have been exiled from the public square of religion for millennia. These values include such long-forgotten "feminine" elements common to both genders, like dreams, psychic phenomena, the wisdom of the body, child care, the subjective realm of emotions, and the divinity found within the natural world. "The Goddess' coming does not mean a rejection of ethics," writes Jungian Edward Whitmont in *The Return of the Goddess,* but "a new ethics more deeply rooted in individual conscience."

> *Success is in store for the faithful, for faith ensures success.*
>
> HAZRAT INAYAT KHAN

Faith is often the quality associated with miracles. I believe the greatest miracle wrought by the newfound feminist spirituality movement in our time has been this: it has restored to us our faith in life itself—in the awesome processes of birth and death, and in the wisdom of the natural world within which we are all merely creatures. But most of all, it has given women the faith to believe in the truth of their own experiences, to trust the voice of their innermost hearts, and to value the firsthand knowledge they have gained on their own. The following stories from my own life, from women religious from the past, and from women seekers in the present is a small offering showing the miracle of faith at work in women's lives.

LOSING AND FINDING FAITH

The simplest definition of faith is the innocent trust that, despite all the bad things that can happen, everything, in the end, will work out for the best. Faith gives us reason to live, when most of us, most of the time, have little idea why we are alive and why we must suffer as we do. "For we walk by faith, not by sight," says the Bible (11 Corinthians) sagely. Implicit within faith, for instance, is a constancy of belief in something invisible and even what some might call impossible, such as faith in the lofty ideals of world peace or an end to hunger despite all evidence to the contrary. Thus, the Old Testament (Hebrews 11:1) holds that faith is "the substance of things hoped for, the evidence of things not seen." Equally implicit within faith is the notion that while we are blind to the reason why things are the way they are, we must somehow find it within ourselves to accept the destiny life hands us. Like Job, the faith of even the strongest believer is tested by circumstances that do not go our way. "We are at the mercy of time, culture, family, even love," writes Thomas Moore in his commentary on *The Book of Job* (Riverhead, 1998). "We have the choice either to live with a controlling ego, where we feel we must understand ourselves and our world, or to submit to a greater design that we don't understand and over which we have little control." I have come to think of faith as a quality that is refined like gold through the "yin and yang" process of loss and rediscovery, skepticism and confidence, courageous defiance and willing submission.

Twice in my own life, for example, I have come to the edge of the abyss of total doubt and darkness, only to be pulled back at the last moment by the saving grace of faith. The first time this occurred was at the age of thirty-four. A young mother with three sons, I had just moved with my husband from the lovely Southwest city of Santa Fe to the highly charged East Coast metropolis of Washington, D.C. It was a move that entailed a separation from many of my Sufi friends with whom I had shared the closest spiritual bonds. I had been used to living in places like Marin County, California, where I had lived before moving to Santa Fe, where the eccentric and the unusual was accepted. Now I suddenly found myself at cocktail parties confronted by two questions: "Where did you go to school?" and "What do you do?" Still just a struggling writer, a full-time mom, and a closet mystic, I had no college degree and didn't "do" anything, or so it seemed.

For the first time in my life I tried to "go straight." I concealed my past as a spiritual seeker and made up stories about my name, Pythia (a name I had received from my Sufi teacher, Pir Vilayat). I threw myself into decorating my house, raising my kids, and toyed with notions like fox hunting and stock investments. I gave up my interest in all things magical, like the tarot and astrology. But the more I tried to cut off my innate spirituality, the more depressed I became and the louder and more insistent my dreams grew. Repeatedly I dreamed that I was going mad; that I was homeless, abandoned, poor; that I was being taken away in a straightjacket to the mental asylum. I couldn't write or meditate, and I fell into a deeply melancholic state.

> *O thou of little faith, wherefore didst thou doubt?*
>
> MATTHEW 14:31

Feeling desperate, cut off from my network of emotional support, I turned to books for guidance, stumbling in the process upon *Memories, Dreams, Reflections,* the autobiography of the Swiss psychologist Carl Jung. Because Jung valued the spiritual world and treated spiritual and psychic phenomenon as real rather than as signs of pathology, and because he regarded dreams as messengers from a person's "Self," or soul, I decided to go into Jungian therapy to seek help for my problems adjusting to a new city. Like my initiation into the Sufi Order, my initiation into the underworld of the psyche was a profound juncture on my personal spiritual path. This important turning point in my life was marked by a dream. In it, I awoke to see Carl Jung sitting, his back to me, at the foot of my bed. In his hand he held a thermos of hot coffee—nourishment for the long "night sea" journey that lay ahead, and a symbol of awakening. Prompted by that dream, I sought the guidance of a Jungian therapist, a woman who eventually helped to heal the faith in life I had once enjoyed in lush abundance, but which had now become broken.

She did this by helping me rediscover the meaning hidden like a treasure in my own individual life, rather than the transpersonal dimensions of my spirit I had explored in Sufism and other Eastern traditions. Finally, I began to glimpse the answer to those timeless questions: What was the meaning of my life? Why had my spirit been incarnated in a body on earth? For what purpose did I exist? Ever so slowly, like the design of a Chinese hexagram, the archetypal pattern underlying my life began to emerge. Through my dreams and my psyche, I once again became connected to the invisible spirit of guidance that had always been at work behind the more visible scenes of my life. I began to cultivate an attitude of sacred reverence for what are called in Indian and African cultures "Big Dreams" as the voice of the Divine. The faith I had once placed in the hands of others, I now entrusted to an inner wise woman—an oracle, or seer, you could say. I began to write again, taking on assignments that dealt more with the soul and psychology. Like a key fitting into a lock, the "right" publications appeared. Energy for life flooded back, and I took up my studies in astrology again. But most important, I learned to become deeply attuned to the psyche, the natural world within my own self. I slowed down and enjoyed the "nonproductive" moments of chatting, eating, and hanging out with my kids. I began to spend more time within the solitude of nature, discovering along the river trails I hiked a quiet reassurance in the steady presence of Mother Nature. As the Jungian thinker Edward Whitmont wrote, I had discovered the "Goddess as guardian of human interiority." For while the patriarchy regulated the externals of human behavior, devaluing "individualized instinct, feeling, and intuition," he wrote, the new orientation valued "the indwelling source of authentic conscience and spiritual guidance, the divinity within."[2] Slowly, over the years, my spirit became reborn and refreshed through an entirely new source of faith—one that has complemented my spiritual practice of meditation.

Like the first test, the second challenge to my faith came as a complete shock. For most of my adult life, I had longed to write and publish a book. After many years of writing successfully for various publications, I finally signed a contract with a major publisher. I poured myself into conducting lengthy interviews and extensive research. Then, quite unexpectedly, my father became ill, eventually dying from cancer. Taking care of him in the final stages of his illness and handling his estate delayed me from meeting my book deadline. After finally completing the book, my agent phoned to tell me my book had been cancelled. I was devastated. For the second time in my life, I found myself unable to get out of bed. Next to raising my children, writing a book had been the most important thing in my life, and I had failed. I stopped writing and lost faith that I would write again. I contemplated other careers.

One in whom persuasion and belief
Had ripened into faith, and faith become
A passionate intuition.

WILLIAM WORDSWORTH,
"The Excursion"

THE COLOR OF FAITH IS GOLD

The color of faith is gold, forged through the dark doubts and confusions that are common to the human condition. If you find that faith is lacking in your life—that your spirit is weakened from doubt and worry—place a gold cloth on your altar. Light gold candles in your home. Find a piece of gold jewelry, and either wear it, or simply rub it to get the feeling for how substantial and strong faith is. Put sunflowers around your house; wear bright-yellow clothes. Each morning, look a the golden disk of the sun in the sky and let the warmth of its rays fill you with faith in the goodness of life. Pay attention to the cycles of the sun as it rises through the sky during the day, sets during the evening, then arises once again out of darkness. Let your spirit be strengthened by the cycles of the sun rising and setting with reassuring regularity. Finally, you may want to concentrate on the color of gold as a yellow light suffusing your body, heart, and soul, radiating the light of faith throughout your whole being.

Then one night I dreamed that I was walking along a beautiful beach at night. The stars were out, twinkling like jewels, although the ocean waves swelled with turbulence. Suddenly, a helicopter painted in brilliant hues with intricate designs landed on the beach before me. A Coptic priestess, tall, regal, shimmering in light, and clothed in luminous yellow robes, emerged. Putting her arm around my shoulders, she drew me close to her and then bent my head over, helping me to vomit out all my doubts, fears, and confusions—a stream of darkness literally poured out of my body as I wretched and heaved. When I looked up, the turbulent ocean waves had become calm and placid.

When I awoke from this dream, I felt physically healed of my despair, as if the Goddess herself had placed her healing hands on my soul and cured it of its illness. As, in fact, she had. Once again, my energy bounded back. I recovered my sense of faith that things would work out—even if I had no idea what that might mean and even if I had lost the thing in life that mattered the most! Indeed, not long after that dream, I met my publisher at Tarcher, who discovered my connection to the Sufis and asked me to help Pir Vilayat write a book on his life's teachings. The process of writing his book *Awakening: A Sufi Experience* was one of coming full circle and instilled in me even greater faith in the hand of fate guiding my life.

If life is about learning a form of higher wisdom, then what I gleaned from these experiences is the importance of accepting the unacceptable, to trust that there is a purposeful design in the limitations that block or constrict our efforts to move in a certain direction. For if there are any constants in life, one of them is that we will surely fail—whether it is a life goal that has been abruptly aborted or a relationship that has ended, we will come to a place where we have been driven to our knees, stripped clean of any pretense of pride or self-righteousness. A defeat for the ego, Carl Jung said repeatedly, is a victory for the Self, for then a genuinely spiritual attitude is born out of that failure. Indeed, if, as Pir Vilayat has taught his students, the soul's journey is about manifesting the Divine Qualities, then perhaps it is through the process of failure, loss, and confusion that the Universe cultivates within us the quality of religious faith.

There lives more faith in honest doubt,
Believe me, than in half the creeds.

ALFRED LORD TENNYSON

In many ways, for example, faith is a quality that is first understood through its absence. I know what faith feels like, for instance, when I have lost it, when I have suffered a terrible disillusionment or betrayal of some kind. Then, it is as if the world has suddenly drained of all color; the meaning of life has vanished; an animating spirit has departed. The person I loved is not the person I thought he or she was; the job I worked toward for so long is suddenly boring; the teacher I have studied with is not the wise, all-knowing guru after all. Yet ironically, it is in the midst of just such moments that the possibility for true transformation exists. If we stay with our feelings of emptiness and disillusionment and allow ourselves to become humble before the awe and mystery of existence, then another layer of reality transpires and a deeper dimension of meaning that had previously been hidden emerges. "Job's life and possessions are restored to him after he discovers the virtue of silence," writes Thomas Moore in his commentary, and only then does the voice of God speak to Job from the whirlwind.

The voice in the whirlwind that brings an end to Job's troubles is the sound of meaning that creates harmony out of the turmoil of our life. For if courage gives us the spirit we need to fully engage life's challenges and kindle the spark of life in others, then faith is the quality that imbues the struggles we endure along the way with meaning. For without faith, the inevitable failures and tragedies of everyday life can appear random and senseless. Those who lack the quality of faith answer Einstein's famous question—"Is the universe a friendly or unfriendly place?"—in the negative. For those who lack faith altogether, life is hostile and unforgiving; death is an unequivocal end. But those who have both tested and proved their faith answer Einstein's question with a positive yes, trusting that though they may not know all the answers to the riddle of existence, God's creation rests upon the ground of essential goodness.

> Faith is "the sense of life by virtue of which man does not destroy himself, but lives on. It is the force by which he lives."
>
> WILLIAM JAMES,
> *The Varieties of
> Religious Experience*

For this reason faith is a life-shaping quality: through its prism, the seeming chaos of the universe falls into an elegant pattern. All the disorganized puzzle pieces of our lives assemble into a recognizable picture, and what seems incomprehensible suddenly makes sense when viewed through the eyes of faith. Faith is also an active, intuitive sense, a homing device that allows a person to feel their way forward through life's dark passages. Placing their faith in the unseen hand of destiny, the faithful trust that, no matter the particular outcome, reality will ultimately right itself according to God's overarching design. If heaven and hell are states of mind, as some contend, then faith and doubt are the paradise and inferno of our souls.

Getting to the state of faith, however, is the exacting journey of a lifetime. That is why, though faith comes in many forms—faith in one's country, one's family, or a political cause—religious belief offers valuable insights into the nature of faith itself. In a delightful story taken from his own life, Hazrat Inayat Khan, the Sufi mystic who was the founder of the Sufi Order in the West, sheds light on the religious function of faith. Every time he parted from his spiritual teacher, he writes, Abu Hashim Madani would offer this blessing: "May your iman [faith] be strengthened." A young man at the time, Khan wondered why his teacher, a revered murshid in the Sufi Chisti mystical tradition, would offer such simple advice. Why, Inayat Khan asked himself, did his teacher not say, "May you become illuminated," or "May your powers be great," or "May you become perfect"? As he pondered his teacher's advice, however, the realization began to dawn on him that "no blessing is more valuable and important than this. For every blessing is attached to a conviction. Where there is no conviction, there is nothing. The secret of healing, the mystery of evolving, the power of all attainments, the way to spiritual realization all come from the strengthening of that belief which is a conviction, so that nothing can ever change it."[3]

Women Faithful from History:

❖

Rābi'ah and Perpetua

Most of us have learned about the spiritual power of faith from the examples set by the world's great prophets. Buddhists think of the Buddha, for instance, who had faith enough to abandon worldly wealth and prestige in order to follow the inner promptings of his soul. Jews and Christians meditate on the Old Testament prophet Abraham, who so trusted the voice of God that he was willing to sacrifice his own son; or on Jesus, who so believed in his Father in heaven that he was able to make the blind see, the dead live, and turn water into wine. Muslims reflect upon the life of Mohammed, whose belief in his nightly revelations was so complete that a timeless religious text, the Holy Koran, was born from him. There literally would be no religion without the originating faith of their founders—no prayers to repeat, rituals to perform, services to attend, or meditations to practice.

It could be said, however, that behind every great prophet stood a woman of equally great spiritual stature: Gautami, the aunt who raised Siddhārtha Gautama, the Buddha, after his mother died and who later founded the first order of Buddhist nuns; Mary, the mother of Jesus, whose example of unshakeable faith in her son still inspires; Sarah, long-suffering, patient wife of Abraham; Khadījah, the wife of Mohammed, whose own faith helped her husband believe in his visions. Indeed as miraculously inspiring as the faith of Jesus, Buddha, Mohammed, Abraham, and other great prophets might be, all the more wondrous and incredible is the faith of women religious throughout the centuries. Excluded from positions of authority, their voices all but ignored, women saints, martyrs, and mystics have believed with a fervor and practiced with a discipline often exceeding that of their male counterparts.

The faith journeys of women have differed from the faith journeys of men

That state of confidence, trust, union with all things, following upon the achievement of moral unity, is the faith-state.

WILLIAM JAMES,
*The Varieties of
Religious Experience*

because they have had to practice their faith within the confines of patriarchal religious doctrines that have doubted, diminished, and undermined the very essence of their feminine being. But as Gerda Lerner has written in her landmark work, *The Creation of Feminist Consciousness: From the Middle Ages to Eighteen-seventy* (Oxford, 1993), there were certain advantages that the religious life offered women. For one thing, life in a convent or as an ascetic freed women from the responsibilities of marriage and child-raising, providing them the opportunity to study and pray. In addition, the ancient tradition of mysticism allowed for a different mode of enlightenment within which the feminine form of spirituality might flourish. Individual inspiration, sudden revelatory insight, and rapturous experiences of unconditional love were the hallmark of all mystics, male and female alike. Thus, if they could not be bishops, roshis, or rabbis, women could find acceptance as mystics. Among these spiritual stars in an all-male firmament were visionaries such as the Christian mystics Hildegard von Bingen and Catherine of Siena, the Hindu saints Mīrā Bāī and Sri Sarada Devi, and the Buddhist saint Sanghamitra, daughter of the emperor Aśoka. Women seekers of all religious traditions owe an enormous debt to these soul sisters who have gone before them. The faith they upheld during the long, dark centuries when women were mostly regarded as "World Mistresses" tempting men away from their religious duties helped illuminate the path for woman religious today.

FAITHFUL PRACTICE

The timeless practices of prayer, meditation, chant, and yoga all help to enhance the quality of faith. Indeed, the many kinds of spiritual discipline could be said to be the key that unlocks the door to the temple of faith. Inside this temple is a sacred well that springs from the intimate knowledge of God. Every prophet and mystic, for example, has left behind some form of a spiritual attunement that emerged from their direct experience of the divine. Over the centuries, like a city that sprang up around this well, layer upon layer of religious practice began to accumulate around a saint or prophet's original inspiration. Faith seekers can turn to this rich repository to help construct a daily discipline, drawing upon the sacred texts of the different faiths for instruction, as well as the wisdom of teachers and instructors in the various traditions.

Therefore, one way to strengthen the quality of faith in your life is to build the foundation of a regular, rhythmic practice. Whether thoughtfully repeating a prayer while attending to its hidden meaning, reciting a sacred phrase, sitting in silence, listening to a sublime piece of music, or attending a yoga class, try to make sacred time a daily ritual. Even walking in nature can be a way to turn your attention toward the deeper side of life and the contemplation of God and the divine. While it is often the case that thoughts and emotions can distract you from your practice, a positive energy builds with repetition and commitment over time. Some say, in fact, that the angels are already there to greet you when you sit before your altar. In time, you may experience a blessed moment of knowing God within the deepest recesses of your soul. It is this wordless experience of grace, the immersion in the sweet nectar of divine being, that is the living source of faith. The miracles that occurred to the holy mystics—the visions, ecstasies, and even psychic and physical phenomena such as the stigmata—all occurred to those whose hearts and minds were finely attuned through spiritual practice. For in seeking to know God directly, we are granted trust, knowledge, and belief.

Rābi'ah

One of the great figures of early Sufism is the eighth-century mystic Rābi'ah al'Adawīyah, often referred to as "Rabi'a pure and simple" and as a "second spotless Mary."[4] Highly respected by all the great Sufi mystics, she is credited as being the representative of the first development of mysticism in Islam, and was considered an authority by her peers, who were mostly men. Within Sufi mysticism "neither male nor female" existed before God as, said the poet 'Attār, it is not "the outward form that matters, but the inner purpose of the heart,"[5] proving that sainthood was open to women as well as men. Still, according to the custom of the time, Rābi'ah's biographer 'Attār wrote of her that "when a woman walks in the way of God she cannot be called a 'woman'" but a "man" whose devotional example should be revered as "manly."[6] Today we might describe Rābi'ah as an extraordinary example of "womanly" faith.

I have faith that yields to none, and ways without reproach, and unadorned simplicity, and blushing modesty.

OVID, *Amores*

According to scholars, Rābi'ah was born into a poor family in Basra, Turkey, in 717 A.D. She was the last of four daughters (her name means "the fourth"). Legend has it that there were no swaddling clothes in which to wrap the newborn child. In great distress, her father fell asleep that night and dreamed that the Prophet Mohammed appeared to him and said, "Do not be sorrowful, for this daughter who is born is a great saint."[7] He then instructed him to go to the local wealthy emir, to remind him that he had forgotten his Friday prayers, and to direct him to pay 400 dinars to Rābi'ah's father as a penance. In spite of this stroke of fortune, Rābiʻah was later orphaned as a young girl after the death of her parents, then sold as a slave to a cruel master. She worked hard cleaning and cooking during the day, then spent the night in prayer. Awakening from sleep suddenly one night, her master happened to look through his bedroom window, where he spied a praying Rābiʻah. A lamp without a chain hung over her head, illuminating her and the entire house in brilliant rays of light. Awed by the magnitude of her religious devotion, her master set her free the next day. Rābiʻah immediately went into the desert, where she lived the life of a recluse; even after her return to the city of Basra, she remained apart, immersing herself in prayer and works of devotion.

> *A faithful friend is the medicine of life.*
>
> *The Apocrypha,*
> ECCLESIASTICUS 6:16

Like her Christian sisters, Rābiʻah turned her back completely on the world, renouncing its pleasures and commitments in service to God. As the years passed, her legend as a saint grew. Day and night, disciples sought her prayers and spiritual counsel. And though she received many offers of marriage—enamored of her piety, even well-known ascetics sought her hand—she refused them all, replying that "My peace, O my brothers, is in solitude, and my Beloved is with me always. For His love I can find no substitute, and His love is the test for me among mortal beings. . . ."[8] Perhaps the most moving element of Rābiʻah's faith is how her passion for the Divine Beloved transformed even the hearts of the most austere Sufi renunciates of her time. In addition to being one of the earliest Sufi mystics, Rābiʻah is credited with being the first to introduce the element of love into Sufism. As Margaret Smith writes in her book on Islamic women saints, most of the early Sufi were motivated by an overwhelming dread of judgment and fear of Hell. Rābiʻah was a strict renunciate herself who voluntarily embraced poverty, refusing even to accept money from her many friends and claiming complete dependence on "Him to whom the world belongs."[9] More radical still, Rābiʻah's faith was not practiced as a means of gaining the reward of Heaven for herself, but of overcoming separation between her soul and the Beloved. Communion with the Divine was the sole aim of Rābiʻah's devotional life.

A famous story about the nature of Rābiʻah's faith illustrates her love for God. According to a popular legend, she ran through the city of Basra one day with a bucket of water in one hand and a burning torch in the other. When asked about her actions, she replied, "I want to pour water into hell and set paradise on fire, so that these two veils disappear and nobody shall any longer worship God out of a fear of hell or a hope of heaven, but solely for the sake of His eternal beauty."[10] Many other miracles are associated with the great saint Rābiʻah, among them that the Kaaba (a Muslim shrine in Mecca) once moved toward her as she made her pilgrimage, that her prayers brought back to life a camel that had died while bearing her on pilgrimage, and that her fingertips glowed like lamps at night. My favorite story about Rābi'ah, however, is a beautiful illustration of the wondrously steadfast quality that characterized the childlike faith she placed in her Beloved.

According to this parable, two well-known religious leaders arrived one day to pay a visit to Rābi'ah. Because they were hungry, Rābi'ah placed two loaves of fresh bread before them. Just before they could begin to eat, however, a beggar passed by and, quite inexplicably, Rābi'ah gave him both loaves. Next, as the story goes, a girl came by bearing many loaves of hot bread. Before serving the bread to her ravenous guests, Rābi'ah counted them; finding that there were only eighteen, she questioned the slave girl, insisting that there should have been twenty, then sent them back. Soon, the girl returned with twenty loaves, which Rābi'ah accepted. Duly puzzled, her guests inquired about the reasons for her odd behavior. Rābi'ah explained that as she had felt humiliated to serve two loaves to her esteemed guests, she had prayed for twenty loaves—"ten for one" to be sent by God. So implicit was her faith, that when the eighteen loaves came, she knew that they were not meant for her, and so sent them back. As it turned out, the slave girl had taken two loaves out for herself, which she then returned after Rābi'ah had questioned her.

> As for those who have faith in God and His messengers and make no distinctions between any of them—to them, in time, will He grant their recompense.
>
> THE KORAN, 4:152, *The Light of Dawn: A Daybook of Verses from the Holy Qu'ran*

Rābi'ah the "pure and simple" lived long into old age, dying in 801 around the age of ninety. Esteemed by many Muslims as the equal to Mary, and compared to Christian mystics such as St. Catherine of Genoa, her faith was the flower of her love for God—a faith that lingers yet like a rare perfume. In the example of her life and in her teachings can be found timeless wisdom on the quality of faith. Even as Job learned through his ordeal the value of patient submission to God's will, so Rābi'ah extolled the same virtue, believing with the Sufis al-Ghazali and al-Qushayri that patience is as "necessary to faith as the head to the body."[11] By patiently enduring the losses, sufferings, and hardships that came her way, Rābi'ah arrived at a humble acceptance of the will of God. Not just patience for life's adversities, but also joyous gratitude for life's gifts is part of faith as "Faith must accept the fact that all benefits come from God and are His free gift...."[12] Rābi'ah could not know that her exemplary life of faith would help pave the way for the full acceptance of women religious centuries later. Because of her unshakeable faith, Rābi'ah stood up to the men in her life—and became legendary as a woman of God.

Perpetua

Among the many stories of Christian saints and martyrs, I have always been drawn to the little-known story of St. Perpetua. On March 7, 203 A.D., she was killed by animals in a prison in Carthage, Africa, for refusing to deny that she was a Christian. While I cannot say if I would give up my life or leave my children for a religious belief—or even if that is a healthy expression of faith today—I find poignant meaning in her story of self-sacrifice according to the historic times in which she lived. Like Joan of Arc, Perpetua was willing to go to the death for her inner convictions. Like Joan of Arc, her faith was marked by a childlike innocence and trust. Even more amazing, her story comes down to us in her own words as she describes the extraordinary vision she received on the eve of her death. As historian Pauline Schmitt Pantel writes in *A History of Women: From Ancient Goddesses to Christian Saints* (Harvard Press, 1992), there are precious few texts that contain the authentic expression of women's feeling throughout history. This autobiographical shard of a 2,000-year-old testimonial written by Perpetua's own hand on the eve of her martyrdom is among them.

She was only twenty-two years old when she was arrested after an edict had been issued banning all forms of proselytism in the Roman Empire, writes Monique Alexander in her introduction to Perpetua's text. The daughter of loving parents, Perpetua was of "distinguished birth and liberal education," and had been married according to the rules for the "marriage of matrons." At the time of her imprisonment, she also had an infant son whom she loved very much. After questioning and a "confession of faith," she was sent to military prison to await the Games held in honor of the birthday of Caesar Geta, the emperor's son. While in prison, her parents visited her. As Perpetua writes, "My father tried to talk me into forsaking my vows. Out of love he stubbornly sought to shake my faith." Perpetua then points to a vase on the ground, asking her father if he could call it by anything other than its true name. When he asserts that he cannot, she replies that "I am the same. I cannot call myself anything other than what I am: a Christian."[13]

Her father's visit, however, paled beside the anguish she suffered over her infant son, writing that she was "tormented by worry for my child." Eventually, after bribing the guards, she was allowed to nurse her child within the prison and

> *A faithful friend is a strong defense: and he that hath found such a one hath found a treasure.*
>
> *The Apocrypha,*
> ECCLESIASTICUS 6:14

comforted her brother by promising him that he could take the child after her death. Still, she writes that she was "consumed with sorrow" at the sight of the suffering she had caused her loved ones.

Perpetua's remarkable testament concludes with an account of a heavenly vision on the eve of the day set for combat—the day of her death. In it, a revered deacon enters the prison and takes her into the amphitheater where he instructs her to have no fear, for "I am with you and will help you." At that point in her vision, the deacon disappears, and she finds herself in the midst of combat, surrounded by beasts and confronted by a "terrifying Egyptian." Suddenly in her vision, she writes, she "became a man." A supernaturally large "Master Gladiator" carrying a green branch with golden apples for the victor appears. Suddenly, she is "lifted up into the air" where she rains down blows on the Egyptian. After smashing his head in victory, the Master Gladiator bestows upon her the victory branch, and she heads for the Gate of the Living. At that moment, writes Perpetua, she awoke from her vision with the sure knowledge that she was fighting the Devil, not animals—and that she would win.

> *Let my faith be as firm as mountains, Lord, standing unshaken through wind and storm.*
>
> HAZRAT INAYAT KHAN

What wisdom can a modern woman of today take from the story of the early Christian martyr Perpetua or the Sufi mystic Rābi'ah? For one thing, the certainty with which both women believed in something invisible, unpopular, and which brought them hardship shows evidence of the dynamic of faith at work. While we may not practice our faith in just the same way today, the ability to trust in one's inner voice and visions regardless of the suffering that engenders, or the criticisms of the outer world it sparks, is what connects women faithful of the past with women faithful in the present.

The Story of Taj,
❉
a Soul Sister

In the Sufi tradition, God is frequently referred to as the "Friend." This is reflected in the tradition of spiritual sisterhood or brotherhood, where two people accompany each other along the path. One of my oldest companions in this regard is my dear friend Taj Glantz. Since I first met her that evening thirty years ago at Unity Village, she has been a constant guide and gentle source of support. Though outwardly she leads a life dramatically different from mystics of past eras, two things remain the same: her unwavering trust in God to guide her life and her faith in the teachings of the Sufi Order.

My friendship with Taj is many layered, ranging from the everyday world of children to the sublime realms of altered consciousness. It was through attending her classes in the early days of the Sufi Order in California that I first learned the art and skill of meditation. As young mothers, we had a lot of fun together raising our children in a Sufi community. Later, as we passed through middle age, we shared our psychological explorations as well. Throughout the years, I have always admired the way her belief in the teachings of Hazrat Inayat Khan has remained unshakeable and undimmed. Today, she is what is called a "Murshida," or woman Sufi teacher. To me, and to many others, she is a woman of exemplary faith.

A petite, youthful-looking woman in her late fifties with corn-golden hair, Taj has large, clear blue eyes that seem to reflect the sky. When I asked her to examine her childhood for hints of the direction she was to take in later life, she replied that her upbringing wasn't particularly religious, and neither was she. Like so many others during the counterculture movement, Taj's first direct encounter with God came during a drug experience in the early sixties. A college student at the University of Iowa, her boyfriend had returned from a trip to Mexico with some psilocybin and, she says, "from one minute to the next there was a complete knowing of spiritual matters. It felt like the veils from my perception were removed and I could see things as they were. I saw that life is about spirit and that there is a life beyond the obvious physical world and an inner connection between everything that exists. It was like the Zen experience of direct knowing through reality instead of through a concept of reality."

Soon after that, Taj and her boyfriend, Mansur, began actively searching for a spiritual path. So when a couple with whom they had been friends in college wrote to them from San Francisco that they had found a teacher, they packed up and drove across country. Their first night in town, their friends took them to visit the Sufi teacher Murshid SAM, where he was reading out loud from the collected works of Hazrat Inayat Khan. "And that was it," recalls Taj of that memorable evening. "I've never had another path or teacher than Inayat Khan, except recently, to study with Hameed Ali, the founder of the Diamond Heart School." Those two simple steps, says Taj—becoming conscious of the spirit behind reality and then finding a teacher and a path—completely shaped the rest of her life. And while it may sound deceptively simple, she says, "it didn't feel simple at the time. I didn't know what I was doing, because I was just following the bread crumbs, following the trail without knowing where it was leading." Still, she says, "There has always been something in me that knows when to move forward in a certain direction. If there is anything about myself that is unadulterated by my personality, it's an inner sense of how to take the next step in life—even if I'm afraid or don't know if I'm doing the right thing, this inner compass has always been there to guide me."

Two years after taking up her studies with Murshid SAM, recalls Taj, she met Pir Vilayat Inayat Khan, the head of the Sufi Order International. By then, she and Mansur had married and started a family. Her regard for Pir Vilayat as a great teacher and as the successor of Hazrat Inayat Khan served to deepen her commitment to the practice of Sufism.

A devoted student of the inner life, Taj's growing knowledge of Inayat Khan's teachings began to attract other Sufi initiates. Soon, she began to offer meditation classes. Because there was little organizational structure in place to guide her, Taj says she feels that she "began to teach precociously, because the situation called for it." As Pir Vilayat was always away travelling, attending to the broad vision of the Sufi Order, his followers, she says, "needed help in understanding the teachings. So I was responding to what seemed to be the need of the situation." Therefore, Taj was often left to her own devices, both as a meditation teacher and also during her own solitary retreats.

"Perhaps you can picture me in a little hut, my children in the care of a babysitter, and the instruction I had [from Pir Vilayat] was 'do some Dhikr' [the repetition of the Arabic phrase 'la ilaha, illa 'llah hu' or, Nothing exists save God]," she says. "This challenging situation turned out to be just the conditions that were necessary for me to learn how to mine the depths of my own self, to become deeply resourceful and find my inner guidance." Over the next decade, guided only by her faith in the teachings of Hazrat Inayat Khan as articulated by Pir Vilayat, says Taj, she was left to "discover the inner world, the inner process with all its strange twists and turns, its pitfalls and glories, for the most part, on my own." Out of this process was born her faith, not just in the teachings of Hazrat Inayat Khan, but also in the value of staying close to her own actual inner experience rather than an external map. The wisdom she gained from her odyssey proved useful to others and over the last several decades Taj has acted as a trusted retreat guide to many others as well.

For Taj, the greatest challenges to her faith have not taken the form of doubting Sufi teachings or questioning the path she has chosen. Rather, she has been tested by the fires of personal relationships. Like many modern women seekers—and unlike her more ancient mystic sisters—Taj was walking the path of interior contemplation while juggling marriage, then divorce and single motherhood. Like the shattering of a crystal that reveals its true shape, however, this unusual life course led Taj in an entirely new direction: the study of human emotions. She went into therapy to deal with her own "human shadow side." Enrolling in college, she began taking courses in psychology with an eye to applying this modern body of knowledge to the age-old teachings on spirituality.

"Acknowledging the very personal pain of my inner struggles and finding the way through them led me in a new spiritual direction which culminated in a deep study of human psychology," she says. Looking back today, she says that this added knowledge proved invaluable as having both perspectives deepened her insight into the goal of spiritual awakening in life—the aim of the Sufi. Likewise, psychology, with its emphasis on healing through connecting to one's authentic feelings, validated the experiences she had had while on meditation retreat as well. It was a perspective that she introduced into her work with her own students: "Working with the actual stuff of our lives (attitudes, feelings, beliefs, self-images)," she says, "is the prima materia of alchemy which is turned into the gold of awakened mind and heart." Indeed, in working with her students, writes Taj, she came to see that guidance is present right in the middle of the experience we are actually having if we can stay "present, aware, curious, open, and non-rejecting . . ."

> *'Tis not the dying for a faith that's so hard, Master Harry—every man of every nation has done that—'tis the living up to it that is so difficult.*
>
> WILLIAM MAKEPEACE
> THACKERAY

Taj's efforts to bring psychology, as well as an awareness of the vestiges of patriarchy and the notion of the Divine Feminine into the more traditionally oriented Sufi Order, however, were initially met with skepticism. "Now it's part of the mainstream. But back then this had never been done before. It wasn't just the Sufi Order, but many groups—Buddhist, Tibetan, and others—were working on the same issues within their own spheres," she says. Persisting in her mission to integrate the psychological with the spiritual, however, other Sufi teachers joined in, and gradually the integration of the emotional life and an appreciation of the Divine Feminine has become more of an accepted part of the Sufi Order.

Nearly thirty-five years later, the sometimes risky adventure of Taj's faith journey has come full circle. Married for the past thirteen years to her husband, Richard, she is enjoying watching her three sons enter adulthood. In addition to the Sufi Order classes, retreats, and seminars that she regularly leads at her home in California and around the world, Taj is also a student of the Diamond Heart and Training Institute where she continues her quest to bring together the spiritual and the psychological. Looking back over her life today, Taj notes that, in spite of the uncertainty and suffering that has marked her life at certain intervals, she has always felt "held by God in a kindly way." Through the experiences of her life, she says that she has come to define faith as a basic trust in the "rightness of reality that is not dependent on any particular outcome—an underlying resting in the goodness inherent in existence and the sense that things are moving in the right direction in spite of all life's contradictions and setbacks." Yet though she has always possessed an uncanny compasslike faith, says Taj, it has been the process of aligning herself with it that has proved difficult. Until recently, for instance, she says, following the promptings of her heart has felt like "stepping into the abyss and then, suddenly, the ground comes up to catch you. But because I never knew that beforehand, I had to take that first scary step into the unknown without knowing where it would lead me."

> *Self-confidence is the true meaning of faith, and in faith is the secret of the fulfillment or non-fulfillment of every desire.*
>
> HAZRAT INAYAT KHAN

After years of feeling as if she were risking her life by faithfully following her heart, however, says Taj, she has experienced a shift in how she experiences faith. "Now I am ninety percent confident of living in the 'not knowing.' I trust that the Universe is safe. The outcome of my life may be a mystery; still, I can live in a day-to-day way resting in the knowledge that whatever happens, it will be good and right. And that is beautiful! A simple, but real, gift. This is the way the teachings become real; they offer instructions and guidelines for transforming into a divine person."

Suffragan Bishop
✿
Jane Holmes Dixon

The story of Jane Holmes Dixon's rise to her present position as the second woman Suffragan Bishop within the Episcopal Church is a parable of faith made visible. As proclaimed in the Bible, she has steadily endeavored through her work to "Fight the good fight of faith, lay hold on eternal life, whereunto thou art also called, and hast professed a good profession before many witnesses." (1 Timothy 6:12). Nowhere was this more in evidence than during the memorial service held at the National Cathedral in Washington, D.C., the Friday following the September 11 terrorist attacks. As Bishop Dixon, somber in the robes of her office, stood before the President, members of the Senate and the Congress, and military personnel to give the opening remarks, I felt pride at the sight of a woman in such a position of religious authority. Of course, men have been fighting the "good fight of faith" for centuries with the benefit of one another's firm support, while women have struggled just to be able to join the fight in the first place. Thus, for women of all religious backgrounds, Dixon is the new face of feminine faith.

When I first visited Bishop Dixon in her office on the grounds of the imposing National Cathedral, I was struck by the commanding aura of her presence: a tall, imposing-looking woman in her early sixties, Dixon's black robes only served to underscore the aura of religious tradition she radiated. Amid the many objects of Christian symbolism decorating her office, I was struck by a small figurine of the Egyptian jackal-headed god, Anubis, on her desk. She explained that it was a souvenir from a recent trip abroad that, for her, carried deep personal meaning. "Thirty years ago a man in the local parish I belonged to labelled five of us [women] who were friends the 'jackalettes,' or female form of the jackal. While it was done in humor, it was not complimentary," she explained. "So when I visited Tutankhamen's tomb in Egypt and saw the spectacular figure of this ancient god, I thought to myself that while this may have been a derogatory term used against us, the fact is this was a beautiful thing. So I brought one home for myself and each of my friends."

Indeed, it could be said that Dixon herself has done much to transform the derogatory ways women in positions of religious authority have been viewed in the past into a very "beautiful thing." The origins of her journey to the position she holds today have their roots in her childhood, where she grew up in a devout Presbyterian family. "I first understood faith through the Church," she says, "so faith and the church have always been inseparable for me." After she married, she and her husband, a Methodist, made the decision to include a life of faith as a part of their marriage and, together, they chose the Episcopal Church. Confirmed forty years ago, she says she has had both a "long faith and a long marriage."

As much as she loved the Episcopalian liturgy, however, Dixon never considered a profession within the church. Instead, her focus was on her young and growing family. Then, during the late sixties and early seventies, with the culture in upheaval around her, she entered a period of intense soul-searching. "I was on a quest for what I would do professionally. But my stirrings were unclear, and I rejected one thing after another—whether working on Capitol Hill, or following in my father's footsteps as a doctor with a career in medicine." At around the same time, recalls Dixon, she was appointed by the local bishop of her diocese in Washington to a task force on Christian education. There, she struck up a friendship with a woman who was a lay theologian and Bible scholar, Dr. Verna Dozier. Putting aside her own dreams, Dixon says she suddenly decided that her twelve-year-old son should be ordained to the priesthood. "This was clearly a case of projection. And when I mentioned it over lunch to Dr. Dozier, she was wise enough to tell me to leave my son alone. If I wanted to be a priest, she told me, then I should be one—not him." It was a bold statement that immediately, recalls Dixon, "rang true." After turning it over in her mind, Dixon confided this radical idea to her husband, fully expecting him to reject it as an absurd undertaking. Instead, he replied, "I think that's it. I think your friend is right."

"That was like a second jolt," says Dixon. After nearly a year digesting the import of such a move, she finally got up her nerve to enroll in the Virginia Theological Seminary. At the time, she was a full-time mother of three young children; in order to study, she went to bed early, then got up at two or three in the morning when her house was quiet. Eventually, Dixon was ordained to the priesthood in 1982. Prior to her election as Bishop, Dixon served parishes in Maryland and Virginia, cochaired a task force on human sexuality, and was a member of the Committee on Constitution and Canons, the Bishop's task force on women's ministries. She was also selected by *Washingtonian* magazine four times as one of the 100 most influential women in the capital city.

Looking back on the unique turn her life path took, Dixon reflects on the mysterious ways she was guided to her destiny occupying a position of religious authority that had for centuries been reserved for men. "External forces came to me at the right time of my own interior searching within the place I had always been a part of—the church. So I considered it to be the hand of God. I will never know for sure in this life if this is what God intended for me. But the church has certainly affirmed my ministry. During the ordination ceremony, the Bishop asks the person being ordained, 'Do you believe that God and the Church are calling you?' and that is a wonderful thing because I pray it's what God wanted for me and that I was reading those signs correctly."

When I ask her to go more deeply into the underpinnings of her faith, Dixon replies that her theology "says that because we are creatures and God is Creator, we don't ever fully know the mind of God. So we live on a faith journey praying that we are interpreting correctly what God is calling us to do—looking for the signs that confirm that, but knowing at the same time that we'll never have the kind of certainty we seek, because that is just not the human experience. My faith does not take me to a place of total assurance. Faith is a risky business."

The solid core of her inner faith, says Dixon, has been repeatedly challenged by outside forces. In her role ministering to the suffering of others, she has been distressed by the tragedies that strike people's lives, such as the sudden and unexplained deaths of family members and loved ones. "Many nights I go to bed and wonder how evil can exist in a world created by a gracious God." In addition, she

says, she gets "irritated with the institution of the church itself—with the way it
continues to miss the mark. Sometimes I wonder if (attending to church business)
is just something we do to keep busy, avoiding what God is really calling us to
do to make the world a place of justice." Then, says Dixon, there are those days
when she is plunged into doubt about the very existence of God. As with my friend
Taj, however, Dixon feels that God has been "very good" to her during her occasional dark nights of the soul, often sending her a sign of reassurance to guide her
way back.

One such incidence occurred following a six-month sabbatical from her official duties as Suffragan Bishop. To celebrate their fortieth wedding anniversary,
she and her husband had travelled with friends to Israel, Greece, Egypt, and
Turkey. It was, she says, the "trip of a lifetime." Yet with the realization of that
dream came sadness. Possessed by a "bland mood of ennui," the notion of returning to work seemed bleak; Dixon doubted whether it was even worth it. Then, she
says, God intervened in the form of a telephone call "out of the blue." A member
of former Vice President Gore's staff had phoned her to see if she would moderate
a panel at the Democratic Convention. Old friends of the Gores, Dixon was
nonetheless stunned. "It was a startling jolt—I was
blown away by it." For Dixon, this was an unparalleled
opportunity for "those of us who have a different perspective on the faith than those who are members of the
Christian coalition" to stand up for their beliefs. Because
this departed from the more moderate stance of the

> *Why are ye fearful, O ye of little faith?*
>
> MATTHEW 8:26

Episcopalian Church, however, Dixon's decision was discouraged by her peers.
Encouraged by family and friends, and by her own strong feelings, however,
Dixon agreed to Gore's request, compelled by her conviction that until more people
stood up to proclaim the gospel as they understood it in the public sphere, conservative Christians would continue "to be the only voice." In short, the time had
arrived for her to put her faith on the line.

Dixon tells this story, she says, as a way to show how God has worked in her
life during times of doubt and despair. "I had said to God, 'I need something to get
me energized again.' And there it was! Something I could never have manufac-
tured myself." Speaking further on her own personal dynamic of faith, Dixon says
that she prays "that God will either put people or things in my life in the time that
I need them. The doctrine of the incarnation—God taking on human flesh—is
one of the central doctrines in the Anglican tradition. Thus part of our life is to
incarnate Christ to each other. I have found through the years that when I have
needed people to do that for me, if my eyes are open and my ears are willing and

the mind is interested, someone appears." Her faith, she says further, is clearly "trust in that which I cannot prove. I am willing to stake my life on that which I cannot empirically prove."

As Dixon describes it, faith for her has been forged from both willing acceptance and assertive discipline. "I've never been able to will faith. But when I approach it as a mystery, then it becomes something very real for me to live into, and I feel very supported." In contrast, on the days when she is plunged into doubt and despair, says Dixon, "I'm not open to the gift of faith—I'm cynical, skeptical, despairing, and even downright rebellious." Then, says Dixon, she takes up the discipline of prayer. "It's important that I pray in those moments when I'm questioning the very existence of God. It's a discipline I do because some part of me knows that I need it. Intellectually, I tell myself that whether I believe or not doesn't have anything to do with the existence of God, because God exists whether I believe or don't." Faith is not passive trust, believes Dixon, but demands something from us as well. "It demands that I get up and come to work and that I try to do what I say I believe in. I can't talk it without doing it. That is what happened with the Democratic Convention—I was called to put my faith on the line, even though I knew I would take a lot of flak for it. It was a chance for me to put into practice the scripture that informs my whole life: 'What does the Lord require but to do justice, love mercy, and walk humbly with your God.'" (Micah 6:8).

EXERCISES IN STRENGTHENING FAITH

Though it may seem as though faith is absent more often than it is present, it is possible to strengthen this quality through meditation and visualization. Like the sun and the stars, faith is a natural part of our soul life—we have only to learn to put our trust in this intuitive sense to begin to feel its healing effects. As the lives of the saints and prophets of old attest, faith is the fountain of spiritual discipline. Then, as now, faith is an inner sense that allows us to bear with patience our doubts and despair, as well as the dry, depressing passages of life, knowing that somehow, some way, we are being led forward in the right direction. In our modern age of technology and materialism it is perhaps even more difficult to cultivate faith in the unseen, invisible dimension of life. It is especially challenging these days to trust that life has meaning when so much of the world seems beset by random senselessness. Yet this is exactly what the spiritual path asks us to do: to become an ardent devotee of the divine mystery, even in the turbulence of life. The following exercises may help to inspire you to deepen your consciousness of the quality of faith.

✿

THE FAITH OF A CHILD

Like trusting children, we are each born believing in the essential goodness of life. Without any more proof than their mother's smile or the sight of a colorful toy, little children possess an inborn faith in life's sweetness. Any parent has seen this when, grinning with delight, a child leaps into the air, supremely confident that a parent will catch them in their arms. Then comes the inevitable day when that innate confidence is crippled by a sudden blow: a parent lets us down, a teacher at school criticizes us unfairly, or a friend betrays our trust. Ever so slowly, as the years pass, our faith in ourselves and life erodes away until, like the Biblical Job, we feel tested to the brink of our capacity to believe in God.

If you feel you have lost your faith in God, the Divine, or even life itself, it is a signal that you have lost contact with your inner child—your core of innocence, purity, and trust. This is not pop psychology. Instead, it is a timeless truth recognized in the mythologies of the ancient world that revered Osiris, Krishna, Jesus, and the maiden goddesses. "The child is potential future," writes Carl Jung of the archetype of the Divine Child. Thus "the 'child' paves the way for a future change of personality . . . It is . . . a symbol which unites the opposites; a mediator, bringer of healing, that is, one who makes whole."[14] For women, the budlike potential of the divine child is represented by the "Kore," the Greek phrase for the goddess as young maiden. The ancient mysteries of Eleusis, in fact, revolved around the relationship between a mother, Demeter, and her young daughter, Persephone.

To reconnect with the hopeful spirit of the Divine Child, recall a time in your life when, as a young girl, you enjoyed supreme confidence and trust. Then, bring to mind a time when that trust received a blow. I remember, for example, being happily self-confident whenever I stood before my class to speak or read out loud. Then one day, at age eleven, I gave a farewell speech to the graduating eighth-grade class and, midway through my talk, forgot every word. It took years before I felt I could stand up and speak before people.

When the adult in you has grown pessimistic and gloomy, go within your heart and allow yourself to be led from darkness by the hand of a trusting child. You may wish to imagine going back in time to the naturally optimistic person you once were. Or, you may wish to meditate on the image of a Divine Girl Child, such as the young Mary, Isis, Kuan Yin, or Persephone. Feel buoyed by the innate strength and positivity of these images of the Divine Feminine—and the faith She conveys to your soul. For in the child, as in faith, lies the secret to the miracle of life.

✺

FOLLOWING ARIADNE'S THREAD OF FAITH THROUGH THE LABYRINTH

In the Greek myth of Theseus and the labyrinth, the young hero is sent by his father to the island of Crete. Along with the other youths of Thebes, Theseus is to be offered as tribute to the cruel King Minos—to die fighting the beastly Minotaur who lies at the heart of the underground labyrinth.

Theseus's courage and bravery help him accomplish the superhuman task of slaying the Minotaur. But it is Ariadne, the daughter of King Minos, whose gift of a thread wrapped around a pine cone helped guide Theseus back through the labyrinth to safety and his flight to freedom. The myth of Theseus is repeated in our everyday lives, as, like Theseus, we often feel trapped in a labyrinth with Byzantine twists and turns. The figure of Ariadne represents the feminine voice of intuition. Thus, if we learn to trust our inner voice—the slender thread of inner knowing guiding our lives—we can learn to feel our way through life's confusions to greater and greater clarity. As the stories of Rābi'ah, Perpetua, Murshida Taj Glantz, and Suffragan Bishop Dixon show, trust in one's intuitive, knowing self is the hallmark of feminine spirituality.

Put your trust in God for support and see His hidden hand working through all sources.

HAZRAT INAYAT KHAN

To strengthen your faith in your own inner voice of guidance, picture yourself in a labyrinth as dark as the one in which Theseus found himself. You may even wish to imagine that a beast, or a Minotaur, lies in wait at the heart of this labyrinth. Sometimes life feels just this way: one wrong turn, one step in the wrong direction, and the dark rises up to take us. Now, see this labyrinth as the reflection of a situation in which you find yourself—a situation that feels blocked. Closing your eyes, imagine next that the knowing, feminine spirit within you has placed a gift within your hands: a strong cord or thread that is attached at the end to the exit of this labyrinth. Keeping firm hold of this thread, feel yourself guided through the dark. As you do this, imagine that you are being edged along by a radarlike sense of guidance that knows the way ahead for you. Continue to feel pulled toward the light until, finally, you emerge forth from confusion and darkness into daylight, clarity, and a resolution to your problems.

✧

CREATE A TESTAMENT OF HOPE AND FAITH

Faith is the force that allows us to believe, as the Bible says, in "the substance of things hoped for, the evidence of things not seen" (Hebrews 11:1). Thus, faith is interwoven with our highest ideals as well as our deepest convictions. Because it may take decades to see our dreams bear fruit, creating a "faith testament" is one way to help sustain us in our lifelong journey toward a particular goal.

What, for example, do you believe in most strongly? Perhaps you have an underlying commitment to being a good mother to your children. Or, maybe you have an abiding passion for healing environmental devastation. It could also be that you have high hopes to raise consciousness around issues of human rights. It might be that you believe strongly in awakening humanity to the message of the Divine Feminine, and the values She stands for such as compassion, mercy, and interdependence. The star that shines brightest for you may be the message of religious harmony and tolerance.

Whatever your beliefs and convictions, create a testament of faith. Then, in times of darkness and disillusion, let this testament be your polestar—the light by which you steer your ship to shore. The following, for example, is a testament of those things I believe in most strongly and will continue to have faith in over the course of the rest of my life:

1. I believe in the essential goodness of people.
2. I have faith that my children are protected by the Divine Mother.
3. I believe that each life has meaning, purpose, and divine intent.
4. I believe that everything that befalls me reflects the design of the Divine Intelligence at work in my life.
5. I have hope and faith that things will always work out, if not for the best, then at least for a very good reason.
6. I trust in the inner voice of my heart to guide me through life's difficulties.
7. I have faith in my own eclectic spiritual path, as unusual and unconventional as it may be.

8. I have faith in my creative vision.

9. I have faith in the seen and the unseen spirit of the divine, creator of all life.

10. I have faith in my friends, who support me in times of doubt and dis-illusion.

MEDITATION ON FAITH

Perhaps because she is from the Midwestern state of Iowa, Murshida Taj Glantz recommends cultivating faith within oneself through small steps, rather than taking "one big leap." "Faith is like a plant that grows and develops over time, nurtured by spiritual practice and psychological insight," she says. To begin with, a person might want to examine their beliefs about reality, as, she says, "our beliefs are like crusts over life." By doing this, a person can discern whether they trust that life is good and trustworthy or whether they have grown cynical as a result of childhood disappointments or repeated failures in work or love. Based on such experiences, many people reach the conclusion that life isn't safe and that they have to look after their own interests. Yet, says Taj, "all those beliefs are ways of separating from the natural flow of life. In order to stay in harmony with the larger reality, a person needs to learn how to say 'yes to yes and yes to no.' It's a complete yes to the whole remarkable catastrophe that life is—that in spite of all the pain and heartache and losses, a deeper, abiding, and positive reality exists. Faith in this sense is choosing to live life in spite of all the pain and heartache—because the bigger hurt arises from closing down and refusing life's gift."

Faithfulness has a fragrance which is perceptible in the atmosphere of the faithful.

HAZRAT INAYAT KHAN

Next, to help soften the spirit hardened by life, Taj recommends the spiritual practice of "evoking positive states of consciousness. When we look at the flowers and trees and planets and stars, we become conscious of the intelligence and wholeness animating nature. That is helpful, because once we experience that, we are given resources that help melt resistances in our unconscious." A spiritual friend along the path can strengthen our faith as well, says Taj. "Whether the friendship of the teacher on the path, the sangha, or community, of faithful, or an individual companion, the friend is a reflection of the friendliness within the Universe itself—it gives us a feeling for the benign support underlying everything."

And last, the practice of faith, says Taj, is forged in the choices we make. Is our trust in the Universe great enough, for example, to choose truth over security? Can we believe, like Christ in the miracle of the loaves and fishes, that our needs will be met? Even though a loved one has let us down, do we have faith enough that love is still possible? To tap into the power of faith this way, it helps to meditate on the examples of the great saints and mystics, or to think of the example of a prisoner of conscience who has risked his or her life to speak out against injustice. With those examples to guide us, says Taj, "we discover within ourselves faith to stop living a lie—and begin living the life we were meant to live."

RECOMMENDED READING

The Book of Job, with Commentary by Thomas Moore (Riverhead Books, 1998)

Dynamics of Faith by Paul Tillich (HarperPerennial Library, 2001)

Enduring Grace: Living Portraits of Seven Women Mystics by Carol Lee Flinders (HarperSanFrancisco, 1993)

Essays on a Science of Mythology: The Myth of the Divine Child and the Mysteries of Eleusis by C. G. Jung and C. Kerényi (Bollingen Series, Princeton, 1963)

Inner Knowing, edited by Helen Palmer (Tarcher/Putnam, 1998)

Miracles: The Extraordinary, the Impossible, and the Divine by Carol Neimar (Viking Studio Books, 1995)

My Soul Is a Woman: The Feminine in Islam by Annemarie Schimmel (Continuum, 1997)

Mystics, Visionaries, and Prophets: A Historical Anthology of Women's Spiritual Writings, edited by Shawn Madigan (Fortress, 1998)

Rabi'a The Mystic and her Fellow Saints in Islam by Margaret Smith (The Rainbow Bridge, 1997; first printing Cambridge Press, 1928)

Return of the Goddess by Edward C. Whitmont (Crossroad, 1992)

Saints, the Chosen Few by Manuela Dunn-Mascotti (Ballantine Books, 1994)

Women's Ways of Knowing: The Development of Self, Voice, and Mind by Mary Field Belenky, et al. (Basic Books, c. 1986)

Your Sixth Sense: Unlocking the Power of Your Intuition, by Belleruth Naparstek (HarperSanFrancisco, 1998)

SUGGESTED MUSIC

Alleluia to the Pachelbel Canon in D/Kyrie by Robert Gass & On Wings of
  Song, audio CD

"Amazing Grace" performed by Judy Collins on *Forever, An Anthology*,
  audio CD

Bach Mass in B Minor (especially the choruses) performed by New Philhar-
  monia Orchestra, conducted by Otto Klemperer, audio CD

Hebrew Songs from Israel and the Orient by Ora Sittner and Youval Micen-
  macher

"Here Comes the Sun" by George Harrison, performed by The Beatles

"He's Got the Whole World in His Hands" and "Amazing Grace," from
  Amazing Grace, Jessye Norman, audio CD

The Lama's Chant, Songs of Awakening by Lama Gyurme & Jean-Phillipe
  Rykiel, audio CD

My Lord What a Morning by Marian Anderson, audio CD

Miserere by Allegri, by Magnificat, audio CD

Soul Chai by Giora Feidman and the NDR Choir, audio CD

CHAPTER THREE

The Feminine Face of Beauty

Tucked away in a corner of my writing desk is a photo of myself taken nearly twenty-five years ago. In it, I am standing outside on an idyllic summer day in a tree-ringed meadow, engaged in an animated conversation with two of my soul sisters, Taj and Zuleikha. We are young, our hair is long and lustrous, pulled into braids or knotted in buns on top of our heads. We are dressed in colorful blouses and bright earrings. The subject of our conversation, memorialized in that light, laughing photo, however, had nothing to do with anything spiritual or metaphysical. Instead, we were discussing the benefits of a particular line of face creams. I love this photograph because it is a scene that is as archetypal as childbirth or dancing. The joy of our friendship combined with the softness of our youth and the simple pleasure of our conversation suffuses the whole tableau with a graceful loveliness. It is a scene, I am sure, that has been replayed across the ages in various settings and among women of all classes and ethnicities.

Truth be told, I have always enjoyed the feminine arts of beauty. Too, my personal experiences have gone against the popular stereotype of women competing against one another or undermining one another's physical attributes in the

> *The soul's natural inclination to love beauty is the trap God most frequently uses in order to win it and open it to the breath from on high.*
>
> Simone Weil, "Forms of the Implicit Love of God," from *Waiting for God*

quest for a man. Rather, I have enjoyed many sweet moments with my girlfriends sniffing perfumes and oils and trying on jewelry and clothes. Unlike the classic fairy tale *Cinderella,* no wicked stepsisters have marred my path. Instead, there have been only supportive soul sisters who have delighted in my natural attributes, as I have delighted in theirs. Perhaps this is because I came of age during the height of the counterculture; after the wool plaids and polyester pants of the fifties and sixties, many women revelled in the sensual joy of dressing in vividly colored silks and velvets, Indian saris, Moroccan and Israeli robes, Guatemalan dresses, as well as adorning themselves in ethnic jewelry such as turquoise rings; brass, copper, and silver bracelets; and coral and amber beads. In addition, many of the rituals that emerged during the spiritual renaissance of that time celebrated the divine beauty of the Goddess—whether as Sita, Mary, Tara, Aphrodite, or Lakshmi.

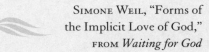

Beauty is eternity here below.

SIMONE WEIL, "Forms of
the Implicit Love of God,"
FROM *Waiting for God*

Even after the counterculture merged into mainstream society, the subject of beauty continued to fascinate, embroidering the tapestry of my friendships with a golden filament of magic. Especially as women have grown busier with the demands of juggling both personal and professional lives, slow, idle chat around cosmetics and clothes has become a wonderful respite from the competitive demands of everyday life. I have helped girlfriends dress for special occasions, for instance, and have been helped in turn: from Mimi, a pair of borrowed antique earrings to wear to Lis's daughter's wedding; to Sylvia, my grandmother's amber-and-black beaded necklace to wear to her friend's wedding; from Ann, a gown borrowed to wear to President Clinton's inaugural ball. In addition to exchanging clothes and jewelry, I think, too, of the gifts I've received: the pale silk sweater from Lis; the palette of eye shadows from Nancy; the silver evening bag from Janet; the purple glass heart from Susan; the sparkling scarf from Tatiana. Hanging on the wall of my bedroom is an exquisite Afghan woman's coat from my friend Sylvia. Each morning when I wake up, the ikat pink-and-purple dyed stripes and flowers inspire my day. Just looking at it makes me want to write beautiful words. Such exchanges go counter to the widespread notion that only a man can make a woman feel beautiful—women, too, bring out the feminine soul of loveliness within one another.

Indeed, as secular as such ordinary rituals around dressing and "looking pretty" may seem on the surface, they have their source in the timeless, mythic realm of Aphrodite. This is the Greek goddess of beauty of whom it was written: "She was clothed in a robe more brilliant than gleaming fire and wore spiral bracelets and shining earrings, while round her tender neck there were beautiful necklaces, lovely, golden and of intricate design."[1] The Greeks were wise to create a divinity to act as the sole personification of beauty. In doing so, they recognized the sacred function of that quality within our everyday lives; by linking the physical world of appearances to the invisible presence of the gods and goddesses, they invested beauty—as well as women—with soul. "Was woman as object considered more precious in previous times than she is today?" asks Jungian thinker Ginette Paris. "And could religion have had something to do with this devaluation? Has the loss of our Goddesses changed our status from that of a sacred object to that of a domestic convenience?"[2]

Sundered from its spiritual dimension, beauty is indeed a hollow charm at best. Even the fashion designer Coco Chanel recognized that outward beauty must be connected to something deeper, remarking once that "Adornment is never anything except a reflection of the heart." Thus, unless a woman takes seriously Plato's injunction in the Dialogues to "give me beauty in the inward soul; and may the outward and inward [wo]man be at one," her appearance will simply be a glittering imitation of external codes of fashion rather than a genuine expression of her own inner spirit.

The tension between outward appearance and inward reality, however, has long bedeviled women's relationship to beauty. In the not-so-distant past, women have felt compelled by societal expectations to choose between developing the beauty of their talents or cultivating themselves as embodiments of beauty to be admired. Thus, the primary relation of women to beauty was as a passive object or consumer of beauty rather than as an active creator of beauty herself. From Helen of Troy, whose legendary loveliness sparked the Trojan War, to Beatrice, whose beauty inspired Dante's *Divine Comedy*, to Leonardo da Vinci's hauntingly mysterious Mona Lisa, women and beauty have been conflated into a single ideal. With rare exception, for instance, a woman could be the subject of a painting—but not the painter. She could be the ideal elaborated upon in a sonnet or an ode, but not a poet. She could be the object of a man's desire, but was forbidden to feel sexual desire herself. She could be set like a jewel in a house of fine furniture and clothed in the finest gowns, yet never design a house, craft furniture, or market a line of clothing herself.

With the advance of feminism, however, women began closing the gap between submitting to how others saw them and reimagining themselves as they

> Let the beauty we love be what we do.
> There are hundreds of ways to kneel and kiss
>   the ground.
>
> RUMI

wished to be seen. Rather than clothing themselves in stereotyped images of beauty, women became independent image-makers in their own right. Coco Chanel revolutionized women's fashion by designing clothes that were elegant as well as comfortable and functional. Adrienne Rich wrote poetry as universal and profound as any man's. Dancers Ruth St. Denis and Isadora Duncan helped restore pagan delight in the unfettered and spontaneous beauty of the female body. Photographer Dorothea Lange shifted the camera away from perfectly posed models, toward the stoic suffering of women who bore the traces of poverty and oppression on their grim faces. Artist Kathe Kollwitz revealed a darker side of motherhood dramatically different from the idealized mother-and-child portraits of the Victorian era; likewise, Georgia O'Keeffe, Frida Kahlo, and Helen Frankenthaler created art that awakened passions, revealed grim realities, and challenged assumptions. "Never in history," writes Anne Higonnet in her essay "Women, Images, and Representation," "have the images both of and by women changed so radically and so quickly." After centuries of being denied their own creative power, she writes, women have learned to cultivate "new attitudes about themselves, their bodies, and their place in society"[3] revisioning the feminine experience through the various mediums of fashion, art, photography, and literature.

> *In beauty is the secret of divinity.*
>
> HAZRAT INAYAT KHAN

Yet even as women have taken control of their own creativity, producing imagery that reflects how they see themselves and the world rather than how the world sees them, the historically complex and complicated relationship between women and beauty continues to persist. Images of models are used by the media to sell everything from pizza to cars. Young girls starve themselves in order to fulfill impossible ideals of thinness. Youth has become the holy grail of the cosmetics industry. Thus, at the same time women in the West have been liberated from outmoded ideas of beauty that once pinched, confined, and bound their souls along with their bodies, a new culture of beauty has emerged through the mass media that is as restrictive as it is liberated from outworn taboos. After centuries of working to free themselves from strictly defined codes of beauty, women still must struggle to define their own individual relationship to beauty.

This modern beauty drama is vividly acted out by women in the public arena. After the inaugural ball for President Bush, for example, Laura Bush's red ballgown was the topic of a spirited exchange between NPR radio host Diane Rehm and fashion maven Joan Rivers on *Larry King Live*.[4] While Rehm congratulated the new First Lady on the graceful beauty of her appearance, Rivers mocked her for wearing a dull dress that a "grandmother" might wear. Not long after that, Senator Hillary Rodham Clinton was criticized because her new, more relaxed hairdo was not as formal as while she had been First Lady.[5]

Not every woman is forced to endure such scrutiny as First Ladies and women politicians. Still, almost every woman I know has experienced this conflict around outer appearance and inner worth. At some point in her life, every woman has had to contend with the issue of how she is "seen"—both by the public and by her own inner fashion critic. "Many women look in the mirror today and see Medusa," says Jungian analyst Marion Woodman, referring to the Greek myth of the goddess who turned those who looked at her to stone, "in 200 pounds of fat, or the ten pounds of fat they cannot get rid of . . . Women obsessed with Medusa look in the mirror and they are turned to stone by what they see. It is tragic because they are faced with their own rejection of themselves. . . ."[6]

Woodman has written poignantly of society's need for a sacred femininity firmly grounded in the physical world, rather than frozen in rigid standards of idealistic perfection. With the reemergence of myths, statues, and paintings of the Great Mother from cultures of antiquity, women today have been given a powerful image of divine beauty that harmonizes the disparate parts of themselves—physical, sexual, maternal, spiritual, and creative—into a single whole. These sacred images of the Divine Feminine, ranging from fertility figures with large hips and pendulous breasts to tiny-waisted, high-breasted priestesses are strikingly powerful. In turn, the rediscovery of ancient images of womanhood has created a renaissance of new art and literature celebrating the reemergence of the goddess. Such positive imagery makes it more possible for women to delight in their physical beauty as a reflection of a sacred dimension of the divine—as well as artists and creators celebrating the beauty of the Divine Feminine.

Practice random kindness and senseless acts of beauty.

ANNE HERBERT

The Swiss psychologist Carl Jung once wrote that problems are rarely solved. Rather, they fade into the background when something else comes along to take their place. In the same way, the centuries-old conflict women have inherited around beauty will never be resolved; it can only be replaced by something more compelling. That one thing might be the image of God as a beautiful woman, a Goddess of many faces and forms and of all colors and sizes. But it might also be the dawning awareness that beauty extends far beyond surface appearances: beyond physical beauty, for instance, there is spiritual beauty, creative beauty, healing beauty, and beauty found in principles of compassion and fairness. Like a river whose full force has been dammed up behind a dike, the healing waters of beauty ought to be let loose—allowed to flow freely into those areas of life that have become withered from its absence: nature, cities, relationships, and justice.

Only the "recovery of beauty as a movement," writes Ronald Schenk, can heal the wound in the modern psyche caused by the separation between "appearance and being." The following myths, stories, interviews, and reflections of women past and present are intended to show that just such a movement is well underway. For once we recognize that a beautiful woman, as well as a holy temple or a hushed forest of redwoods, reflect different facets of the same quality, then we realize that beauty is not limited to how we look, but is an enlivening essence animating the world around us. Indeed, a sense of beauty, wrote the philosopher Simone Weil, makes the "total incarnation of faith possible."[7]

Why is this so? Because ultimately beauty is a spiritual organ of perception, a kind of magic inner vision that, by seeing the flower in the seed or the adult in the awkward teenager, allows the Goddess's creative genius to flourish on earth. In the presence of beauty, whether a lyrically curved seashell intricately etched with colors, a cherubic child wide-eyed with wonder, a silver-slivered moon glowing against the ebony canopy of night, a scented summer garden, or a painting whose harmonious perfection of form takes our breath away, we experience a mysterious presence suffusing all created things. Seeing beauty, we cannot help but have faith that the hand of an artistic creator is at work in existence. The capacity to embody, see, and be moved to awe by the beauty of life makes believers—and artists—of us all.

> *Beauty is the object which every soul pursues.*
>
>
>
> HAZRAT INAYAT KHAN

GOLDEN APHRODITE AND THE LOST MYTH OF BEAUTY

As elusive as the quality of beauty can sometimes seem, we can gain insight into its mysteries through the myth of Aphrodite, the Beautiful One. Her origin is ancient. Said to be older than Time, she immigrated to Greece from the East, where she was worshipped as Asherah or Astarte, goddess of the oldest continuously occupied temple in the world. In Rome, she became Venus where she was revered as the ancestral mother of all Romans.[8] The legends that arose over the centuries around the escapades of Aphrodite are wise parables that illustrate beauty's paradoxical nature: jealousy, betrayal, and deceit, as well as harmony, pleasure, and joy all follow in the wake of this potent goddess. Yet without full knowledge of Aphrodite, there can be no true understanding of beauty's deepest secrets.

Even the birth of Aphrodite reveals the light and the dark aspects hidden within beauty, an event the poet Friederich Schiller describes as a "dark birth out of the endless sea." As the story goes, Uranus, the god of heaven, had just spread himself lovingly over earth when he was suddenly and violently castrated by his son, Cronus. White foam swirled around his male member as it floated in the sea; in it a young woman took shape. Entranced by her beauty, Zephyrus, the god of the west wind, blew her softly across the sea while the waves gently buoyed her in a seashell. At dawn's rosy light, she was swept ashore on the island of Cytherea, where, upon the first touch of her foot, the earth blossomed in a carpet of grass and flowers. There she was greeted by the Seasons, as well as the three dancing Graces—Joyous (Euphrosyne), Flowering (Thalia), and Brilliance (Aglaia). After bathing and anointing her in perfumes, her attendants adorned her in jewels, then placed her in a golden chariot drawn by white doves, where she was taken to the gods and goddesses on Mt. Olympus. Each year at springtime, Aphrodite returns to the island of Cytherea, where she dives into the sea that gave her birth. Rising from the waves, her youthful beauty is restored, dewy fresh and sparkling with drops of sea.

> *Beauty is the life of the artist, the theme of the poet, the soul of the musician.*
>
> HAZRAT INAYAT KHAN

According to later versions, Aphrodite's beauty was so dazzling—and threatening to the established order—that upon her arrival in Olympus, Zeus immediately married her to the plain, crippled craftsman Hephaestus in order to prevent jealous competition for her hand among the gods. It was ugly Hephaestus, the goldsmith, who wove the fabled golden "girdle of Aphrodite," the source of her bewitching magic to stir love and desire in all who beheld her. Indeed, it wasn't long before Aphrodite was causing trouble. Among her lovers were Zeus, king of the gods; Ares, the handsome warrior brother of Hephaestus; and the young god Adonis. Counted among her children are Eros, the capricious god of romance, and Harmonia, or Harmony. According to myth, just three goddesses among the Olympians were immune to Aphrodite's enchantment: Artemis, Hera, and Athena.

THE RAINBOW COLORS OF BEAUTY

Because beauty and color are twin spirits, the color of beauty is embodied in the image of the rainbow. A symbol of the link between heaven and earth, the seven colors of the rainbow also represent the seven heavens. Thus, the colors of the rainbow reflected here on earth are a reflection of the beauty found in heaven. There are many ways to think of a rainbow in connection to beauty: as a palette of the colors found in nature or as reflections of the shimmering isles of paradise. God sent the rainbow after the flood as a sign of his covenant with Noah. I like to think of the rainbow as the scarf of the Goddess: she trails her scarf across the skies, glistening with lovely iridescence, reminding us of the covenant of beauty she shares with all creatures.

The symbolism in the myth of Aphrodite is richly layered with meaning. Peering into the mirror she holds before us, we see reflected the dynamic principles of beauty. In her marriage to Hephaestus, for example, can be seen the connection between craftsmanship, skill, and artifice to beauty. Just as Aphrodite arose into existence from unspoiled nature, so, too, do objects of beauty have their origin in earth's raw materials. From clay, the potter crafts cups and plates of delicate porcelain; miners extract gold from veins of precious metals layered in rock that artists then fashion into rings, necklaces, and earrings. Perfumes and incense are distilled from the essence of flowers and herbs, while paintings imitate nature's beauty.

What is the meaning of Hephaestus's repellant appearance? Perhaps it is the inextricable link between beauty and ugliness—in one is the shadow of the other.

A thing of beauty is a joy forever:
Its loveliness increases; it will never
Pass into nothingness; but still will keep
A bower quiet for us, and a sleep
Full of sweet dreams, and health, and quiet
Breathing.

JOHN KEATS, *Endymion*

When residents in impoverished neighborhoods transform empty lots into gardens, repair the façade of abandoned homes, and plant flowers, for instance, crime often diminishes, vanquished by beauty's civilizing force. At the same time, perfectly landscaped suburban neighborhoods can sometimes seem devoid of life; they cry out for a touch of Hephaestus's less-than-perfect, earthy reality. There is something of Hephaestus in every act of creativity, too. When I am working hard, whether weeding my garden or writing a book, for example, it is as if every ounce of beauty in me goes into my work rather than into my appearance; I forego makeup, wear baggy sweatpants, and have little interest in shopping for clothes or arranging my hair. Too, the process of making an object of beauty is often messy: the paper-strewn desk of the writer, the piles of weeds and garden tools of the gardener, the smeared paints and dirty brushes of the artist at the canvas, the spilled sauces and spices of the chef. There is a longstanding tradition, in fact, that quilts, rugs, and weavings are incomplete unless they have a small imperfection said to create an opening for the spirits to enter.

And what of Aphrodite's love affair with Ares, that virile god of war who later became known as Mars? To Jungian thinker Ginette Paris, the bond between Ares and Aphrodite represents the link between love and aggression, peace and strife. In its positive expression, Ares represents the independent spirit of courage necessary to meet life's demands. Beauty without courage or assertiveness would pale into lifelessness—the charmingly helpless woman or the handsome yet ineffectual man who lacks strength or conviction. According to Thomas Moore, Aphrodite represents the civilizing force necessary to tame aggression from turning to violence. "Venus was placed in the centre of heaven next to Mars," Moore quotes Pico della Miran-dola, "because she must tame his impulse which is by nature destructive and corrupting." One of my favorite paintings hangs in the National Gallery of Art: In it, a

Simplicity is the living beauty.

HAZRAT INAYAT KHAN

voluptuously lovely Venus sits beside a reclining Mars. While the Roman soldier's sculpted muscles, breastplate, and armor emanate raw power, Venus's beauty softens his hardened warrior stance into philosophical reflection. It is as if the fight has literally "gone out of him." At the same time, the union of Venus and Mars, says Moore, represents the paradox of any human relationship where conflict and disagreement coexist on a daily basis with love and harmony—the fight before breakfast, the make-up kiss before bed.[9]

The coupling of Aphrodite with various gods shows that she represents the archetype of civilization—the essence of a culture's capacity to refine humankind's aggressive instincts through art, music, poetry, cuisine, fashion, and architecture. A society that is civilized keeps a sacred place for beauty in its pantheon of ideals: honoring beauty in the shape of its buildings, for instance, as well as caring for its artists, lavishing public funds on public gardens or tree-lined boulevards. Cathedrals, temples, and mosques are expressions of civilization past and present: the flickering candles, soaring ceilings, stained-glass windows, and incense-perfumed atmosphere reflects the beauty of the Divine on earth. Too, civilization reveals itself in the way a culture appreciates the arts associated with love and romance. As her friendship with the three Graces indicates, Aphrodite civilizes by charming; wherever she goes, roses blossom, music plays, graceful laughter ripples, and the pleasures of wit, conversation, and seduction abound.

Yet Aphrodite's veil of beauty conceals a dark side that humans ignore at their peril. Reject her, the myths warn, and she will wreak vengeance, causing impotence, lovelessness, and loneliness. I take this to mean that beauty is a quality that we cannot excise from our lives: in some form, our souls must have beauty, or we may suffer depression or emptiness of the spirit. Making a place for Aphrodite in our lives, however, does not mean simply owning beautiful things or clothes. Among Aphrodite's symbols is the white dove, an image of peace. Thus, beauty can mean creating an atmosphere of harmony out of the fractious notes of our busy lives, whether through taking time to have a thoughtful conversation with a loved one with whom we have fallen out of sorts, cleaning a disorganized room, or working to bring peace to a divided neighborhood or community. It means finding a means of expressing the principle of beauty in our lives through our creative talents, such as writing a poem or planting a flowering bush. It means bringing beauty into the lives of others—cooking our friends a fine meal; buying a small but lovely object for a relative; or taking an inner city child to the opera or the museum.

> *God is the essence of beauty; it is His love of beauty which has caused Him to express His own beauty in manifestation.*
>
> HAZRAT INAYAT KHAN

Finally, making Aphrodite a reality in our lives means recognizing that love is a work of art that lasts a lifetime. In the story of Eros and Psyche, for instance, we see love made authentically beautiful through what have been called "the works of Aphrodite." In this timeless fairy tale of love lost and regained, a king and a queen were blessed with three beautiful daughters. The last, Psyche, was so beautiful she was regarded as an incarnation of Aphrodite; no mortal dared approach her. When her father consulted the Delphic oracle for advice, he was told to abandon her on a mountaintop. At this point in the tale, a jealous Aphrodite makes her entrance, instructing her son, Eros, to punish the maiden by making her fall in love with an unworthy suitor. Yet when he sees her, Eros himself is smitten, and wisks her away to his castle where he conceals his true identity as a god by visiting her only at night. When Psyche's two sisters visit her in her new home, they become suspicious of the situation and persuade Psyche that her husband must be a horrible monster. They concoct a plan whereby, with the aid of a sharp knife and a lantern, she will kill the beast her sisters are sure will devour her. Yet as Psyche lifts the candle that fateful night, she sees that her lover is indeed a beautiful god and not the ugly monster her envious sisters had warned her about. Too late, however, a drop of oil falls on his shoulder. Awakening, Eros flees—as he had warned her he would do if she sought to uncover his identity. Abandoned, betrayed by her sisters, Aphrodite once again reappears, ordering her daughter-in-law to undertake certain labors in order to regain her husband. After years spent wandering the world fulfilling these tasks, Psyche's last ordeal involves a descent to the underworld, where, unaided, she must retrieve Persephone's beauty box. On her return, she sinks into a deathless sleep; touched by her devotion, Eros persuades Zeus to intervene. Finally, Psyche and Eros are reunited for eternity.

There have been many interpretations of this classic story with its echoes of the familiar children's fairy tale *Beauty and the Beast*. While most agree that it is about coming to consciousness through love and relationship, there is at the same time a recognition of the role beauty and appearances play in the rituals of love and romance: Psyche's beauty that stirs Aphrodite's jealousy and steals her son's heart; Eros' insistence on hiding his godlike visage from his wife; Persephone's beauty box. It tells us about beauty's power to seduce. Who, for instance, has not glimpsed a person on the street, whether man or woman, and not felt that familiar tug at the heart or weakness in the knees? Thus, beauty, the myth tells us, is one of nature's ways of drawing us into relationship with another human being. A lovely woman or an attractive man draws us out of our lonely solitude into the earthly and human realm of love and commitment.

Yet as Psyche's sisters prove, and as men and women both know, appearances can also prove deceptive, stirring confusion and envy and sowing the seeds of discord. It is Psyche's sisters' disbelief over a situation that looks "too good to be true," for instance, that prompts Psyche to take a "better look" at her new husband. As Christine Downing points out, the two doubting women helped sister Psyche in her journey to selfhood through questioning the nature of her marriage. "The story of Psyche and her sisters serves as an initiation into the mysteries of sisterhood, opens us to an appreciation of how our sisterly relationships challenge and sustain us—at the same time that we inevitably also fail and

> *Beauty is hidden in every soul, however wicked; and our trust and confidence in the beauty of the soul helps to draw out that hidden beauty which must shine out one day.*
>
> HAZRAT INAYAT KHAN

betray one another."[10] Though it is a strange ritual to men, most women are familiar with the role girlfriends play in relationships: probing and analyzing the surface "appearances" of a romantic attraction, women help one another enter into a relationship as fully aware as possible. All too often, I have had women friends involved with married or otherwise unavailable men. Inevitably, it falls to a close girlfriend to ask, as Psyche's sisters asked her, the difficult questions about these powerful attractions: Is this man for real? Is he truly who he says he is, as Eros claimed in the myth—or is he nothing more than a fleeting illusion?

Finally, Persephone's beauty box, retrieved from Hades's underworld, reveals that true beauty is not about glittering surface appearances, but has depth of soul. What makes a person most appealing is beauty of character. A pleasing personality, a generous and forgiving heart, are as much expressions of beauty as fairness of form and face. After all, as Ginette Paris writes, "The cult of Aphrodite is not the cult of oneself and of one's own beauty; it is the artful giving of oneself. It is not a bag of tricks to capture another."[11]

The Healing Art of Beauty

Elise's Story:

The artist Henri Matisse repeatedly said that he wanted to make paintings so beautiful that, when a person saw them, all problems would suddenly subside. What Matisse described with regard to his art is the feeling I have whenever I enter my friend Elise Wiarda's home: Stepping across the threshold of her tiny bungalow nestled along the banks of the Potomac river, I am enfolded in an atmosphere of beauty so serenely peaceful, any worries I have immediately dissipate. The unique environment she has created reflects her twin passions as both artist and healer. Her home is decorated in spare, subtle colors of browns and beiges, muted red rugs, antique furniture in dark wood, and, hanging on the walls, the delicate, oyster-colored silk tapestries that bear her tiny, trademark stitching. The alcove off the living room is mostly bare, save for the massage table set up in the center where she does her healing work as a Rosen therapist, and an altar with a candle and icon. Surrounded in summer by a wild, lush garden, the whole environment is like a tiny shrine set in the woods.

Beauty is a pledge of the possible conformity between the soul and nature, and consequently a ground of faith in the supremacy of the good.

GEORGE SANTAYANA,
The Sense of Beauty

Elise was born in Holland just before World War II to parents who belonged to prominent cultural and intellectual circles. Her father, Gerard Wiarda, was chief justice of the Supreme Court of the Netherlands, and later became president of the Court of Human Rights in France; her mother was for many years an anthroposophist, following the spiritual tradition founded by Rudolph Steiner. From the very beginning, art, music, and poetry nurtured her life; she was always, Elise says, "in love with beauty." Yet her passion for beauty was colored by darker emotions of terror stirred by her experiences during the war; then, the German occupation transformed the city around her into a sea of gray, uniformed Nazis. At the age of six, her parents arranged for her to be sculpted by an artist who had refused to sign allegiance to the Germans—as all artists at the time were required to do.

Returning from a session one day with her older sister, a young, blond German soldier who wanted to hug her picked her up. As she struggled to escape his embrace, says Elise, an intense revulsion unlike anything she had experienced before swept over her and "hatred soared through my veins, and an overwhelming sense of violation." In 1944, in an attempt to destroy a German headquarters just two blocks from her home, the Allies bombed Amsterdam and bombs fell around her home. Once again, terrifying emotions of fear swept her being. In 1945, however, Amsterdam was liberated by the Canadians and Allied tanks swept into the streets. In order to impress upon her young daughter the significance of that moment, her mother lifted her up on one of the tanks and, says Elise, "I learned in that victory ride about ecstasy."

Her experiences at such a young age of deprivation, hatred, and fear, says Elise, proved pivotal in shaping her life story as a healer and an artist. It led her on a lifelong quest away from the terrors of war, toward beauty as a path to heal suffering. These tendencies showed early in her life; when the Unicorn tapestries came from Paris to the museum in Amsterdam, she was so taken with the exhibit that she begged to be taken back again and again. The other side of her character, however, influenced by her grandfather who was a famous social worker in Europe, felt drawn to go to Africa to work with Albert Schweitzer. Arriving in Washington, D.C., as a young woman of twenty-two with plans to become a social worker, however, Elise fell in love instead, married, and had two children. She spent the next twenty years of her professional life "in the service of beauty," working for museums and art galleries. As she helped mount exhibitions, Elise says, her eye for beauty grew sharper, influenced by her friendships with some of the area's finest artists, such as her close friend, landscape painter Dale Haven Loy.

> *Beholding beauty with the eye of the mind, he will be enabled to bring forth, not images of beauty, but realities (for he has hold not of an image but of a reality), and bringing forth and nourishing true virtue to become the friend of God and be immortal, if mortal man may.*
>
> PLATO'S DIALOGUES:
> *Symposium, 212*

Elise's appreciation for art and artists of all eras and traditions expanded as well; among others, she grew to love the early Greek Cycladic goddess statues, the Renaissance paintings of Pierro della Francesca, Giotto di Bondone, and Fra Angelico, and the works of modern artists like Helen Frankenthaler and Daniel Brush. The art that called forth a response from her seemed filled with pathos and intensity, and conveyed something of the spiritual state to which she aspired to connect. Beauty, it seemed, brought solace to her suffering and inspired every aspect of her life. "It would be impossible for me to live without beauty," says Elise. "Even if I were in prison I would put a rock out. I crave it; it's like food. Sometimes I will attend an exhibition, and something about a composition or a sculpture will just send me into a state of ecstasy."

After completing a course in Reiki healing in 1979, however, Elise's life course began to shift. Slowly, the two sides of her nature began to draw closer. "After my Reiki course, I had to view two sculptures for purchase by a museum. Suddenly, I realized that I was looking at them in a totally new way. I had to decide between them—and I let my body make the choice. Since then, I experience art differently. I still have the same critical taste, but I also allow the vibrations of the art to guide me in my body. When art is truly great, I have no doubt in my judgment because I feel it in my body. Kandinsky said that if an artist is good and true he can put his or her vibrations in the artwork. And, in turn, the vibrations of the artwork will touch the vibrations of the viewer." Thus, art at its best, says Elise, "should transport us or act as a mirror that reflects our souls—because great art stirs what is the best and truest in us."

Another turning point came when Elise's second husband became ill and died of cancer. Disgusted with the commercialism corroding the art world and grieving over the loss of her husband, she decided to devote herself entirely to healing, becoming a practitioner of Rosen Method bodywork. Always deeply mystical, Elise had studied various spiritual disciplines and undergone years of psychotherapy—perspectives she now brought to bear on her healing work. Before beginning a session, as she describes it, she places her hands on her client and prays silently for "the pure, white light of Christ to come in. I ask to be used as a channel for healing, and that the session be for the highest good and growth of my client. . . . While I work, I hold the Jesus prayer as a mantra on the in and out breaths." Then, gliding her hands over the body, she looks for areas of dis-ease, or where breathing is absent. Soon, long-held emotions—including rage, shame, fear, guilt, hatred, and sorrow—begin to surface. "The body is very honest. Often, simply by allowing the feeling or the pain to be there in a state of emotional awareness, a kind of letting go will occur naturally. This is what healing is about," she explains.

In addition to prayers and breathing practices, Elise will use a beautiful holy image to support her healing work. "I have an old Russian icon of a saint, which sits on the altar in my healing room. A client of mine who is married to a priest in the Russian Orthodox Church told me that it probably had not been blessed properly for a long time. A blessed icon is no longer ordinary, she told me, but becomes

> *Beloved Pan, and all ye other gods who
> haunt this place, give me beauty in the
> inward soul; and may the outward and
> inward man be at one.*
>
> PLATO'S DIALOGUES:
> *Phaedrus*

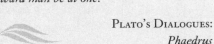

a holy object, a window to God. So my icon was blessed by her husband with holy oil. Recently returned to my altar, it is infused with a new sense of sacredness. I now often focus on the gold halo around the saint's head and feel myself encounter a holy presence." In one incident, for example, says Elise, a client who had been diagnosed with cancer neared the end of their session while still in an unbearable, "dark hole" of suffering. "As I held her head, I looked at the icon and at a Coptic cross that is lying on my altar table. Internally, I began to beg for help. Help us. Help us. At that very instant, something changed. I could feel it in my hands, a powerful energy. I felt I was in the presence of an awesome grace. Then in that same instant, I heard my client say, 'I see a hand and it is pulling me out of the hole. . . .'"

Indeed, her Rosen bodywork, says Elise, has allowed her to use all the gifts she has been given in this lifetime, including the healing power of love and beauty. "If you connect to the essence of another person, you are in the presence of beauty. Most of the time my eyes are closed or I am looking down at my hands. Sometimes when I open my eyes, however, and look at the faces of my clients, I think I've never seen anything so beautiful. In their true essence, everyone is exquisite. The Sufi teacher Pir Vilayat Inayat Khan once said that we have to look at each other's eternal face. And because we live in such a critical society where people are judged according to what they do, rather than as a child of God, simply to see someone's inner beauty is profoundly healing." The creative power of emotional healing to reconnect a person to their original state of beauty and wholeness, says Elise, is reflected in these words of Simeon the New Theologian, the tenth-century Russian Orthodox monk: "And everything that is hurt, everything that seemed to us dark, harsh, shameful, maimed, ugly irreparably damaged, is in Him transformed and recognized as whole, as lovely, and radiant in His light. We awaken as the Beloved in every last part of our body."

Yet though healing satisfied Elise at a deep, soul level, the muse of beauty had not finished with her. One day she realized that if she never found the courage to make something of beauty herself, she would be "lying on my deathbed one day and I would be really sad." So, always an accomplished needlewoman, she began creating tapestries. Because she loved minimal art, she chose white silks, stitching ancient symbols like a triangle or a square as a still point in the center. Finally, using the finest gold thread, she embroidered a haiku, such as this one by Dogen: "Midnight. No waves, no wind, the empty boat is flooded with moonlight." Occa-

For beauty being the best of all we know
Sums up the unsearchable and secret
aims of nature . . .

ROBERT BRIDGES, *The*
Growth of Love, SONNET 8

sionally, she would feel blocked in her inspiration by her critical inner voice that told her she would never create anything worthy of comparison to the great artists she admired. Then one day, she received advice from a fellow artist, who told her to make her tapestries for God and poetry—and nothing else. Released from her inhibitions, Elise began showing her tapestries at local art exhibits. Soon, she began to receive accolades from friends and fellow artists who recognized the delicacy, intricacy, and complexity of her work.

For Elise, art, beauty, and healing had come full circle.

Bringing Out the Beauty of a Soul Sister

My experiences over the years with my closest women friends have shown that women bring out the beauty within one another's souls. While this may include the graceful rituals around cosmetics and dress, it shows itself in other ways as well.

Perhaps you have a friend who is going through a difficult time financially: If you can afford to, why not buy her an extravagant bottle of perfume, or a pair of silk pajamas? Or, make a plan to have a beauty day with a close friend. Have a manicure, a facial, or be teenagers again and have fun sampling makeup at the beauty counter.

Like the story of Elise and Dale, you can also bring beauty into a friend's life by supporting and encouraging her art or creative projects. Nothing is sweeter to me when I am working than receiving feedback from my friends: the E-mail my friend Susan sent me upon publication of an article I had worked long and hard on; the flowers Taj sent me when I finished my first book; the letter from Dana praising the meditation I had written for a women's new moon ceremony. Likewise, I am proud of the beauty of my friends' creations: Harriett's farm, Elise's tapestries, my sister Colleen's flute performances, Taj's paintings, Lis's newly decorated home, Barbara's article. The beauty soul sisters see in one another's creativity is a wonderful, powerful thing.

Perhaps the best way to bring beauty into a friend's life, however, is to practice seeing her soul shining through her face and personality. Try this meditation, for instance, and see what magic happens: After sitting in silence for a few minutes, stilling the mind and calming the breath, bring to mind the image of one of your closest friends. As you meditate on her physical form, imagine that something else begins to transpire through her. A transparent glow appears to radiate throughout her whole being. Her eyes become windows to the heavens, her hair the halo around

Beauty as we feel it is something indescribable: what it is or what it means can never be said.

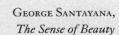

George Santayana,
The Sense of Beauty

the stars. Now, become aware of a particular quality this friend appears to embody—perhaps you feel her core of strength, or maybe you feel the depth of her capacity for compassion and empathy. Maybe you see in your friend the beauty of erotic passion or the brilliance of intellect. Whatever the quality, commit to remaining loyal to that quality you see reflected in her, despite the ups and downs of everyday life. As the Sufi mystic Hazrat Inayat Khan says, "Our trust and confidence in the beauty of the soul helps to draw out that hidden beauty which must shine out one day."

Dale's Story:

"When the people of the world all know beauty as beauty," said Lao-tzu, "there arises the recognition of ugliness." This has been the experience of Elise's close friend and soul sister, artist Dale Haven Loy of Washington, D.C. The beauty we see in nature, believes Loy, "comes with a warning" of its possible demise. An attractive, dark-haired woman in her sixties, Loy's petite build belies the large, dense, darkly apocalyptic landscape paintings that are her signature creation. Themes around the war in Bosnia, as well as images that portray earth's devastation, dominate her exhibits that have been shown at the United Nations and galleries around the country. "Her landscapes please the eye," wrote one critic, "but unsettle the psyche."[12] In part, the direction Dale's art has taken has been shaped by her marriage to former Undersecretary of State for Global Affairs Frank Loy, whose political involvement heightened her own awareness of human-rights and ecological issues. Too, the experience of living in Washington, D.C.—vortex of power and politics—sensitized her to the eternal struggle between the dark and the light forces at work in the world.

Beauty is a terrible and awful thing! It is terrible because it has not been fathomed, for God sets us nothing but riddles. Here the boundaries meet and all contradictions exist side by side.

DOSTOYEVSKI,
The Brothers Karamazov

Although most significant art expresses this universal conflict, says Loy, she ponders whether the forces for light have dimmed dramatically low in our time. "In my paintings in recent years," she said in her introduction to an exhibit influenced by the war in Bosnia, "I have been trying to locate this life force, finding it harder and harder to discover as the environment degenerates in general and as specific disasters such as Bosnia scar the soul as well as the land." Her series, titled The Series Antaeus, Loy says, was inspired by the Greek myth of Antaeus. In it, Antaeus, the son of the god Poseidon and the goddess Gaea, derived his invincible strength from his contact with the earth. Each time Hercules picked him up and threw him to the earth to kill him, he sprang back to life, renewed. Finally, Hercules killed him by holding him aloft above his head. "This said to me that, like Antaeus, we are in danger of dying because we are losing our earth connection," cutting down our trees and razing fields, said Loy with the same intense conviction that marks her art.

Gradually, however, Loy's work has come to reflect more of a balance between the light and the dark forces. In *Path,* part of her Series Trees, which explores the symbolic and mythological aspects of trees, an ebony tree and a silver-barked tree stand on either side of the pathway that stretches toward the horizon between them. In *Archetype*, white and black branches intertwine. Though she is not a religious person, she says, "I find myself looking for things that tell me about reverencing the earth." Loy's quest to develop more spiritual and soul-related subject matter is reflected in a series of images devoted to the discovery of a prehistoric ring of tree trunks that recently surfaced off the coast of Norfolk, England. In this image, now called "sea henge," Loy found a symbol of promise and hope. "Here was this ancient prayer circle that, instead of being made of stones, was made of oak trees—and it survived."

Loy's magical gold-hued triptych of this exquisite Stonehenge-like circle, however, would not have come about without the inspiration of her close friend, Elise Wiarda. Paging through the newspaper one day, Elise saw the photograph of this discovery and thought immediately of her friend. Indeed, if nature is the muse of women, so, too, are women muses for one another. In the arena of art and beauty, soul sisters inspire and encourage the efforts of their friends.

> *Happily may I walk.*
>
> *May it be beautiful before me.*
>
> *May it be beautiful behind me.*
>
> *May it be beautiful below me.*
>
> *May it be beautiful above me.*
>
> *May it be beautiful all around me.*
>
> *In beauty it is finished.*
>
> **The Night Chant**
> *of the Navajo*

Painting the Goddess in Nature:
Meinrad Craighead

Years before the Goddess movement got underway, artist Meinrad Craighead first encountered "God the Mother" as a young child. Lying with her dog beneath blue hydrangea bushes in her grandmother's garden in Little Rock, Arkansas, she had heard "a rush of water" deep within her. "I listened to the sound of the water inside and I understood: 'This is God.'" Thus, it is no surprise that she now lives and paints near the Rio Grande River, the watery guide she describes as "the natural, metaphysical, archetypal symbol which has ruled my life."

Located on the valley floor between the Rio Grande and the pyramidic mountains of Albuquerque, New Mexico, Craighead has designed and built a studio that is a sanctuary for beauty and the creative spirit. Enclosed within the protective circumference of an old grove of cottonwood trees, it is a simple, light space, warmed by a wood-burning stove. Dogs sleep in corners, and a profusion of geraniums blooms in the ceiling-high windows. A worktable stands in the center of the room. Here Craighead, like a medieval craftsman, paints image after holy image of God the Mother. In paintings such as *Tree Mother* and *Changing Woman,* the body of woman and the body of earth are woven, through symbol and image, into lush, tapestrylike icons that celebrate the immanence of the Mother God in creation.

> *Oh, thou art fairer than the evening air*
> *Clad in the beauty of a thousand stars.*
>
> CHRISTOPHER MARLOWE,
> *The Jew of Malta*

> *O world, as God has made it! All is beauty!*
>
> ROBERT BROWNING,
> "THE GUARDIAN ANGEL"

Once a cloistered religious, Craighead brings a contemplative focus to her life as an artist. Her day begins outside with a walk along the riverbank, or before her altar where she builds a fire in the belly of a gourd-shaped vessel, gathering in the energy of nature so it will be with her as she works. Moving inside, she then makes a ritual circumambulation of the altars she has placed around her studio, each one honoring a sacred direction. Dusty with the cornmeal that she sprinkles on her animal fetishes and cluttered with stones, pots, postcards from friends and photographs—of the Black Madonna, Carl Jung, Thomas Merton, and family members—these "living" altars reflect the rich mythology of Craighead's life, the creative cauldron out of which her work emerges. They are paradigmatic of one of the most powerful statements in her book *The Mother's Songs:* "I am born connected. I am born remembering."

This sense of connection began for Craighead in the close childhood bond she shared with her mother, grandmother, and sisters, an intimacy that extends back through her foremothers. "She passes on to me the meaning of religion because she links me to our origin in God the Mother," Craighead once wrote of her mother. This intuitive grounding in the Divine Feminine flourished within her, like a seed in fertile soil, throughout a childhood and young adulthood imbued with rich images from the Catholic liturgy.

Raised in Chicago, Craighead attended Catholic schools from elementary school through college. After graduating with a Master of Fine Arts degree from the

University of Wisconsin in 1960, she taught at the art department at the University of Albuquerque. Two years later, she left to teach in Florence—and remained abroad for the next twenty-one years. While in Europe, her veneration for God the Mother led Craighead to Spain, where she lived at Montserrat, the mountaintop monastery near Barcelona famous for its shrine to the Black Madonna. Then at age thirty, following a deep yearning to live a contemplative life, she left her life as a teacher and entered the seventeenth-century Benedictine monastery Stanbrook Abbey in England. Over the years, however, her love of the rituals and daily rhythms of monastic life were insufficient to overcome a growing disillusionment with the sisters' "narrow and rigid expectations of what life should be."[13] Thus after fourteen years, moving once again on the strength of an interior understanding, she left the monastery. "I knew by then that this was exactly what I was supposed to do, and I did it. I had nowhere to go; I had to be supported by friends. But I have always had the sublime understanding that God was going to take care of me."

And in fact, almost immediately, Craighead received a generous grant from the Arts Council of Great Britain, allowing her to continue painting for several years before returning to New Mexico. Out of this period evolved her work with images of the Divine Feminine. These images, along with her own prose commentary, have been published in books such as *The Mother's Songs: Images of God the Mother*, and *The Litany of the Great River*. Currently, she is at work on a retrospective of her life work. According to Craighead, her main source of inspiration comes from a desire to give thanks for the wonder and beauty of creation. "When you wonder, you give thanks, and giving thanks is a ritual. Ritual is the need to do beautiful actions with beautiful things in order to say thank you for this divine beauty we all share. My own upbringing in the Catholic Church gave me a great love of ritual." Indeed, while she does not consider herself to be a "Catholic artist," the tradition has nonetheless nourished her. "Anyone who has grown up in the womb of the Catholic Church is given a very early understanding of the sanctity of the Great Mother figure in Mary, the Mother of God. In the history of art, she takes over where the early images of the Great Mother were pushed aside." Craighead points out the way the Church, over the centuries, has used the energy of the Divine Feminine symbolically. "The Church is called the Mother, the womb, the source." The image of the Black Madonna, in

> *What to the mind is shameful is beauty and nothing else to the heart. Is there beauty in Sodom? Believe me, that for the immense mass of mankind beauty is found in Sodom. . . . The awful thing is that beauty is mysterious as well as terrible. God and the devil are fighting there, and the battlefield is the heart of man.*
>
>
>
> DOSTOYEVSKI,
> *The Brothers Karamazov*

particular, has inspired her both inwardly, and in the images she paints. "I recognize in her the face of the abyss, which is infinite, beautiful darkness, without an edge. To me, it's a sign of truth, a sign of abundance, a sign of mystery. It's a sign of light shining in the darkness. The original Black Madonna is black-Isis holding Horus on her lap. That's the paradigm that came into medieval craftsmanship. Isis holding her son became Mary holding Jesus."

Craighead's creative process, as she describes it, is an act of worship that arises out of seeing and giving expression to the divine beauty around her. She doesn't have visions; her visions are in her paintings. Indeed artists, she says, are like "see-ers" who "see" for the rest of us, and bring back a great treasure. "As an artist, I'm the first to see the treasure which has never existed before. But the treasure is never for yourself. You are just the agent to receive it and bring it back." The creative process, she says, is "endlessly regenerative.... An artist is a transformer; transformation is what our work is about. It's the work in the cauldron: You throw in anything and it all comes together as something delicious. It's like there's a centrifugal force in us, and everything that comes in each day is spun

> *He hath a daily beauty in his life.*
>
> SHAKESPEARE,
> *King Lear*

around. Most is flung off, but the rich stuff drops right down to the bottom. You know what a compost heap is like: It seethes, makes noises, stinks, bubbles, and emits gases. All of that is transformation. So when your imagination gets in there, it's growing in the most incredible, rich earth. No wonder the images come out; they've been trapped in there. The work of the spirit is in each of us. All we've got to do is just do it. That is the incarnation, that is making the invisible visible."[14]

BEAUTY THAT WILL SAVE THE WORLD

Beauty, said the Russian novelist Fyodor Dostoyevski, will save the world. Certainly, that was the example set by Mother Teresa, whose work with the poor and dying of India inspired the title of the book *Something Beautiful for God* by Malcolm Muggeridge. Beauty as a tool to heal humankind's suffering was also the intent of Simone Weil, the French theologian and philosopher who devoted her life to serving beauty through the principles of fairness and justice. Though she is a relatively little-known figure, I find in her story and in her writings a profound understanding of beauty as a creative force for social transformation. Through Weil's intellect, the example of her short life, and above all her soul, beauty becomes the medium through which we go about making heaven on earth.

"... We must have faith that the universe is beautiful on all levels," she wrote. "The beauty of the world is the co-operation of divine wisdom in creation."[15]

Beauty entered Weil's life at a young age, yet in a way that would alter her life forever. As a girl growing up in France during World War I, the story goes, Simone Weil felt intellectually inferior to her older brother, a mathematical genius—even though she herself was considered a remarkable student by her teachers. One day she overheard a chance phrase of a visitor to her mother. "One is genius itself," said her mother's friend, pointing to her brother; then, indicating Simone, "the other beauty!"[16] These words left an indelible impression on the young Simone. In order to cultivate the beauty of her mind and soul, she forever avoided the trappings of traditional feminine adornment. An oversized brown beret, shapeless cape, and large, floppy shoes were her typical costume as an adult. "Only in her writing," writes Leslie A. Fielder in his introduction to Weil's collection of essays, *Waiting for God,* "is Simone Weil betrayed into charm; in her life, she made a principle of avoiding it."

Though she died a mystic at the young age of thirty-four, writes Fielder, Weil began life as the cherished daughter of an agnostic, bourgeois Jewish family in Paris, France. She excelled in school, studying philosophy under a well-known French philosopher, and eventually became a teacher of philosophy at a girls school. Despite the security her French family provided her, she commiserated from a very early age with those who were born to less privilege. At the age of five, she refused to eat sugar, as long as the soldiers fighting on the front were unable to eat it; later, she refused to wear socks in solidarity with the children of the workers who had none. Gifted with an incredible intelligence, she nonetheless suffered such intense unworthiness that she felt pushed to suicide by the age of fourteen. Her health, as well, was frail, and she endured acute migraine headaches for most of her life. Influenced by Karl Marx as much as the Greek philosophers she loved, Weil became a committed left-wing political radical. At the age of twenty-two, while working at her first teaching job, she picketed with the unemployed workmen of the town and began writing for *La Revolution Proletarienne.* Her devotion to the working-class life continued throughout her life: at various intervals she worked in the fields, in a Renault car factory, and alongside the soldiers on the front in the war in Spain. Yet always, ill health intervened, forcing her away from her political activities to seek out rest and medical attention.

Though she had never prayed or entered a church, Weil later said that she had always been a Christian. This she credited to her experiences with the work-

The most general definition of beauty . . .

Multeity in Unity.

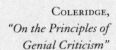

Coleridge,
*"On the Principles of
Genial Criticism"*

ers in the fields at the factories, and on the battlefront. While recuperating after her Spanish experience while on holiday with her parents in Portugal, however, Weil experienced the "joy and pain" of Christ's passion while listening to a Gregorian chant. "I felt, without being in any way prepared for it . . . a presence more personal, more certain, more real than that of a human being . . ."[17] Incredibly, five years passed before she took up prayer as a practice; then, each time she repeated the Lord's Prayer, Christ himself, she wrote in her journals, "descended and took her." She experienced mystical raptures of communion until the day of her death. Yet though solitude and her inner life grew in magnitude, Weil still remained inseparable from the misfortune of others. During World War II, she refused to leave Paris until it had been declared an open city; she then moved with her parents to Marseilles, where she worked at a Catholic agricultural community under the direction of the lay theologian Gustave Thibon. There, working alongside the peasants in the vineyards—even sleeping and eating alongside them—she gave lectures on the Upanishads. It was during this time that her spiritual progress blossomed under the influence of her friendship with both Thibon, to whom she entrusted the journals that were published after her death, and Father Joseph-Marie Perrin, with whom she was able to confide the deepest secrets of her soul.

Beauty is truth, truth beauty—that is all
Ye know on earth, and all ye need to know.

JOHN KEATS,
Ode on a Grecian Urn

When the people of the world all know
beauty as beauty,
There arises the recognition of ugliness.

LAO-TZU,
The Way of Lao Tzu

It was with Perrin that she addressed the question of whether or not to become baptized in the Church. Central among her objections was her concern over whether Christianity denied the beauty of this world. In ancient times the "love of the beauty of the world had a very important place in men's thoughts and surrounded the whole of life with marvelous poetry," she wrote in her journal. And though Weil took note of expressions of beauty in the writings of St. John, as well as certain parts of the Old Testament and in the Gospels, she concluded that, in general, "we might say that the beauty of the world is almost absent from the Christian tradition. This is strange. It is difficult to understand. . . . How can Christianity call itself catholic if the universe itself is left out?" Ultimately, Weil never resolved her dilemma. She decided to wait for a sign or a command from God, believing that searching and seeking for God led only "to error"; rather, she wished to wait in patience for his command.

When health reasons compelled Weil to leave the Catholic agricultural community, she set off for a trip to America with her parents. After a brief stay there, she returned to England, but, because of the war, could not return to France. There, once again, she wished to share in the hardships of her fellow compatriots in France and refused to eat any more than the rations allotted her countrymen in occupied territory. The deprivation of nourishment seriously weakened Weil's health, only this time she did not recover, and she died in August 1943. The letters and essays Weil had entrusted for safekeeping to her friends Father Perrin and Gustave Thibon were published posthumously. Through them she became known as a kind of "outsider saint," a mystic at the crossroads between "Christianity and everything that is not Christianity," thus ensuring her universal appeal among seekers of all faiths. Her chief mission, writes Fiedler, was to those still submerged "in materialism." She called for a "new kind of saint," one whose universality combined both love of God and love of the "city of the world."

> *. . . We have given you garments to cover your nakedness, and as a thing of beauty; but the garment of God-consciousness is the best of all.*
>
> KORAN 7:26, *The Light of Dawn: A Daybook of Verses from the Holy Qu'ran*

Weil's status as an outsider and a social activist, coupled with her tendencies toward worldly renunciation, make her writings on beauty all the more potent. For Weil, beauty was both a state of the soul and a moral response to the beauty lacking in the lives of her fellow human beings. For what was the horror of poverty, she wondered in her famous essay "Forms of the Implicit Love of God," if not "a horror of ugliness. The soul that is prevented by circumstances from feeling anything of the beauty of the world . . . is invaded to its very center by a kind of horror." To thrust human beings in cities down to the state of social outcasts, she wrote, "was to sever every bond of poetry and love between human beings and the universe . . . to plunge them forcibly into the horror of ugliness."

At the same time, however, Weil found beauty in the kind of poverty chosen by saints as a way to feel the presence of God, just as, she wrote "Saint Francis needed to be a vagabond and a beggar in order to feel it (the universe) to be beautiful." Not only is St. Francis' poetry perfect, but, she writes, "all his life was perfect poetry in action. His very choice of places for solitary retreats or . . . his convents was in itself the most beautiful poetry in action."

Simply to read Weil's passages on beauty are to feel moved to the depths by her mystical participation in reality: "All these secondary kinds of beauty are of infinite value as openings to universal beauty." But, she writes, "with the exception of God, nothing short of the universe as a whole can with complete accuracy be called beautiful." God created the universe, she continues, and "his Son, our first-born brother, created the beauty of it for us. The beauty of the world is Christ's tender smile for us coming through matter." Thus God created the beauty of the earth, imagines Weil, as a way for us to be enticed into loving his creation.

Zainab Salbi, the founder of Women for Women International, who was profiled in chapter 1, shares the way a small gesture on the part of one person brought beauty to a woman who had suffered its absence because of war's injustice. She tells the story of a woman in the states who was sponsoring a nurse living in Sarajevo. In one letter, the nurse wrote of her experience standing in line to get water, when suddenly a sniper killed the person standing in front of her. Even so, the nurse remained in line, because she couldn't return home without water. In response, her American sponsor wrote back to her describing the garden she was planting— the colors and smell of the flowers, the beauty of springtime. "Some people feel guilty writing about the positive, wonderful things in their lives to those who are suffering. But I met the nurse in Bosnia who was receiving these letters," said Zainab. "And she told me that these letters were the only colors in her life. They reminded her that somewhere, people were living a normal life and that one day she, too, might have that normal life again."

> *Beauty is nature's coin, must not be hoarded,*
> *But must be current, and the good thereof*
> *Consists in mutual and partaken bliss.*
>
>
>
> JOHN MILTON,
> "L'ALLEGRO"

If more people made the commitment to make the world a more beautiful place, society might have the makings of a real beauty myth. If women seek to cultivate their appearance as beautiful, for instance, then let them do so as a way to celebrate their unique styles of beauty as expressions of the many faces of the Goddess. If women make art, then let them make art in imitation of the glory suffusing the universe—art that awakens the eyes of the soul to the sacrament of life. And if women seek to bring principles of fairness and justice to those who suffer, then let them do so in the cause of creating a city of the world that is a reflection on earth of the beauty of the city of God in heaven.

MEDITATIONS ON ENHANCING THE PERCEPTION OF BEAUTY

✵

Amid the genuine terror and horror that so often shadows life, the experience of beauty, no matter how impermanent, can resurrect faith and give us courage. One day after September 11, for instance, I walked outside and was instantly captured by the sight of a lofty white cumulus cloud piling up in the blue sky vaulting above me. Suddenly transfixed, I was overcome by the precious wonder of life, existing even in the heart of despair. Beauty, wrote the Islamic scholar Henri Corbin, is "the supreme theophany, divine self-revelation." If beauty is a form of revelation, then meditation is one way we can awaken its sleeping presence within ourselves and in the world around us. By stilling the voices of pragmatism and necessity for just a few moments each day, and by allowing ourselves to open, as a flower, to the miracle of the creation, we incarnate the soul of beauty in our everyday lives. The following are some exercises to help enhance the presence of beauty in your life.

✿

Walking Meditation on the Sacrament of Beauty

One way to receive the sacrament of beauty into your life is to step outside the limitations of your self by stepping outside for a walk. Whether you live in a city, the country, or the suburbs, beauty is all around. There is no need to go anywhere; creation itself is a temple of beauty.

Before you begin your walk, set your intention toward receiving the quality of beauty, repeating within your heart the simple phrase, "the beauty of the world."

*Tis not a lip, or eye, we beauty call,
But the joint force and full result of all.*

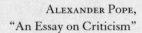

Alexander Pope,
"An Essay on Criticism"

Perhaps you would like to identify with a mystic like St. Francis, Hildegard of Bingen, or Sita—holy beings who revelled in earth's loveliness. Then, opening the door of your house or office, open the doors of your bodily perceptions by throwing open your physical senses: Drink in the sights around you through your eyes. Hear the sounds of life. Smell the fragrance of nature. Feel the elements against your skin. As you walk, begin to open to the world around you; become aware of the way the beauty in creation nourishes and feeds your soul.

Slowly, such ordinary things as the countenance of the mailman, the people in the street, the children darting and playing, or brightly colored cars begin to appear as awesome and transfigured as a magnificent painting hanging in a museum. The gardens and trees you pass seem effulgent with color. Clouds chase birds in the blue bowl of the sky. Like St. Francis, you are so taken with the beauty of creation that you feel like singing and dancing. A part of you feels called to respond to the beauty that pours over you like a golden river of life. You want to write it all down, say a prayer, compose a poem, or cook a dish to express this beauty that fills you with creative energy.

As you continue to walk along, your senses are even further heightened. You can feel the river winding its way along, called by the beauty of the ocean. You can even hear the birds singing in the tropical rain forests long distances away; watch a silent snowfall on a remote mountain peak; or witness a comet sail through space, trailing a brilliant plume of light.

Through opening to the beauty of the world this way, you have entered a transfigured landscape, a visionary world. But it is not a fantasy world in a land far away. It is the real world you live in—yet have never really seen before. In this way, receiving the holy sacrament of beauty through your physical senses has transformed you. The soul of beauty penetrates the very cells of your body, and you have become wholly beautiful in the image of the Goddess reflected in creation.

✿

MEDITATIONS ON APHRODITE

Where can Aphrodite be found today? A glimmer of the goddess may be found in the enchantingly bejeweled movie stars who promenade down the red carpet for the annual Academy Awards show. Or she can be felt, seen, smelled, and touched in the perfumes and creams, clothes and shoes, and bracelets and rings that line the aisles of boutiques and department stores. These places lure because they promise that frisson of frivolous charm so utterly lacking in our utilitarian culture. For all its commercialism, there is a symbolism to be found in these superficial forms of beauty: the notion that beauty reveals itself in the appearances of the world. We are drawn first to beauty through the sight of something that catches our eyes, or through the senses of our bodies: a bright scarf, the scent of perfume, the touch of silk, an orchid, the smell of a summer's evening, the feeling of water on dry skin. Like Psyche in search of Eros, the sight, sound, smell, and touch of beauty beckons us forward along the pathway of beauty and love.

To open one's physical senses to the presence of beauty in the appearances of the world, it helps to meditate on the archetype of beauty as it is reflected through Aphrodite. Begin your meditation by creating an atmosphere of loveliness and serenity that will attract her presence. You may, for instance, wish to adorn your altar with some flowers, as well as photos of loved ones; you may also want to play a piece of music that, to your ears, is soothing and peaceful.

As you sit before your altar to beauty, allow the music to still the jangled edges of your aura: You can almost imagine the Goddess's hands smoothing away the tension of the day. Through her being, your subtle body—the magnetic aura that surrounds you—becomes as still as the surface of the sunlit sea. Next, let the rhythmic feeling of the ocean fill your heart, as the waves rise and fall. Then, imagine that this ocean of feeling has given rise to an emotion of sublime beauty: This is Aphrodite, emerging from the depths of your heart. She is the essence of beauty, the perfume of loveliness, the embodiment of grace and joy. She is all lithesome light and laughter. Bathe in her being, as she herself ritually bathes in the ocean once each year to restore her sense of wholeness. Feel wholly beautiful, inside and out.

After immersing yourself in the being of Aphrodite, open your eyes and survey the environment around you. Practice seeing the world through her eyes, rather than your own narrow vision. As you do, life appears transfigured, lit from within: the flowers on your altar radiate color; the photos of your loved ones reveal an inner dimension of soulful depth that you had never experienced before; the window opening to the sky outside is a vision of glory. This is the precious pearl that is the gift of Aphrodite—the vision of beauty animating all creation.

As your meditation comes to a close, make an offering of thanks appropriate to the goddess of beauty—a dance, a smile, or a graceful gesture. To continually renew the spirit of beauty in your life, choose an article of loveliness—a scarf, a scent, a flower, or a treasured object—to use as a talisman to re-invoke the goddess in your heart. Or, you may want to initiate a daily "beauty ritual" in honor of Aphrodite, such as taking a scented bubble bath, tending an exquisite flower, or complimenting a different person each day on something nice you have noticed about him or her.

❖

MEDITATION FOR ARTISTS

Artists are devotees of beauty. The chef who creates the sublime signature dish, the writer who strings words together like pearls on a necklace, or the musician who composes sounds that stir the soul are each endeavoring to reflect something of that quality in their work.

> *Adornment is never anything except a reflection of the heart.*
>
> COCO CHANEL

> *Beauty in things exists in the mind which contemplates them.*
>
> DAVID HUME,
> "Of Tragedy"

Yet to be a creator of beauty in any form requires both discipline and concentration. Because every artist begins with an image of an ideal, one's whole attention must be focused to make that ideal a reality. In this sense, creativity and meditation are closely linked. In order to do their work, for example, artists, like meditators, must first establish a safe zone of quiet where they can work undisturbed by outside distractions—what author Virginia Woolf once described as a "room of one's own." Once inside this safe zone, however, artists must then create an inner calm so that they can be free from the intrusion of nettlesome thoughts and feelings—"It's time to go the dentist," or "I have to buy so-and-so a birthday present," or "I should call my mother back"—that will inevitably arise to distract them from their process.

In the art of meditation, there exist many different techniques to help focus one's concentration. Similarly, visualization combined with meditation can enhance creativity. While I was working on this book, in fact, two images came to me in separate dreams to help center my concentration. At the time, many issues in my life were distracting me from my work; I could not get to that quiet place necessary to write. Through the images in these dreams, which I pass along to you, I was able to still my mind to finally drop down into a deep place and begin to work. If these images don't speak to you, then you may wish to come up with your own images: What is important is the way the image can be used to help create an inner sanctum for creativity.

In the first dream, I was told by a dream teacher to stand before a black-and-white painting hanging on a wall. The painting was very simplistic—a paint-by-number depiction of a winter landscape of a farm and a road. The teacher in the dream guided me to keep staring at the picture and to pay no attention to the people on the periphery of my vision. At first, I felt restless. But as I continued to stare, the landscape before me opened up into a living scene. Like a character in a fairy tale, I stepped through the black-and-white painting into a complex world of color, smell, people, and animals. It literally "opened up" through the power of my concentration. Now, I work with this image as a "warm-up" to writing. My computer screen may seem at first like a flat gray screen with

In art economy is always beauty.

HENRY JAMES,
The Altar of the Dead

And the true order of going, or being led by another, to the things of love, is to begin from the beauties of the earth and mount upwards for the sake of that other beauty, using these steps only, and from one going on to two, and from two to all fair forms to fair practices, and from fair practices to fair notions, until from fair notions he arrives at the notion of absolute beauty, and at last knows what the essence of beauty is.

PLATO'S DIALOGUES:
Symposium, 211

black letters on it; but as I focus my attention on it, looking beyond its surface and into the depths, new worlds open up.

In the second dream I had, I was taken by the same "dream teacher" to the beautifully landscaped grounds of a private school. He then led me inside an old brick building that stood on these grounds, where I suddenly found myself in a high-ceilinged, book-lined library with tall windows. The atmosphere was hushed and still. Old manuscripts lay open on polished wooden tables, and a few students were quietly reading. Inspired by the atmosphere in the dream, I, too, began to study. Like my first dream, the imagery in this dream has proved helpful in my creative process. Now, when writing becomes difficult, I sit down at my desk and imagine myself in the hallowed atmosphere of an old, old library set apart from the rest of the world. In this "private" world, like the private school in the dream, I can think and write and give free rein to my creative imagination, undisturbed by the demands of the outside world.

> *Beauty is the gift of God.*
>
> ARISTOTLE, FROM
> *Diogenes Laertius: Lives*
> *of Eminent Philosophers*

THE LUNAR PHASES OF BEAUTY

The quality of beauty is, like the six phases of the moon, many faced. Each stage is marked by a way of being or a quality of energy.

. . . Like the new moon, there is beauty that is in the process of becoming: the artist at her easel, the architect at the drawing board, an adolescent girl or boy, the first snatch of a poem or song, or the taste of a new recipe. This phase is full of promise and excitement.

. . . Like the waxing first-quarter moon, there is beauty that is near completion: the half-finished manuscript, the outline of a picture sketched onto a canvas, the dish baking in the oven, or the half-built house. This phase is marked by hard work and discipline.

. . . Like the full moon, there is beauty that has reached the fullness of perfection: the finished poem, the ripened apple, or the sublime piano concerto. It is that moment when the writer sends off her manuscript, or the painter steps back from her easel and sighs with satisfaction. This phase is marked by a feeling of completion and wholeness.

. . . Like the waning third-quarter moon, there is beauty that pours itself out, like balm from a vase, making the world a more lovely place: the teacher who inspires

her students; the social activist who beautifies the quality of life for the poor and suf-
fering; the spiritual healer who, through seeing the innate beauty within each indi-
vidual soul, draws it forth; the master artist teaching her students; or the chef
sharing his recipes through a book. This phase is marked by feelings of generosity, a
"pouring out" of the creativity within oneself.

. . . Like the dark of the moon, there is beauty that is empty, waiting to be filled up
again with the light of creativity and the spark of inspiration. This phase is marked
by a feeling of waiting and of complete receptivity.

✿

BALANCING THE SCALES OF HARMONY AND BEAUTY

In the astrological zodiac, the sign that rules beauty is Libra, whose rulership is the planet Venus. "Love develops into harmony, and of harmony is born beauty," says the Sufi mystic Hazrat Inayat Khan. And though it may seem at first glance as if the two qualities of beauty and relationship are unrelated, anyone who has watched a true Libra in action has observed the natural skill with which the "diplomat of the zodiac" is able to skillfully balance their individual needs with those of "the other." It is this rare ability to create harmony out of the jangled notes of a fractious world that is a source of true and lasting beauty—and a sure sign of "Libra magic" at work.

> *. . . but I have loved the principle of beauty in all things . . .*
>
> JOHN KEATS, *Letter to George and Georgiana Keats*

While Eros, or love, was among the children born to Aphrodite and her lover, Ares, so, too, was Harmonia, or harmony. Indeed, among the symbols that represent the sign of Libra, the most significant is the set of scales. One of the symbolic functions of the scales of Libra is to see how skilled we are at the art of living harmonious lives of relationship. According to the teachings of Hazrat Inayat Khan, rhythm, balance, and harmony are not only the foundation for music but also the secret of health and happiness.

To invoke the spirit of harmony in your relationships, bring to mind a person with whom you are engaged in some kind of conflict. Clearly outline the differences between the two of you: what "she" did, or "he" said, and how you feel otherwise. Then imagine that person is seated across from you. Next, open your heart to that person; if you do not love him or her, at least cultivate a sense of respect for his or her individual autonomy. To deepen the feeling that the person across from you is not just your opponent, but also a child of the Divine, address him or her silently as "thou."

Cultivating such an attitude of respect opens the door of empathy; putting yourself in their place, you begin to see how things appear from their perspective. Slowly, like the dawn of a star, you begin to glimpse how the impasse has prevented the two of you from seeing each other's point of view. After you have thoroughly immersed yourself in the viewpoint of the person opposite you, return to your "side" of the argument, then review your disagreement in light of the understanding you have just gained. Similarly, imagine that the person opposite you, in body and in point of view, has undergone a similar process and is now able to see things from your perspective.

> *Without charm there can be no fine literature, as there can be no perfect flower without fragrance.*
>
> ARTHUR SYMONS,
> *Stéphane Mallarmé*

Now imagine that throughout this process, some alchemical magic greater than the two of you has been working to sort through your differences. In this heart-opening process, you have conceded something; so, too, has your partner. This mixing and matching of views has resulted in an open flow of energy between you. Now, instead of the chasm that has separated you, a current of warm feeling streams between your hearts. The two of you have somehow managed to retain your individual perspectives; yet at the same time your relationship has been magically balanced so that you have achieved a momentary equilibrium—a heaven of harmony.

Conclude your practice by contemplating once again the symbolism of the scales of Libra, and the harmony and beauty of Venus. Then bow to "the other" in your life, and give thanks that this situation has come into your life as a wise teacher who has taught you how to live in right relationship with others.

MEDITATIONS ON CREATING A MORE BEAUTIFUL WORLD

According to the Sufi teacher Pir Vilayat Inayat Khan, the aim of the Sufi mystic is to "build a beautiful world of beautiful people." In contrast to the ascetic who seeks to renounce the world, Sufis consider such an ideal "the fulfillment of the Divine Purpose on earth."[18] In the same way artists are inspired to bring beauty into the world, so, too, do social activists feel compelled to bring beauty into the lives of those who have suffered the ugly wrongs of injustice. All too often in our modern-day world, beauty is the province of the rich and powerful and not the poor.

In order to help make the vision of a beautiful world an equal part of all people's lives, spiritual seekers can begin by making it a regular part of their daily meditation. You may wish to do this at the conclusion of your contemplation as a way of grounding your experience back into the world. After completing your concentration, rest for a few minutes in the beautiful feelings that you may have experienced during your meditation. Perhaps you felt the beauty that came with feeling peaceful and at ease. Perhaps you felt the beauty that arose from being in the presence of God. In almost every religious tradition, for example, heaven is pictured as a place of unbelievable loveliness: crystal rivers, streets paved with gold, bubbling brooks, trees laden with food, and flowers blooming everywhere in a perpetual springtime.

Now, bring your attention back to earthly reality. Then consider the neighborhood that you live in, then the suburb or precinct, then the larger city of which you are a part. Does beauty live in this environment? Where do people breathe good air and enjoy spacious sidewalks and trees—and where do they live in crumbling-down houses beside garbage-choked streams where the air is too polluted to breathe? Where has the ugliness of racial tension sent the spirit of harmony and beauty into hiding? Where has greed selfishly hoarded beauty for itself?

Rather than feel hopeless or overwhelmed as you allow all this into your consciousness, continue to rest in the peaceful beauty of your earlier meditation. As you breathe in and out, however, inhale the beauty of your heavenly encounter—then exhale the spirit of this beauty into those parts of your neighborhood or city that are suffering the wounds of ugliness. As you do this, imagine how a dirty river or a rundown street might look transformed. Like seeing the beauty of a person's soul, so, too, can we practice seeing the beauty of the soul of a place. In this way, we make our prayers real by bringing heaven on earth.

As you bring your meditation to a close, think of one thing that you might do this week that can help make your vision a reality. Whether it be attend-

Beauty is . . . associated with reticence, with stubbornness, of a number of kinds. It arises somehow from a desire not to comply with what may be expected, but to act inevitably, as long as some human truth is in sight, whatever that inevitability may call for. Beauty is not a means . . . it is a result; it belongs to ordering, to form, to aftereffect.

EUDORA WELTY,
The Eye of the Story

Soul is born in beauty, and feeds on beauty and requires beauty for life.

JAMES HILLMAN,
*The Thought of the Heart
and the Soul of the World*

ing a city council meeting to stop construction of an ugly building that blocks the sky from view, or vowing to protect your local river from the effects of pollution, let the vision of heavenly beauty that could be a reality on earth be your guide.

RECOMMENDED READING

The Artist's Way: A Spiritual Path to Higher Creativity by Julia Cameron (Tarcher, 1992)

The Education of the Heart, edited by Thomas Moore (HarperCollins, 1996)

The Goddess: Mythological Images of the Feminine by Christine Downing (Crossroad, 1981)

The Litany of the Great River by Meinrad Craighead (Paulist Press, 1990)

The Mother's Songs: Images of God the Mother by Meinrad Craighead (Paulist Press, 1986)

On Beauty and Being Just by Elaine Scarry (Princeton University Press, 1999)

The Once and Future Goddess: A Symbol for Our Times A Sweeping Visual Chronicle of the Sacred Female and Her Reemergence in the Cultural Mythology of our Time by Elinor Gadon (HarperCollins, 1989)

Pagan Meditations: Aphrodite, Hestia, Artemis by Ginette Paris (Spring Publications, 1983)

The Re-enchantment of Everyday Life by Thomas Moore (HarperCollins, 1996)

Saving the World with Soul: The Reimagination of Modern Life by Robert Sardello (HarperPerennial, 1992)

The Thought of the Heart and the Soul of the World by James Hillman (Spring Publications, 1992)

Turn, The Journal of an Artist by Anne Truitt (Viking, 1986)

Waiting for God, by Simone Weil, with an introduction by Leslie A. Fiedler (Harper & Row, 1973)

Women as Mythmakers: Poetry and Visual Art by Twentieth-Century Women by Estella Lauter (Indiana University Press, 1984)

SUGGESTED MUSIC

Clarinet Quintets by Wolfgang Amadeus Mozart, audio CD

I Am the True Vine by Arvo Part, audio CD

Libera, Libera, audio CD

Luminosa by Libera, audio CD

Migration by Peter Kater and R. Carlos Nakai, audio CD

Pavane by Gabriel Fauré, audio CD

Rapture by Nusrat Fateh Ali Khan

"Sanctus and In Paradisum," from Fauré's *Requiem,* Fauré, audio CD

11,000 Virgins by Hildegard von Bingen, performed by Anonymous 4,
audio CD

BEAUTIFUL HEALING MUSIC

Ave Maria, sung by Benedictine Nuns of St. Cecilia's Abbey, audio CD

Rivers of One, Traditional Sufi Healing Music, Oraf Guvenc & Tumata,
audio CD

Spirals by Barry Berstein and Steve Gorn, cassette

CHAPTER FOUR

The Feminine Face of Love

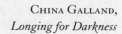

ONCE, MANY YEARS AGO, MY YOUNGEST SON, THEN JUST A TODDLER, TURNED me with his wide brown eyes and asked, "Mommy, what love is?" Caught off guard by his sweetly misphrased sentence, I struggled to find simple words to explain life's most complex mystery. Suddenly the answer came, and putting my hand over my heart, I said, "Love is that feeling you have inside for people or animals— like what you feel for me, or your dad, or your best friend." When he gestured to his own heart and nodded knowingly in response, I knew I had hit the mark—just as his words had left their imprint on me.

Indeed, though love could be said to be the great unsolved riddle of the ages, the truth may be that it is as simple a matter as keeping faith with our heartfelt emotions for another living creature. Every wisdom tradition has taught that the answers to life's questions lie within. This is never more true than with the quality of love. We may strain to enhance our relationship skills by reading books and attending seminars. Yet love is not learned, but deepened through opening to those feelings that, spontaneous and unbidden, well up from within like an underground river rising to the surface of the earth.

Our choice is to be in love or to be in fear. But to choose to be in love means to have a mountain inside of you, means to have the heart of the world inside of you, means you will feel another's suffering inside your own body and you will weep. You will have no protection from the world's pain because it will be your own.

CHINA GALLAND,
Longing for Darkness

RIVER OF LOVE

*If you feel that love is a quality that has run dry in your life, then try this visualiza-
tion. Imagine that your heart is like a riverbed, drained dry of water, and dusty in a
drought. Just as you feel that there is no love within you to give, and no love without to receive, so there is no life stirring at this desolate spot. Next, imagine, that you
decide to undertake a journey to the source of this river. You trek long distances
along the banks of this empty river until one day you reach a green oasis of trees and
brushes. There, at the center of this oasis, a small stream of water gurgles up from
the depths of the earth. Sitting beside this well, you begin to feel refreshed and
restored. Soon, the outpouring of water begins to increase, and the wellspring of
water turns into a gushing torrent, filling the riverbed with water and happily
splashing the animals and vegetation. Likewise, your heart becomes a gushing fountain of water; having travelled to the headwaters of love, your whole being becomes
flooded with feelings and emotions of affection, warmth, and cherishment. Like the
river that has returned to fullness, so too has the uprush of love within your heart
transformed the arid desert of your former life into an emerald garden of love and
beauty.*

The paradox of love is that although it originates in our hearts—the spiritual
epicenter of our being—it immediately overflows the limits of our individual
selves, joining us to an "other." Thus, you could say that,
like the Ganges or the Nile, our hearts are the headwaters of majestic rivers that carry us forward on lifelong
journeys of human connection. Just as the earth's rivers
interlace its surface, opening trade routes among cultures, facilitating the free-flow exchange of goods and
ideas, so, too, are each of our lives tributaries of deep-
flowing currents of feeling that join us to the larger soul
of humankind. "Love alone is capable of uniting living
beings in such a way as to complete and fulfill them,"
wrote the Catholic theologian Pierre Teilhard de Chardin in *The Phenomenon of Man,* "for it alone takes them
and joins them to what is deepest in themselves. . . ."

Love's fluid quality, along with its capacity to stir ecstasy, has led some poets
and writers to compare it to wine. Just as there are many vintages of wine, so, too,
are there varieties of love. Centuries ago, for instance, the Greeks distinguished
different types of love: *eros, storge, philia,* and *agape,* among others. Erotic love, for

*From birth to death, love is not just the
focus of human experience but also the life
force of the mind, determining our moods,
stabilizing our bodily rhythms, and changing
the structure of our brains.*

THOMAS LEWIS, FARI AMINI,
AND RICHARD LANNON,
A General Theory of Love

example, is the fleeting passion and romance we feel when we "fall in love." It is exactly as portrayed in the myth of Eros, or Cupid: glancing at another, an arrow pierces us in the heart, and we feel as if we have found our missing half. Eros, too, is the bodily electricity that generates sexual desire, and that sometimes leads to marriage and family. Just as often, however, it is tinged with the tragedy of thwarted fate, as in the classic story of Romeo and Juliet—or when two people fall as suddenly out of love as they fell in love. In marked contrast to previous centuries when romantic love unsanctioned by family or church was forbidden, erotic love is the predominant form of love in our time.

Far less regarded these days are those other forms of love that were once the mainstay of ancient cultures. *Storge* is the cherished affection a parent might feel for a child, for instance, or even what one might feel for a beloved companion animal. While parenting books and even books on pets cram store shelves, they nearly always fall in the category of strategies for discipline and management, rather than as one of life's highest expressions of love. *Philia* marks the enduring brotherly or sisterly love between best friends; likewise, the art of friendship rarely receives the same regard as partnered love. *Agape* is the selfless love unconditionally lavished on the world by those whose lives revolve around service. Appropriated by the early Christians, agape also came to describe that sweetness of feeling among those with a shared spiritual bond.

> *For Mercy has a human heart,*
> *Pity a human face,*
> *And Love, the human form divine,*
> *And Peace, the human dress.*
>
> WILLIAM BLAKE,
> "The Divine Image"

Just as rivers make their way to the ocean, so do these various streams of love—romance, affection, friendship, and selfless love of humanity—flow eventually toward union with God. "The fountain stream of love rises in the love for an individual, but spreads and falls in universal love," said the Sufi Hazrat Inayat Khan. Love of God is the impetus behind the world's great religious traditions, which seek to remind us of the greater reality that exists behind the curtain of everyday life. For as the Biblical psalmists, the Hindu "bakhti" teachings, and the Sufi poets remind us, there is no greater love affair than that of the soul seeking to be reunited with the Divine Beloved.

If there is a commonality among these disparate forms of love, it is the desire to join together with that from which we feel separated, fragmented, or driven apart. Indeed it could be said that the plot driving all our lives stems from the wish to weave the separate thread of our individual selves into some kind of bigger picture—whether family, religion, or the public sphere of the polis. Once, when I took a pre-Columbian textile fragment to be appraised by a rug dealer, I marveled as he and his assistant peered closely at its design, keenly studying the direction of the thread's warp and woof. In the same way, love in all its varieties forms the warp and woof that weaves the pattern of our destinies; every life is a grand tapestry of a "love story" of one kind or another, whether failed or fulfilled, tragic or glorious, ordinary or extraordinary. Perhaps this is the reason why we so readily respond to love stories at the box office or in novels. The narrative of relationship of one kind or another is the universal subtext of all our journeys.

Someday, after mastering the winds, the waves, the tides, and gravity, we will harness for God the energies of love. And then, for the second time in the history of the world, humankind will have discovered fire.

TEILHARD DE CHARDIN

The course of my own life is a thick cross weave of varieties of love. Each one traces a line of connection leading from myself to another person, purpose, or ideal, drawing a distinct design of fate in the process. The earliest memories of love I can recall were the feelings I had as a young child for my parents and three younger siblings. My recollections are dim and come back to me as impressions, images, and tiny incidents: the smell of my father's TWA uniform; the early morning ritual my father and I shared of waving good-bye to each other as he drove off to leave on a trip; swimming with my mother, brothers, and sister on a hot summer afternoon; watching television together in the family room; my mother's beautiful black hair and watermelon paintings on old wood.

My parents were both passionate romantics. Like them, I have always been a lover of love; as a schoolgirl, I still recall the way I pined after the beautiful boy with olive skin and ebony eyes who sat across from me in class. For him, I wrote letters, composed songs, and dreamed of his kiss. His face, I think, is etched forever in my imagination, as are the faces of all the men I have ever loved. Like everyone, however, I have suffered when it comes to romantic love. Often, I have felt cheated by the experience—something once so golden with promise, suddenly becomes tarnished. For some years, I thought of romance as a hoax—a thief who stole hearts only to leave them empty. Now, I think of romance as one of love's seasons—like the rapturous flowers and scented breezes of springtime, that fade naturally into summer, fall, and winter. Any true and lasting relationship, I think, weathers many seasons within its cycles of love. At the same time, there is romance and magic to be found in other kinds of relationships as well.

One of my most memorable experiences of romantic love, in fact, was as a new mother. Perhaps it was the innocence of our youth, but I'll never forget the rare moment that occurred after my first son's birth. Gazing down at this incredible new being in awe, my husband and I felt so overwhelmed with love for our new family and for the whole world that we simply couldn't believe what we were feeling. Babies were born everyday—still, we wondered, how could there be war or any kind of violence in the presence of such living miracles?

Nothing, in fact, has so completely defined the course of love in my life as the unique path I have travelled as a mother. By the age of twenty-nine, I had three children under six. Because love spins webs of connection, I not only had my own individual relationships with each of my children, but also was drawn into relationships with others through them, especially other mothers. Each of my sons, for example, was born while I was living in a communal household of several families. My midwife, Fatima, lived in the same house, and was present along with a physician at the home birth of each of my sons. Fatima was a true soul sister who for many years helped bring joy to my earliest experiences as a mother. In contrast to many women who are often isolated and housebound with small children, I always had Fatima, as well as my other friends, to cook with, talk to, and share the simple pleasures of hanging out on our large outdoor deck watching our children play together.

Even after I moved into my own home, the bonds that I forged with women while raising my children have been among the most affectionate that I have known. Like the homespun charm of a cross-stitch sampler, the play of women and children has a sweet romance all its own. In Santa Fe, with Sylvia and her three sons, as well as Taj and her three sons, Kristen and her son Adam, Laurence and her children, I recall afternoons fragrant with after-school snacks, tea and long chats, snow days, and school holidays. In Washington, D.C., I have the fondest memories of my friendships with Ann and Shannon, mothers of the two best friends of my oldest son. Together, we helped one another navigate the chaotic teenage years—the middle-of-the-night phone calls, the school pranks, and the speeding tickets. One of the things I have appreciated the most about my women friends is the way we help "see" for one another during those times when we are blinded by worry or anxiety, calming or reassuring one another that, somehow, things will be all right.

The ripening love that grows over the years through the interlocking relationships between women and children extends as well to close friends who have no children of their own. Many single women have shared with me the ups and downs of raising my sons. One memory sums up the kind of loving support I have received: After my oldest son had left home to live abroad in Taipei, Taiwan, I was

The crown of these
Is made of love and friendship, and sits high
Upon the forehead of humanity.

JOHN KEATS, *Endymion*

preparing dinner for my friends Harriett, Susan, and Mimi. As they were about to walk in, I turned on the television to watch the news and was stunned by the news of a major earthquake in that small island off the coast of China. The initial reports were sketchy; the grainy images of destruction sent cold chills of fear through my whole body. As we sat around the table, Harriett led us all in a prayer for my son's well-being and safety; holding hands in a circle, I felt strengthened by their supportive net of friendship. Not long after, I received the news that my son was fine. It is a story that I often tell, because to me it is an example of how mothering is never the task of one woman alone, but can be shared among friends.

That best portion of a good man's life,
His little, nameless, unremembered acts of
kindness and of love.

WILLIAM WORDSWORTH, "Lines
Composed a Few Miles
Above Tintern Abbey"

Like beads on a rosary, I have more tales of mothering-sistering than I can share in this book. As my sons enter adulthood, it is a narrative that continues to unfold. Hardly a week goes by that my close friend Sylvia and I don't talk on the phone about our children. Astrology, dreams, psychology, and spirituality all weave their way into our conversations, enriching me as a mother and also deepening our friendship. And although love has constantly pushed me to grow larger as a person, what has surprised me the most is the small scale upon which the great work of love takes place. "Work is love made visible," said the poet Kahlil Gibran. And in fact, most of what goes into loving a child are the humble tasks of everyday life: the chores of cooking, cleaning, laundry, or meeting with teachers, as well as the dogs, pet snakes, and friends crowding the house. Leaving aside for the moment the fact that housework (still mostly women's work) is unfairly compensated by society, I have felt deeply rewarded by the satisfaction that comes from lovingly keeping a house for family. The poet William Blake may have seen heaven in a grain of sand; I found it in my Comet cleanser–scrubbed sink. Monks and nuns may love God through repetition of sacred phrases; I patiently repeated to the boys over and over again to close the front door, brush your teeth, put your dishes in the sink. I read the same books out loud, night after night. "You will not find me in stupas, not in Indian shrine rooms, nor in synagogues, not in cathedrals ..." wrote the poet Kabir. "When you really look for me, you will see me instantly—you will find me in the tiniest house of time...."[1]

Indeed, most women know that love is permanently grounded in fleeting gestures and mundane rituals—the warm glance, the kind word, twenty minutes of uninterrupted listening, the shoulder rub, the home-cooked or take-out meal. They are on intimate terms with the fact that love is the art of thousands of such seemingly inconsequential particulars that yet, when painstakingly put together over a lifetime, results in something lasting. And they are aware of the way love is forged in the living space of certain unplanned-for moments. On countless occasions I have stood with each one of my sons in the heat of an emotional encounter— in anger, disappointment, grief, happiness, wild rebellion, or the frustration of school work or jobs. This is the tedious work of intimacy, the netting together of two human beings that results in unbreakable bonds. Once, when she was having a difficult time resolving a problem with her husband and sons, for instance, my friend Sylvia dreamed of making a rug with intricate stitches—a metaphor for the work she was engaged in with her family. And although I have been divorced from my sons' father for over twelve years, I have taken similarly tiny steps to work together with him and his wife, Anne, to raise our children together. Though we had our share of hours of therapy working to heal the wounds caused by our divorce, the supportive family we have today is as much the result of the daily round of yearly rituals of birthday dinners, conversations, Fourth of July barbecues, graduations, and Christmas parties than anything else. While it hasn't always been easy, I think that the three of us have been guided by a larger vision that has helped put into perspective any minor discomforts or disagreements.

The fountain stream of love rises in the love for an individual, but spreads and falls in universal love.

Hazrat Inayat Khan

Because of society's almost exclusive preoccupation with romantic love, we are often unprepared when it crops up in the unlikeliest of places. I learned more about love than I ever thought possible, for instance, when my father became ill with cancer and died. From the time I arrived on his doorstep after his diagnosis, I became wholly absorbed into what my sister and I called "the zone." Because he had chosen to die at home with the assistance of the local hospice in Corpus Christie, Texas, my stepmother, sister, and I became responsible for his physical care. The rest of the world fell completely away as I met with lawyers and helped arrange his will, monitored his morphine, helped him to the bathroom, brought him his favorite dishes, and slept by his bedside at night, reading aloud or talking with him when he woke up. I had always adored my father; his alcoholism, however, had riddled our relationship with bitterness and sadness. For many years I had cut off my feelings for this difficult, chaotic person who happened to be my parent. But as he lay dying, the love I had felt as a child broke through again in the most powerful way possible. As I sat beside him and watched him wrestle with his soul, I loved him as a father again, but also as a human being on the brink of a momentous transition to a new world. How could I not care, and care deeply?

"You must tend your father as if you were Mary caring for the body of Jesus," said the Mexican priest Father Eddie, a large-hearted man who limped with polio, who came to counsel my father in his last hours. Through those simple words, spiritual love intersected with personal love, breaking my heart open to a new depth of feeling for the precious humanity in my father—and in myself, as his daughter.

Love does break our hearts—it breaks them to expand them, to shake them loose from the constrictions that have bound them closed. It breaks our hearts in order to release us from those artificial expectations that blind us to the full and beautiful autonomy of a person's whole being—teaching us to love others for who they are, rather than who we want them to be. It breaks our hearts open to the miraculous joy of life on this tiny planet in an infinite dark space. Indeed, the hallmark of love is the way that it shifts the balance of our attention away from ourselves, outward to life. Many times in my life I have felt the relief that comes from not bearing the burden of a life alone. I recall how I felt after my first book was cancelled, and how profoundly I appreciated being in the presence of my friends and family. Not to think about myself and to watch those around me carry on with their lives was somehow comforting and healing. Whether I was a successful writer or not didn't really matter—what did matter was connection with others.

At the same time, there have been many times when I have felt like I have failed at love. Being divorced and a woman alone has sometimes led me to feel as if I know nothing about the art of sustaining intimacy. Then, I have taken refuge in my writing, finding satisfaction in work, though wondering sometimes whether writing was a form of escape. Yet over the years, as I have studied the writings of feminist psychologists and theologians, I have gradually arrived at a more complex view of love. Now, I am more conscious of the ways in which Western culture has split love in half. On one side of the divide lie personal bonds of kinship; on the other side exists the public domain. But isn't love of the world the inspiration of activists and saints that was celebrated by the Greeks as agape or *caritas*? As my children grow older and move farther from home, I find myself increasingly drawn toward forms of affection that lead from the individual toward loving solidarity with humanity.

Greater love hath no man than this, that a man lay down his life for his friends.

JOHN 15:13

I felt this most recently, for example, after months spent working on an article exploring the deeper side of the place where I live: Washington, D.C. I found I loved my city—its rivers, neighborhoods, history, and people—as much as I had loved any person. I began to reflect on different ways to care for its soul, much the same as I had tended the souls of my children. Too, perhaps this new direction opening in my life was an expression of that form of love Jung called *"amor fati,"* or love of one's fate. Often I have thought that the reason I have not been able to sustain a long-term relationship is because I was unable to be a mother, a partner, and a writer all at the same time. As the talk-show host Oprah Winfrey is fond of saying, a woman can have it all—just not at the same time. It takes enormous energy for a woman to remain true to the larger work she has been called to do while at the same time nurturing intimate connections that sustain her in turn. While men have had women's support sustaining the emotional infrastructure within the home, leaving them free to follow their fate in the world, women have had to juggle both roles at the same time.

Indeed, in the past, the kind of noble love that impacts the public sphere has often been denied women. Men have their own struggles with affairs of the heart. But women's relationship to love has been inevitably shaped by their history. As feminist thinkers have pointed out in recent decades, familial, empathic forms of love have long been regarded as the exclusive province of women. It wasn't so much that women were better nurturers than men, but that that was the role assigned to them by society. In addition, the tasks of tending a marriage and raising children were seen as separate from the larger spheres of business, politics, academia, and religion. Even though women were sentimentally idealized as caretakers, the work they did was unpaid and unrewarded. Even today a woman (or a man, for that matter) who stays home to raise children receives no social security benefits for the years spent at this task. The public sphere suffered from this dichotomy as well, because anything to do with the personal, whether nursing, childcare, or teaching, became trivialized as "women's work." Society became split between power and love. Both sides lost out in this artificial division that divided family and work, public and private.

This long history with regard to love has meant that women, many of whom tend to put the needs of others above their own, have had to struggle not to lose themselves in relationships. They have had to suffer love's double bind—the conflict between self and other—in a way men rarely have had to do. Especially in the early days of feminism, women eschewed marriage and family in order to gain equal power through their careers—a logical move, since there was no power to be gained from staying home. For some, this was a choice well made, while for others, it was a choice that came at the expense of great personal loneliness. Even with all the advances of feminism, most women I know must still deal very consciously with issues around love. Over the years, I have watched as each one of my friends has wrestled within herself over whether or not to marry; have a child; go to work or stay home with a child; or even how to handle such seemingly mundane tasks as household work, children's homework, or elder care with their partners.

The really good news, however, is that love in our time is evolving. As women have taken their place in the public sphere—writing books, conducting research, starting businesses, entering politics, and, yes, becoming rich and famous—a radical restructuring of relationships has taken place. A different set of values has emerged that challenges outmoded gender arrangements. Psychologist Jean Baker Miller and her pioneering group of associates at the Stone Center in Wellesley, Massachusetts, for instance, have spent decades working ceasely to cultivate greater respect for the unsung tasks of caretaking that have mostly fallen on women's shoulders. Rather than ask women to become more like men, they have called upon men, or society at large, to develop "relational" skills of compassion, empathy, and tolerance. In turn, they encourage women to ensure that "reciprocity," or an equal give and take, is a healthy part of all their relationships, whether at work or in the home. As consultants to large organizations, they have also sought to encourage businesses to value the invisible kinds of nurturing, often performed by secretaries or other assistants, that sustain any workplace. And they have documented the complex intricacies of love—the genius!—that go into the dance of raising a child through infancy into adulthood.

> *One opens the inner doors of one's heart to the infinite silences of the Spirit, out of whose abysses love wells up without fail and gives itself to all.*
>
> THOMAS MERTON

New words for love, as well, are entering our everyday language. Authors Elisabeth Young-Bruehl and psychologist Faith Bethelard, for example, have partnered together to introduce to Western society what they call "cherishment," the kind of affectionate love the Greeks called *philia,* the Japanese term *amae*—and for which Western society has no term at all. In their book, *Cherishment: A Psychology of the Heart.* Young-Bruehl and Bethelard write lyrically of the universal human need for affection that "goes heart to heart." This passage is a beautiful summation of the awareness that arose out of their mutual friendship and research into this topic:

> "Cherishment" derives from the French *cher* (dear) and the Latin *caru,* which comes from caritas, a word that means love, but of a special sort: benevolence, well-wishing, presuming goodwill. Caritas has a history in the Christian concept of charity, too, but "cherishment," as we use it, does not imply any moral obligation to give love or be altruistic; cherishment is spontaneous affection. It

also does not imply any saintly transcendence or asceticism or selflessness, but is located right in the roil and broil of emotional life, in the growth and development of a self. And, besides, it is not so much about giving love as it is about receiving love and being able, because receiving, to be benevolent, kind, considerate, indulgent. When you come to think that the precondition for giving is receiving, or talk about how a baby wishes to be wished well, expects to be cherished, to get cherishing, it is natural to say, "That child has cherishment," or "that is a well-cherished child." Or "There is a child who wants cherishing." We now easily think of cherishment as the emotional equivalent of nourishment. Soul food.[2]

The kind of tender love so lacking in our culture described by Young-Bruehl and Bethelard has also been traced to the root of eating disorders by Jungian analyst Marion Woodman. In her books, she has written poignantly about the "sweetness" women long for that has been displaced onto the food they crave. In her view, eating disorders are linked to problems that stem from lack of mothering from either sex. "It's a longing for the archetypal mother. The sweetness, the cherishing, the acceptance, the mirroring by the missing mother—I mean mother with a big 'M.' Because this is not just a longing for the personal mother, but a longing for the Mother Goddess, a being in whom you can have total trust. . . ."[3] This is the inclusive kind of "mother love" celebrated within the feminine spirituality movement: the positive principle of love that honors feelings and that nurtures the spark of life found in all created beings, from the tiniest blade of grass to the hardest-hearted criminal, to the child next door. Indeed, the return of the goddess has often been linked to the return of love itself in a culture addicted to power and perfection.

> *He that loveth not, knoweth not God;*
> *for God is love.*
>
> THE FIRST EPISTLE
> GENERAL OF JOHN 4:8

Reading the works of these groundbreaking thinkers had a revolutionary effect on the way I regarded love. I discovered *Women's Growth in Connection,* a collaborative work from five women psychologists at the Stone Center, for example, during my oldest son's senior year of high school. Their perspective on the important social skills of interdependency and the value of empathic listening had the effect of slowing me down so that I could take time to appreciate his last year at home. Like everyone, I had always been so distracted—always running, running, running toward things that, in the end, weren't nearly as important as my relationship with him. Some years later, when my second son decided to drop out of college and move back home again, the theories of Stone Center thinkers such as Judith Jordan helped me to support his unspoken need for dependency at a difficult time in his life and to weather the criticism I often received for allowing him to live at home. The great wisdom of these women helped steady me in my own strong instincts that were guiding me to allow my sons permission to feel vulnerability and confusion even as young adults in their twenties. As other psychologists have recently shown, satisfying a child's dependency needs is often the precondition for genuine independence.

Finally, feminine spirituality and psychology also changed my relationship to women. While my friends had always been my mainstay, I grew more conscious of just how life-sustaining that link really was. As relationships between men and women continue to be buffeted by the sea changes wrought by feminism and other social transformations, women's friendships often provide the long-term stability and containment once provided within marriage. The truth is, however, that it has always been this way. Only now, as women have begun to reclaim their voices and speak out the truth of their lives, has society begun to value the enduring depths of female bonds and their intrinsic cultural worth. For although historians may have "averted their eyes" from the love of women as they work and live side by side, as feminist scholar Carolyn Heilbrun has written, how often in the past have women "drawn from that love what men draw, not from the friendship of men, but from the nurturing of women?"[4]

The kinds of friendships that have nurtured women for centuries, in fact, may contain within them elements that could be usefully applied to other relationships: equality, intimacy, empathy, and freedom of expression. "Friends, like lovers and saints," writes Heilbrun, "can offer us a pattern of their love."[5] Yet there is one important way in which women's friendships have begun to change. While throughout history male friends have tended to "stand side by side," and affect the outside world, says Heilbrun, women's affectionate relationships have tended to form "societies of consolation" that nourish one another through life's hardships. Only rarely, as in the example of American feminism's founders Elizabeth Cady Stanton and Susan B. Anthony, for instance, have women's friendships turned their attention toward the world of human events. This, too, is changing, however. I think, for instance, of the way women came together during the Million Mom March, linking arms to end gun violence. I think of the women who started Mothers Against Drunk Driving. And

> *What permeates the entire being*
> *Like an inexhaustible stream*
> *Alone can be called love.*
>
> KABIR

I think of the way women have joined together in a global feminist movement to restore women's human rights and to bring an end to the sex slavery and genital mutilation of young girls.

Indeed, when it comes to the quality of love, women have evolved a myriad of expressions that may include men and romance—but do not solely revolve around them as they have in the past. Among the many images that have come to symbolize the meaning of the feminine spirituality movement are the circle and the spiral. Thus, I think of women's ways of love as circles of care that ripple out from one's most intimate group of friends and family to the wider sphere of humanity. Like a spiral, these circles of connection build upon one another, drawing more and more within their all-inclusive embrace. The full measure of women's love is only now being told, recorded for future generations. The following stories of ordinary women relate several examples of these kinds of love stories, ranging from the personal to the political, as well as the historical and the modern.

"TOWER OF MOTHERS"—WALKING THE PATH OF MOTHER LOVE

Love is the Divine Mother's arms; and when those arms are outspread, every soul falls into them." This saying by Hazrat Inayat Khan captures an abiding form of love: that of the mother for the child. So pure and selfless is this form of love in its highest potential that every religion across the ages has likened God's love for creation to a mother's love for her child. Images of the Great Mother can be found in the Egyptian Isis, the Greek Hera, the Hindu Devi, the Buddhist Tara, the Nigerian Ala, and in the Christian Mary. "She is the mother of the thunder, the mother of the streams, the mother of the trees and all things. She is the mother of the world . . . and she is the only mother we possess."[6]

The Sufis have a saying that God is as close to a person as their jugular vein; likewise, God the Mother may be as close to us as the nearest mom on our block. I am not talking here about the positive or negative mothers of our psychological complexes. I am referring instead to the garden-variety behavior of ordinary, well-adjusted mothers toward their children: their gestures offer insight into a kind of spiritual practice that is oriented toward daily life. Trouble is, however, many women devalue their feelings as incompatible with more transcendent spiritual aims. Take the way most mothers worry, for instance. Hardly a mother I know does not think daily about the well-being of her children. I remember the time one of my sons went away on a freezing winter weekend, for example, without a coat. Common sense told me that he was old enough, big enough, and smart enough to keep himself warm. I felt silly letting such a small thing disturb me until I shared it with my friend Barbara. When she told me that she and her son had a running "coat joke" between them, we laughed together—and I realized I wasn't so unusual after all. My friend Sylvia was once so bothered by her unremitting anxiety over her three sons that she sought the advice of Pat Rodegast, the channeler of the spirit guide known as Emmanuel. Believing that fear and love should not coexist together, Sylvia felt that her fears made her somehow less spiritually evolved and that she should be able to maintain more of a sense of detachment. Yet Rodegast reassured Sylvia that her feelings were perfectly natural, and that she should stop being so hard on herself.

The practical dimension of mother love—the concern for children's physical safety and their future—cannot be meditated away. In fact, mothers and other caretakers are only behaving protectively toward their children in the same way the Divine Mother is watching over each one of us. Even the great Hindu saint Sri Sarada Devi, whose story is below, made mother love her path. As her biographer wrote of her relationship to her disciples, "She once remarked that, as was natural to a mother, she always asked the Lord to see that they never suffered from any physical privation. . . . To the disciples she often said: 'Whenever you are in danger or trouble, remember that you have a mother.'"[7] All mothers and caretakers can be helped in their tasks by knowing that their burden is shared by a divine being, that they are not alone. Once, when my friend Taj's son was nervous over being separated from her over the summer, for instance, she allayed his anxiety—and her own—by telling him that, no matter what, he could always turn to the Divine Mother for support. This simple statement helped me to see that there is a loving,

*Last night I learned how to be a lover
 of God,
To live in this world and call nothing
 my own.*

*I looked inward
And the beauty of my own emptiness
Filled me till dawn.
It enveloped me like a mine of rubies.
Its hue clothed me in red silk.*

*Within the cavern of my soul
I heard the voice of a lover crying,
"Drink now! Drink now!"—*

*I took a sip and saw the vast ocean—
Wave upon wave caressed my soul.
The lovers of God dance around
And the circle of their steps
 becomes a ring of fire round my neck.*

*Heaven calls me with its rain and thunder—
A hundred thousand cries
Yet I cannot hear . . .*

All I hear is the call of my Beloved

RUMI, FROM *In the Arms of the
Beloved* (TRANSLATION BY
JONATHAN STAR)

beneficent force who is with each of us at all times, mothers and fathers and children alike, worrying about and tending to our every move.

TOWER OF MOTHERS

Kathe Kollwitz's image of a "tower of mothers" is an inspiring one to incorporate into a meditation on the Great Mother. It is a wonderful image, as well, to use to empower any kind of social activism in which you are involved, or even to help get you through your day as a mother or a teacher.

To begin with, invoke the names of all the human mothers you know, both biological and spiritual. As you name them, see them joining hands in a small circle that begins to slowly spiral outward in successive circles. After listing the names of those mothers and caretakers that you know, add to your list the names of those larger-than-life mothers and honorary moms you don't know, but admire: Oprah Winfrey, Jane Fonda, Hillary Clinton, Madonna, Eve Ensler, Tipper Gore, Marian Wright Edelman, and others less well known.

Next, call to mind the names of all the Divine Mothers from history and mythology that come to mind: Mary, Kuan Yin, Tara, Hera, Diana, Astarte, Eve, Sarah, Ruth, Isis, Demeter, Sojourner Truth, the Black Madonna, Sri Sarada Devi, Laksmi, Kali, and so on and so on, spiraling and spiraling not upward, but around and around and around the earth. This horizontal "tower" of mothers is the strength of life itself, the force of love that binds all our lives as one. This is a wonderful image to use whenever you are feeling alone in all your caretaking duties. By calling upon all the visible and invisible mothers, you can feel your spirit strengthened by their collective presence. Their accumulated wisdom is always available to you as a resource of love to draw upon. For any mother anywhere at any time: remember, the tower of mothers is always with you.

The work of the German artist Kathe Kollwitz conveys this kind of fiercely protective maternal devotion in a different way than the more subtle portrayals of Mary and Jesus in classical art. Kollwitz, too, lost a son, on the European battlefields of World War I. Her drawings, woodcuts, sculptures, and political posters portray a kind of mother love that reflects the soul of the modern era—a time that has seen the ravages of war magnified a thousandfold. Thus Kollwitz's mothers are not ethereal or otherwordly, but muscular, large-boned women with strong hands and square faces. Her earliest drawings show working women as political revolutionaries; later, this fighting spirit became incorporated into her depictions of maternal figures protecting the vulnerability of children against the abuses of poverty and war. Deeply affected by the loss of her own son, Kollwitz's work evolved a new myth, one that asserted the mother's role against oppression and violence in society.

In her drawing *Seed Corn Shall Not Be Ground*, a metaphor borrowed from Goethe to express the fact that children should not be destroyed in war, for example, an old woman extends her powerful arms around several innocent children peaking out from beneath her embrace. Her body acts as a shield, presenting a "larger image of the female human being as a force in a world of forces . . . a force to be reckoned and valued."[8] The work I find most meaningful by Kollwitz, however, is a compact, yet powerful, sculpture entitled *Tower of Mothers*. In it, a group of four women use their bodies as a kind of four-square circle within which children huddle against an oncoming threat. The thickly built woman at the forefront of this sculpture stands with her legs spread, her arms thrust backward around the other women and the children; her face is jutting forward in fierce outrage. It is a striking image of grounded mother love—and of the formidable communal power that comes from women joining together to protect those who are in their care.

> *God hugs you.*
> *You are encircled by the arms*
> *Of the mystery of God.*
>
> HILDEGARD VON BINGEN

Liz's Story:

Taken together, the soul sisters I know make a living "tower of mothers": Liz, Taj, Sylvia, Barbara, Nancy, Martha, Kristen, Elise, my sister Colleen, Shannon, Ann, and others. Just as remarkable are those women I know who have cared for children who are not their own. The story of my friend Liz Wilder, for instance, never fails to inspire those who hear it. I first met Liz over seven years ago when she began dating my good friend Anthony, the single father of three boys close in age to my own. As Liz tells her story, she had been working as a vice president of information systems for a Blue Cross subsidiary. Strikingly attractive, with cascading chestnut curls and velvet brown eyes, Liz was in her early thirties and single. Her well-paid job, she says, was "fun and challenging" and allowed her to travel around the world. Still, she recalls, something was missing. "I felt as if there was no meaning in my life. Corporate America just wasn't very fulfilling. I thought about joining the Peace Corps or going to work with Mother Theresa—anything that would give me a feeling that something mattered rather than sitting in a boardroom arguing over what column a piece of information belonged in."

It was in this mood that, on the spur of the moment, Liz attended a summer barbecue at a friend's house. There she met Anthony—a tall, attractive man with strawberry-blond hair and blue eyes. The attraction between them was instantaneous, and within a month they had fallen deeply in love. By the end of the year, Liz, who had lived on her own since leaving her parents' home, had decided to move in with Anthony—and his three teenage sons who lived with him full time. "At first I had this naïve mentality that they were his children and I wasn't going to really have anything to do with them. But it didn't take me long to realize that both for my benefit and for the boys I was going to have to be involved," recalls Liz. Their natural mother was unavailable and, says Liz, "was unable to put their interests before hers. As they grew up her ability to be a mother figure to them was challenged. The boys would sometimes stay out all night, or if their mom got mad at them she would leave. Because they were children, they wouldn't know when or if she would come home. So when I heard these things I realized that we really needed to pull together. I realized that it wasn't just the two of us, but them, too— it was a package deal."

From the first day Liz arrived, the boys proved a challenge, acting out, drinking, and experimenting with drugs. Accustomed to living alone with their dad and the male housekeeper, there were few rules. "The first time I spent the night I woke up to find a house full of kids sleeping in every corner of the house. From six to seven each morning before school, there was violent testosterone, with yelling matches, banging on doors, and stealing each other's breakfast. The boys shared one bathroom, and either one was taking too long in the shower, or the other was spending too much time looking in the mirror. It was a nightmare! I just huddled in the corner of my room until they left."

Yet, says Liz, even though she had never really wanted children of her own, she found herself willing to take on her new role as stepmother. She began setting rules, as well as doing such "motherly" things as cooking family dinners every night—something the boys were not accustomed to. "They loved that!" she says. "I made the choice that I wanted us to be a family. I developed a close connection to the boys and realized that I had a lot to offer them." Finally, says Liz, she had found something that satisfied her need for meaning. "I didn't need to go and see Mother Theresa. She was right here on Fort Sumner Drive in Bethesda, and she had a project for me with three teenage boys!"

When you love, you wish to do things for. You wish to sacrifice for. You wish to serve.

ERNEST HEMINGWAY, AS QUOTED IN
A General Theory of Love,
BY THOMAS LEWIS,
FARI AMINI, AND RICHARD LANNON

Life did not magically settle down, however; the boys continued to get into trouble. Often Liz would accompany them to juvenile court hearings and monitor their community service or probation. In addition, there were financial problems to deal with. Quitting her job, she assumed more of a managerial role in Anthony's fledgling contracting business. Slowly, over the years, the boys began to mature into creative young adults pursuing their own careers. Anthony's business became so successful that, in 1999, he won the CotY Award for Contractor of the Year and was featured on *Good Morning America.*

When I ask Liz where she found the resources to sustain her love for her newfound family, she replied that her early childhood years had been "phenomenal. I had a loving, caring, good family." The youngest of four children, Liz's perfect "white picket fence" family, however, came crashing down when her mother became ill with cancer and died when she was just eighteen. Her father did not handle the death well and withdrew. This meant that she lost him as well. "Losing my mom so early made me realize how lucky I had been and what a great parent she was. And because I knew how I felt when I lost that, I could understand how bad the boys felt not having a mother be there for them—and I wanted to let that be my gift to them. What got me through was knowing I was helping them and that someone cared about them and wasn't going to leave or be unavailable as a parent to them."

> *Love is, in fact, an intensification of life, a completeness, a fullness, a wholeness of life. . . . Love is our true destiny.*
>
> THOMAS MERTON

Underpinning everything, however, was Liz's love for Anthony. "I always believed that Anthony and I were brought together for a purpose. I think that was part of what let me jump in without thinking about whether or not I was doing the right thing for me. I had many down days when I felt as if I was giving and giving and not seeing any results as a family, but our relationship was the strength that helped me to persist. No matter how difficult it was, I couldn't pull out from him or the boys—I had become so bonded, it just felt wrong. After I met him, I never felt I had any other choice. Did I want a life with him that came with chaos and teenage flailing—or did I just want to play golf?" Like most women, Liz has been sustained in her new family by a close circle of girlfriends—women with whom she talks regularly on the phone and spends time as often as possible. At a time when most people thought she was crazy, says Liz, her friends gave their unconditional support. "I could have made it through without them—but it would have been harder, and lonelier."

LOVE BETWEEN FRIENDS

In her book *Testament of Friendship*, first published in 1940, writer Vera Brittain recorded the dynamic relationship she shared with author Winifred Holtby. Though Holtby died of kidney disease at the age of thirty-seven, the two women sustained each other in their passionate pursuit of feminist ideals, in their desire to make a mark on the world, and in their careers as writers. The two first met as students at Oxford University in 1920, where they were mutually inspired by each other's keen intellect. Brittain was the more fragile of the pair, suffering depression over the loss of her brother and his close friends on the European battlefields of World War I. Exhausted with grief, Brittain writes that she saw Holtby as a "radiant young goddess" whose generous extension of affection helped heal her back to health.

As young women, the two traveled together, and eventually shared a flat in Chelsea. As she recounts in her book, "Neither of us had ever known any pleasure quite equal to the joy of coming home at the end of the day after a series of separate varied experiences, and each recounting these incidents to the other over late biscuits and tea . . . Those years with Winifred taught me that the type of friendship which reaches its apotheosis in the story of David and Jonathan is not a monopoly of the masculine sex. . . ." Indeed it was the beginning, Brittain writes, "of a shared working existence which was . . . to last . . . to the end of Winifred's life," each sustaining the other through the toil of writing and the despair of rejections and bad reviews, as well as defending the other's time for work amid life's claims. Even after Brittain had married and had children, while Holtby remained single, enjoying a widespread reputation as a social activist, journalist, and published novelist, they continued to strengthen each other in both their private and professional lives. Upon a publisher's acceptance of Brittain's classic work, *Testament of Youth*, for instance, she immediately thought of her dear friend, who at the time was seriously ill and caring for her dying father. The following passage is a beautiful summation of the rare love the two women shared:

> Suddenly remembering the debt that I could never repay, I ran to the post office to telegraph to Winifred, and on to a favorite flower shop in Sloane Street to send her a box of white lilac and blue irises and pale pink tulips with folded glistening petals. This change of fortune was her doing, her achieve-

There is only one happiness in life, to love and be loved.

GEORGE SAND, "Letter to
Lina Calamatta"

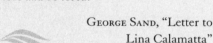

ment; it was she who had made me go on again and again when despair had prevailed. It seemed inconsiderate to feel so happy when she, an invalid herself, was at home watching her father die, but she had once said that what mattered was the existence of happiness . . . and not who experienced it . . . she would be glad, I believed, to know her critical judgment endorsed, pleased with the gay and brave spring flowers." [And pleased Holtby was, writing back to Brittain] "I have become so much accustomed to feeling you part of me that every line of happiness in your letter . . . lights up the candles of my Christmas tree . . . I know now that all my hopes for what you may do with the book are going to be justified. It will be the instrument to give you that power you need to work for the things you care about and fulfill your destiny and yourself. That is the only security and the only happiness.

Reading that passage, I was filled with wonder at the kind of wildly generous connection that existed between these two women. Truly, theirs was a testament to the kind of remarkable love that can exist in a friendship between two women.

LOVING A SOUL SISTER

Like the friendships recounted in this chapter, loving a soul sister as a friend can add untold depth and richness to your life. While one of the following chapters will offer advice on how to find a soul sister, this is a meditation to help deepen an already existing friendship.

First, call to mind the friend you wish to honor. Recall the story of how you met—the events that surrounded your introduction, and what you said and how you felt at the time.

Then, go back in time. Because so many friends feel as if they already know each other even when they are meeting for the first time, it's possible that you have shared lifetimes together. My friend Taj and I, for example, often feel as if we must have shared an Egyptian lifetime together. Don't censor your imagination—just let the stories and images arise in your mind. If you feel comfortable, share them with your friend. These buried memories embroider your relationship with age and meaning. They link you in a long lineage of soul sisters. And they are a part of a momentum carrying you forward into more lifetimes and more adventures together.

In fact, as my friend anthropologist and Jungian psychologist Jan Clanton Collins has pointed out, sharing memories is what keeps any bond of love strong and alive. So make a date with your soul sister. Before you meet, pick out an especially beautiful box that, to you, says something about the quality of your friendship.

*Then make a point during your get-together to share stories from the past—
whether past lifetimes or events you have shared along the way. Harriet and I, for
instance, love to reminisce about our mutual connection to Pir Vilayat Inayat Khan
and the Sufis. And my friend Janet and I love to recall the New Year's Day party
where we first met. At the end of your time together, present your friend with a box
as a container for all the special memories you've shared so far—and are looking
forward to sharing more of in the future.*

The Story of
✿
Carol and Susan

I have been blessed to encounter other similarly great "testaments to friendship."
Among them is a friendship I inadvertly helped to spark. The story of Susan
Kuner, Ed.D., and Carol Orsborn, Ph.D., begins, in fact, with my own longtime
association with Susan through the Sufis. During the 1980s, Susan and her two
children had moved to Nashville, Tennessee, where her husband had found a job,
and where they planned to start a Sufi center. I knew from my phone conversations with Susan that she was lonely and had been unable to make friends. Around
that time, I attended a Common Boundary conference while on assignment for a
magazine. One of the seminars I attended was presented by Carol Orsborn, who
had authored several books on business and spirituality. When she happened to
mention during her presentation that she was moving with her husband and two
children to Nashville, I immediately thought to give her Susan's name and telephone number.

Although she felt "excited and hopeful" at the time, recalls Carol, she also
had her doubts. "When I heard from you that Susan was a wonderful person who
hadn't been able to find anybody to connect to on a soul level in Nashville, I
became very nervous—I thought that she might be my one opportunity and I
didn't want to blow it. So I put it aside and started a lot of superficial friendships,
but nothing that really touched my soul." In the meantime, I had also called Susan
and given her Carol's telephone number. But Susan, too, could not bring herself to
make the call. "I was so miserable that I just didn't take the right step of calling a
friend," she says.

Several years later, however, fate intervened when Carol and her husband
decided to attend a seminar on soul journeys that was being offered at the Unity
Church next door to their home. "I had never done anything like that before. We
weren't even members of the Church," says Carol. Neither, recalls Susan, had she

and her husband—the teachers who were leading the seminar—ever offered public classes on Sufism in Nashville. "At the end of the class," recalls Susan, "Carol introduced herself, and I said 'Oh my God—I've had your name in my book for three years. If only I'd known it was *you*!'" Likewise, laughs Carol as she remembers that evening, she, too, immediately recognized Susan's name. "It was the most amazing thing because we had so much in common," says Susan. "Not only did it turn out that we lived just six blocks away from each other, but our children were just a few years older than theirs, with the same teachers, and the same problems." In addition, both were enrolled at Vanderbilt University, Susan studying for her doctorate and Carol at work on her master's degree in religion. (Since then, they have each received their doctoral degrees, Carol in religion and Susan in education.)

The two got together the very next day and delighted in discovering that they felt as if they had known each other forever. "We realized that we resonated spiritually in a way that transcended both of our personal spiritual histories," says Carol. "We could talk about anything at the deepest levels." As time went by, says Carol, she grew to love the way that she felt when she was with her new friend, feeling that Susan calmed her down and gave meaning to life. For her part, Susan felt as if she could talk about the things that were the "most precious to my heart. Often with other people I would get the feeling that those things were totally inappropriate to speak about. So to have someone to share those things with has meant a great deal to me."

Indeed, despite the differences in their religious backgrounds—although Susan was born into the Jewish tradition, she is a teacher in the Sufi Order, while Carol maintains her traditional Jewish faith—the two friends shared a spiritually based "deep understanding" about life that went beyond abstract religious doctrine. As Susan describes their dialogue, "We may start out talking about something we're dealing with, whether it's a child having a terrible time in school, a parent who's ill, or being frustrated at work. Then as we talk about that, our spiritual perspective begins to weave itself into the conversation."

And now abideth faith, hope, love, these three; but the greatest of these is love.

1 CORINTHIANS 13:9–13

A year and a half after Carol and Susan first met, however, their friendship took a dramatic turn. Following a routine medical checkup, Susan received a suspicious mammogram. Just before she was scheduled to have an excisional biopsy—when a tumor is surgically removed, and then taken to a lab to be tested for cancer—she told Carol the news over lunch. "At the time I was terrified," recalls Susan. To make things worse, when she told Carol the name of the surgeon who was in charge of the procedure, Carol responded dramatically that the surgeon was not to be trusted. She urged Susan to go for a second opinion. As it turned out, Carol, too, had received a suspicious mammogram from the same doctor the previous summer. Yet when she had gone to another doctor for a second opinion, she had been advised that she was fine and to come back in a year.

Uncertain over what to do, Susan wavered. Ultimately, however, she decided to go ahead with the procedure. "I wanted to find out. So I went ahead and had the biopsy—and it turned out that I did have cancer. First, I had a lumpectomy; that didn't work, and then I had to have a mastectomy." Throughout all of Susan's ordeal, her friend Carol was there for her, she says, "every step of the way. After each surgery she gave me a little present. Then she completely focused on me while I was in recovery; she and her daughter would come over and bring me soups. I was worried I wouldn't finish my dissertation and so we'd sit on my bed and go over how to outline it." For anyone going through the "terrifying chasm of an illness," says Susan, it really doesn't matter what you talk about, "just having somebody be there, like a ground to rest on, is vital to recovery."

Meanwhile, as Carol was tending to Susan's healing process, she had begun to worry about her own diagnosis. "I had been told not to come back for a year. So I tried to just be with Susan through her experience. Finally the pressure began to build to the point where I realized I needed to go back to the doctor just to calm myself down." Returning to the same doctor who had told her that she was fine, Carol was now told that there was indeed something suspicious in her breast after all. "I was so upset—at this point I didn't trust this doctor at all. Here Susan had been having a fabulous experience with this other surgeon I had originally mistrusted." That same day Susan e-mailed her surgeon about her friend, who agreed to see her immediately. And indeed, after a biopsy, Carol was diagnosed with breast cancer.

Thus, just as Susan was beginning to exit her ordeal, Carol entered into her own. A mastectomy was followed by months of chemotherapy, but today, five years later, like Susan, she is cancer free. Both women were awed by what they called the "cosmic nature" of their synchronistic connection: four months, as Susan points out, makes a huge difference in the spread of cancer. If Carol had not been alerted by Susan's situation to go back for another checkup sooner than her first doctor had advised, she might not have survived. "It saved my life. Susan mentored me through it, partly because she was a step ahead of me, but also because she knew what I was going through." At various points in their journey, one of them would feel more optimistic and secure, while the other might feel more vulnerable. But, says Susan, "We were always able to talk about it and take it to a deeper level. We brought our souls into it. Even though all these cataclysmic events were happening on the surface, at the same time we were plunged into soul searching: wondering if we were going to die, or what would happen to our children. And then there was the way people treated us—as if we were going to fall over dead any minute."

One incident in particular describes the kind of healing the two friends brought to each other. One spring day, barely able to move because she had been so weakened by chemotherapy, Susan came over to take her friend for a walk. "At that particular moment I felt that I had lost some trust and faith in life and in God. But Susan gently urged me to go just as far as the first redbud bush—and then she ate one of the redbuds! I looked at her in amazement, telling her that she couldn't do that—the flowers were poisonous. But she replied that she had read somewhere that it was all right to eat them—and that she hadn't died yet. Then she placed a redbud in my mouth and it turned out to be delicious and sweet. So we started laughing and nibbling them off the branches, like giraffes. It was as close to a sacramental meal as I've ever had. There was something about that moment of putting something alive into my body in the company of my good friend that felt like an act of faith. To me, it is a visual image that expresses the kind of intimacy that we had."

Together, say Carol and Susan, they were taken to the very depths of their being through their life-and-death encounter with cancer. The intensity of their shared experience was not unlike the bonds forged by men who encounter death on the battlefield. Like an ancient initiation rite, they each were forced to leave behind the safety of their known world and undergo a period of uncertainty until reentering the world again. Even though they both went to breast-cancer support groups, they found that they were not talking the same language the two women shared. "A lot of people who have cancer just want it to be over with so they can get back to their lives," says Susan. "And while that's fine, we saw it instead as an initiation into something very profound and mysterious." Having someone who could understand and express in words how spiritually transformative the experience could be, adds Carol, "was just an unbelievable gift. There were many times when I was being forced to grow and felt out of my depths, only to find that Susan had gone through the same space and had a handle on it—and vice versa."

The two friends, in fact, found little within the mainstream cancer movement that helped satisfy their spiritual needs. And while they may have shared the emotional intensity similar to men's wartime experience, they found nothing inspiring about the "battlefield mentality" that characterized the breast-cancer movement. "We couldn't identify with the war imagery of winners and losers," explains Susan. "So much of contemporary cancer talk draws on the language of aggression, such as 'races for the cure.' While I'm all in favor of taking an engaged approach to one's illness, we experienced a totally different set of values that grew out of our friendship, and the fact that we were having such a rich experience." For the two of them, says Carol, the experience was "more about simply being together, finding love with another in the same experience, rather than 'conquering the enemy' of breast cancer. Becoming victorious over one's circumstances is very popular in American culture. A lot of people are in love with that way of living life, of overcoming obstacles and transcending hurdles. But we found that it wasn't suited for us."

*I was dead and now I am alive
I was in tears and now I am laughing.
The power of love swept over my soul
And now I am that eternal power.*

RUMI

The two also discovered that there wasn't much in the popular culture to describe what they were talking about. So, inspired by what they had been through, Carol and Susan decided to write a book. Together with two other women who represented different religious backgrounds, they coauthored *Speak the Language of Healing* (Conari Press, 1999), a book that aims to present a spiritual dimension to healing from cancer. Today, they are both popular speakers on the lecture circuit; many women have responded with relief to their message. To illustrate how deeply entrenched cultural attitudes remain around healing, however, they tell the story of the public relations firm that contacted them as consultants on a new publicity campaign for the Breast Center in Nashville. "They seemed to love our message of not speaking in terms of war," recounts Susan, "and told us that they had decided to make their campaign about hope. But when the first ad for the campaign came out, it featured Winston Churchill giving the victory sign! This incident speaks to the lack of language, metaphors, and images to describe the feminine way of healing. We leap to war analogies because it's so engrained in us."

And what would their own ad campaign look like? Says Susan, "Instead of a big 'v' we would have our arms around each other," encircling each other with care and compassion. Adds Carol, "The message would be that even though this is a tragedy, we must be there for one another. In the Chinese way of thinking about the world, everyone is tied together with tiny red threads. And the threads get thickest for the people you're closest with. To me, this is finding the soul connection in a healthy way."

✸

Susan and Carol's wonderful image of women encircling one another with care and compassion is an apt description for one of my own experiences with a close friend. The incident involved my close friend Susan and was presaged by a dream in which a voice urged me to be as the biblical Martha had been a helpmate to Mary, her sister.

Not long after I had this dream, I was invited out to celebrate Susan's birthday with two other close friends, Mimi and Dodie. Susan and I had met some years before through our mutual connection to a magazine, where she had worked as an editor. We had felt an instantaneous connection, as not only did we share a passion for writing, we also saw the same Jungian therapist and spoke the esoteric language of dreams and astrology. That night, though, the big topic of conversation at dinner was Susan's recent breakup with her boyfriend, Will. Though it had been intense and loving, it had been a troubled relationship. He had lost his job and had been unable to find another one. In addition, Will had suffered from depression. The three of us that night spent hours helping Susan to digest the breakup and process her emotions. At the end of the evening, feeling hopeful and happy for Susan's future, we hugged one another good night and drove away in our separate cars.

Almost the minute that I walked in my front door, my phone rang. Wondering who it could be at that late hour, I picked up the receiver to hear Susan's voice, screaming in anguish and disbelief that she had come home to the tragic news that Will had killed himself that afternoon. He had chosen her birthday, Susan felt, to let her know he held her responsible. I felt completely stunned, as if I had received an electric shock throughout my entire body. I kept Susan on the phone until Mimi, who lived near her, arrived at her house to stay with her. I couldn't sleep that night, but stayed up praying for Susan, and for Will and the children he had left behind. For Susan, the next few weeks were a blur of grief and horror. Because she had broken up with Will, she had no "official" standing as a mourner, and felt deep shame and recrimination from his family and friends. There was no home for her suffering; only with her closest friends could she reveal her true feelings and get support.

One of the most difficult events for Susan to get through was the evening of the viewing of Will's body. To lend our friend support, Mimi and I decided to accompany Susan. Thus, while Susan kept vigil beside Will's body, praying, we kept vigil alongside her. In the following days, the four of us—Mimi, Susan, Dodie, and myself—would frequently get together to form a circle of support for

Susan. What seemed to help the most was simply being together, talking, talking, and talking. Frequently, I would dream of Will, then pass my dreams along to Susan, as they were healing in nature. In one dream, for instance, Will gave me a crystal bead as a symbol of his soul essence; later Susan made a small prayer bracelet of crystal beads. One weekend about three weeks after Will had died, Susan decided to go away for a retreat. While she was gone, Dodie had the inspiration to do a house purification to help soothe away some of the more troublesome memories and vibrations. With incense, candles, and our own homemade prayers and invocations, the three of us moved from room to room, harmonizing the space and blessing Susan's life with all our good wishes and hopes for her.

Several years later, Susan still feels the healing effects of her circle of friends. As she says today, "That whole chapter of my life was such a nightmare. But there was a blessing in it. Never before had I been so desperately in need of love and support, and so open to receiving it. My friends gave me that. They walked with me through the fires of hell and I cherish them for it. There is nothing so sweet and soothing as the comfort of friends in your time of need."

For the Love of God

❀

Sri Sarada Devi

On December 22, 1853, a holy girl was born in the small Indian hamlet of Jairambati, in Bengal. Her name was Sri Saradamani Devi, and her birth had been foretold to her parents in a vision in which a girl encircled her father's neck with golden arms. She grew up in a simple Indian village, raised by devout Brahmans who shared what food they had with the poor. It was said of Sarada that she was a very serious child who was more interested in her small clay figures of the goddesses Kali and Lakshmi than the typical playthings of other girls. Drawn to the Divine Mother from a very young age, she meditated on her daily and had mystic experiences and visions. At the age of six, according to the custom, she was betrothed and married to a young man named Ramakrishna, who was twenty-three at the time and lived in a nearby village.

As the story goes, Ramakrishna had since an early age been consumed with God. Because he showed no interest in school, his family arranged for him to become a priest at a temple of the Divine Mother Kali. But the intensity of his yearning, the severe austerities he practiced, and his indifference to the world caused them great concern. Alarmed by his behavior, they sought medical and even magical cures to bring him down to earth. When their efforts failed, they made plans for him to marry—but were frustrated in their search. Rather than objecting to his parents' efforts to find him a wife, however, Ramakrishna instead acquiesced, saying "Why are you fruitlessly looking for the girl hither and thither? Go to Ramachandra Mukherjee's house . . . and you will find the girl there . . ."[9] And so they did. After their marriage, the two exchanged visits, gradually coming to know each other as Sarada grew into adulthood.

Taken by his kindness, Sarada grew to love her husband deeply. She was especially moved by his devotion to God and the Divine Mother. By the time she had turned eighteen, however, Ramakrishna's God-intoxicated behavior had provoked rumors that he was insane. Concerned, Devi asked her father to take her to visit him. Becoming ill on the journey—which in those days was taken on foot—she was forced to rest at an inn. That night, she had a vision of a beautiful woman who appeared by her bedside, soothing and stroking her fevered body. When she asked the woman who she was, she replied, "I am your sister" and said that she was from Dakshineswar, the village where Ramakrishna lived.[10] When she awoke, Devi's fever was gone, and she continued on her journey. Upon arriving at Ramakrishna's home, her fears abated as she realized that the gossip about him was merely the speculation of people who could not recognize her husband's spiritual greatness. He, too, was happy to see her and, welcoming her warmly to his side, confided in her that he had "fervently prayed to the Divine Mother to remove all traces of carnality from her mind so that she might remain pure and immaculate." When he asked her if she had come to distract him, she is said to have replied, "Why should I do it? I have come only to help you in the path of religious life."[11]

Love is saying yes to belonging.

DAVID STEINDL-RAST

And so, for the next thirteen years, Sarada Devi devoted herself to the care of Ramakrishna, the growing number of devotees who surrounded him, and her own spiritual practice. Often, Ramakrishna would pass entire nights in samadhi, a state of enlightened consciousness. It fell to her to whisper the correct divine names in his ear to help ease him back to earthly consciousness. An eager student, she readily absorbed his teachings. Soon she, too, passed hours in blissful communion. An essential part of their practice was devotion to the Holy Mother.

During the early days of their stay together, Ramakrishna placed Sarada Devi on the seat intended for the Divine Mother, then invoked in her the Divine Mother through this prayer: "O Divine Mother, Thou Eternal Virgin, the Mistress of all powers and abode of all beauty, deign to unlock for me the gate to perfection.

Sanctifying the body and mind of this woman, do Thou manifest Thyself through her and do what is auspicious." This invoked in Sarada Devi a high state of spiritual experience. "When she came to, she did not lose sense of her identity with the Divine but retained it throughout her life."[12]

This event signalled Sarada Devi's future participation in her husband's growing ministry. "They saw in each other only the Divine Mother. . . . She was holy as he was holy. He was the 'divine man' and she the 'divine woman.'"[13] Even after Sri Ramakrishna's death from throat cancer in 1886, Sarada Devi acted as a mother to his disciples; as her spiritual greatness grew in reputation, people flocked to her for guidance. Often, people came to her to seek purification of their sins; literally laying their sins at her feet, she would frequently suffer their transgressions as burning sensations in her body. When her disciples expressed concern for her health, she replied, "My child, several among those who come here have been up to everything in life. No type of sin has been left undone by them. But when they come here and address me as mother, I forget everything and they get more than they deserve." Indeed, her powers were said to have cured some of drunkenness, and returned many who had strayed back to the spiritual path. Her hospitality and concern for her disciples' everyday needs were also legendary. She extended "mother care and solicitude" to all her guests, cordially greeting all devotees no matter the time of their arrival.

Sri Sarada Devi passed away on July 20, 1920, widely revered as a great guru in her own right and as an incarnation of the Divine Mother. As she said, "Sri Ramakrishna left me behind to manifest the Motherhood of God to the world."[14]

> *Once our hearts are open, all existence appears naturally beautiful and harmonious.*
>
> TARTHANG TULKU

Ruth and
✳
Abby's Story

The story of Sri Sarada Devi's life path as an incarnation of the Holy Mother is an inspiring one for all women. She was a role model of the twin forces of compassion for humanity and spiritual devotion to God. Her life embodied these words of Hazrat Inayat Khan: "The truly great souls become streams of love." Sarada Devi's path of austere renunciation of sex and material wealth may be ill-suited for contemporary women. Still, she can be regarded as a spiritual foremother—a feminine figure who helped pave the way for women devotees who both love God and seek to heal the world's suffering.

Ruth Berlin and Abby Rosen are two women who, over the past several decades, have sought to do just that with their lives. As they tell the story of their years-long friendship, the two first met in San Francisco in 1978, as young women in their twenties studying with the Hindu yoga teacher Swami Muktananda. As Abby recalls, "Our bond was instantaneous. We felt like soul sisters right away." Ruth admired Abby's heart and "her gutsiness" that invariably led the two of them on adventures. Together with another friend, Marilyn, they helped to run Muktananda's San Francisco Siddha Yoga Center. An "incredibly warm, nurturing place," says Abby, the Center was located in a beautiful home they had rented that had a fireplace, a fish pond, and lovely views of the bay. There, they taught classes, hosted enormous potluck suppers for students and devotees, pursued their separate careers as psychotherapists and, with Marilyn, were codirectors of the San Francisco Family Group Institute. As single women, the three shared one another's romantic hopes and fears. "At night, we would hang out in front of the fireplace and talk about our lives. It was a wonderful time of shared work, personal dreams, and spiritual practice," recalls Ruth.

As Muktananda's reputation grew, attracting more and more people, Ruth, Abby, and Marilyn began organizing public conferences. The first event they hosted was at the Palace of Fine Arts in San Francisco, and drew more than 3,000 people. Following this initial success, they were flown all over the country to organize further conferences on Muktananda's behalf; in India, they helped coordinate the seventh International Transpersonal Association conference with Stanislav and Christina Grof, titled "Ancient Wisdom and Modern Science" with the Karmapa, the Dalai Lama, Mother Theresa, and Pir Vilayat Inayat Khan. Because of the extent of their travelling, they gave up their home in the San Francisco Siddha Yoga Center. Eventually, however, their lives led them in separate geographical directions—Ruth with her husband and son to Los Angeles, and Abby to Annapolis, Maryland, with her new husband.

Despite their bicoastal separation, however, the two women maintained a close connection. Following Muktananda's death in 1982, their attention turned more toward their careers in psychology. When Abby encouraged Ruth to move to the East Coast with her family to help with her burdgeoning therapy practice in 1990, a new phase in their collaborative partnership began. "We had done so many things together, and now we had so many ideas," says Abby. So, weaving together their interests in psychotherapy, healing, and spirituality, and drawing on the organizational skills they had honed while working with Muktananda, the two women opened a holistic health, psychotherapy, and education center on the marina in Annapolis. In searching for a name that would capture the identity of their center, they did a special ceremony in the woods during which each came up with a word that was meaningful to them. "One of us came up with the word 'inner,' and the other 'source,'" says Ruth, "so we named our center Innersource. To this day, however, we can't remember which one came up with which word!"

Opening in the fall of 1992, their center was an immediate success. Ruth focused on organizing Innersource conferences, drawing in guest speakers such as the mind/body speaker Bernie Siegel and the Buddhist meditation teacher Sharon Salzburg, while Abby turned her attention to Innersource Center for Psychotherapy and Healing; each maintained their own separate practice as well. In addition, they hosted programs for singles and celebrated holidays with their growing community of friends and clients. Their success changed the dynamics of their relationship. "As we aged and got stronger, our differences became more evident," remembers Abby. "One of the things that happened was the realization that we each needed our own sphere to be who we were. It became clear that it was better for us to honor our individual strengths by doing parallel work rather than doing the same work together. That way, we avoided holding back each other's power."

Not unlike a marriage that starts off with a state of fusion, then gradually separates into a relationship of equals, Ruth and Abby's friendship continued to evolve over time. And even though there were times when they were each off pursuing their own activities, says Ruth, "there was always a coming back together again. Over the years we've been through a lot of life issues together—weddings, my son's birth, Abby's divorce, my mother's struggle with Alzheimer's—and we've supported each other through the great and the difficult life transitions."

> *Love your neighbor as yourself.*
>
> LEVITICUS 19:18

There were spiritual changes they each weathered as well. After Swami Muktananda's death in 1982, "we felt that it was time to move on and go more inward—for each of us it became an opportunity to connect with the inner teacher," explains Ruth. Abby began exploring Judaism, her religion of origin, especially the mystical tradition of Kabbalah. Gradually, Ruth became drawn, as well, to explore the faith of her ancestors. For the past decade, they have celebrated Shabbat together every Friday night—albeit with their own added rituals—and belong to the same synagogue as well.

What remains central to the unique partnership they have forged over the years, say both Abby and Ruth, is their mutual commitment to service. "The passion to serve underlies both the spiritual, transpersonal form of psychotherapy we do that helps people connect with God and their inner selves—their inner source—as well as our separate projects," says Ruth. Abby, for example, has focused on her local synagogue and in addition has conducted a Kabbalah circle for over twelve years. Ruth, who has suffered in the past from environmental illnesses, is a committed environmental activist who has worked to reduce the public's exposure to toxic pesticides. Each feels fully supported by the other in the work they do.

"Part of our strong connection has to do with a similar feeling that we both have in terms of giving back to the world." says Abby. "That sense of being of service to the world came in first through Muktananda and then continued with Judaism through the tradition of 'tikkun olam,' or restoration of the world." Sometimes, says Ruth, the two of them and their old friend Marilyn joke among themselves that Muktananda implanted a "microchip of service" in each of their hearts. "My feeling is that this is how we came into the world, and Muktananda was the catalyst that brought out that passion for service. If something were to happen and I couldn't do service in the world, I would feel like a limb had been cut off—it's my life blood," says Ruth with conviction. Indeed, says Abby, Muktananda used to liken the three women to the confluence of the three rivers in India. "Clearly," she says, "there was a reason that we came together. The energetic connection between the three of us is so strong that I know we will always stay connected."

"We're very aware that we're kindred spirits—sometimes it's hard for us to find other people who are like us," adds Ruth, who says that she can still remember how she felt the first moment she saw Marilyn and Abby. "It's a feeling where you just know. It feels very familiar. Our friendship is our destiny, and everything we've done together has strengthened that. And even though Marilyn is in Los Angeles, she and Abby are the two people that I know that I can really connect to. And that is so precious because the ones who share the same unique journey with you are few and far between. Even despite the fact that I have a husband and a child and we each have a very full life, there is still nobody in my universe other than her that I connect to in the place that we connect. Our friendship is a very special treasure. We're blessed."

MEDITATIONS ON LOVE

✧

Many of the exercises and meditations given throughout this chapter draw on images of nature. Whether the sun, a river, roses, or the Mother of Animals, these images show that love is a natural dimension of the world, intrinsic to all existence. For if God is love, as the mystics say, then love is life itself. And if God as woman is the Divine Mother of Creation, then we have only to honor Her to release that same regenerative power within ourselves. Thus, as we awaken to the world of nature, so too do we discover the universe of love within our hearts. May these exercises help to attune you to the deep love abiding like a precious secret in your soul.

✧

Awakening the Divine Mother Within

To awaken the love of the Divine Mother within your heart, set aside a special time daily or weekly to meditate on her presence. You may wish to do this alone, or with a group of close women friends. Before you begin, create a special altar especially in honor of the Holy Mother. Scatter flower petals, light incense, or include an object that represents a part of your life that is in need of Her succor—a photo of a child, an emblem of a part of your life that is in need of healing, or even a particular political issue that is in need of divine compassion such as homelessness, war, or famine. In my own meditations, I have found that concentrating on a picture of one of the Divine Mother's many forms helps to deepen my attunement. I often begin my meditation by reflecting upon the stories that are associated with Her, as they are revealing of Her loving nature.

One example, for instance, is the Chinese bodhisattva of compassion Kuan Yin, the "One Who Hears the Cries of the World." After many lifetimes, according to legend, Kuan Yin had finally attained enlightenment. Thus liberated from worldly attachments, she began her ascent through the realms. Suddenly, the cries of those she had left behind reached her ears, and turning around, she descended back to earth, vowing never to leave until every living creature had attained enlightenment. I have always loved this story, as it captures that feeling of love we all experience in our finer soul moments—that feeling that says that we can never be truly at peace until those around us are eased of their suffering, as well. Kuan Yin is thus the very essence of selfless love. She is the spirit within who is sensitive to the slightest sadness, the one who pours healing balm onto wounded souls.

To meditate on Kuan Yin, relive the events of her spiritual journey within your heart. Experience her as she finally attains the bliss of enlightenment; then be with her as the cries of children, men, women, and animals reach her ears with their plaintive suffering. Even if a real mother is meditating and her baby cries, for example, she will interrupt her silence to hold her child. In just the same way, Kuan Yin is the mother of the world who will never abandon the children of the earth and who will gladly interrupt her practice to assist them. As you reflect upon her being, imagine that she fills your heart so completely with compassion, that, becoming full, it overflows with mercy, raining love onto all creation.

I sometimes combine the Buddhist "Loving Kindness Meditation" that helps to awaken bodhicitta, or the enlightened heart, with a concentration on Kuan Yin: First, imagine that you are seated before the being of Kuan Yin. In one of the classic images of Kuan Yin, she is pictured in the heavens, slightly turned toward the earth, and pouring droplets of compassion from a vessel onto humanity. As you meditate on this image, experience the bliss that comes from her being. Feel all the hard places within you of resistance, fear, and pain dissolve in her unconditional love and forgiveness. Filled with this love, imagine next the people who are closest to you in your life—your children, parents, and friends. Extend that same loving kindness you received from Kuan Yin toward each one of them, especially those with whom you are having difficulties. Next, imagine the people who live on your street, then in your city, then in your country. Expand your heart to include all of your fellow countrywomen and men in this gradually widening aureole of love; visualize growing numbers of people within the Goddess's embrace. Then, going beyond the boundaries of your country, extend Her embrace of loving kindness to include all beings and creatures who live on this earth: every human being, blade of grass, mountain, and tree. Last, expand this love to include the entire universe, until all of space, all of existence, radiates with the unconditional love of the Divine Mother.

Another powerful image that helps to awaken the Divine Mother within is the Virgin Mary, Mother of Jesus. Many of my friends collect images of Mary, ranging from the Black Madonna to classic Christian images. My favorite image of Mary is the Virgin of Guadalupe who appeared in 1531 to the Nahuatl Indian peasant Juan Diego. I have a beautiful gold medallion of this image given to me by my friend and soul sister Tatiana that, rather than wear, I keep on my altar. I rarely wear it myself, but pass it along to others, whether to one of my sons for protection or to a friend in need. I also find candles with her image on it in the Mexican food section of my local grocery store. When I light these candles on my altar, I think of all the women in this country and in countries around the world who may be evoking Mary their mother at the same time. Then I call to mind the circumstances surrounding the appearance of the Virgin of Guadalupe. I think of the terrible oppression the Indians suffered at the hands of the Spanish conquerers; I reflect upon the fact that she appeared on the site of an ancient Aztec temple dedicated to an Aztec Earth Mother; I feel the poverty of the peasant Juan Diego, and how Mary's appearance to him was a response to the depth of his need of her; then I smile as I think of the flowers she caused to bloom as proof that her appearance was real. In the image of the Virgin of Guadalupe, Mary's arms are folded in prayer over her heart; her head is bent down toward the upturned face of Juan Diego. In many representations, she is surrounded by roses and stands on a crescent moon.

To meditate on the image of the Virgin of Guadalupe, you may wish to play a piece of music that evokes her presence, such as some soothing Gregorian chant. Then call to mind that place within where you feel most powerless and hopeless.

> *Though I have all faith, so that I could remove mountains, and have not love, I am nothing.*
>
> *And though I bestow all my goods to feed the poor, and though I give my body to be burned, and have not love, it profiteth me nothing.*
>
> *Love suffereth long, and is kind; love envieth not; love vaunteth not itself, is not puffed up.*
>
> 1 Corinthians 13:2–4

Maybe you can't come up with the money to pay your bills, your health is suffering, or you've been having a difficult time on the job. Then think of Mary's sweetness, her bright hope, and imagine that she takes you into herself, holding you like any mother would take a child onto her lap and soothe away their cares. As she does this, imagine that all the hurt places within you are healed by her love. Where once there was coldness in your soul, flowers now bloom.

Of course, the flowers of Mary's love are not only for yourself, but also for others in the world whose suffering is even greater than your own. As you grow closer to Mary, imagine that, along with her, you hear the prayers of all those who are at this very moment praying to her for help: "Oh Blessed Virgin Mary, heal my child"; "Oh Blessed Virgin Mary, save my marriage"; "Oh Blessed Virgin Mary, help me to put food on my table"; "Oh Blessed Virgin Mary, comfort me in this prison cell"; "Oh Blessed Virgin Mary, help me to survive this torture"; "Oh Blessed Virgin Mary, forgive me all my sins." Then imagine Mary extending her compassionate love to each one of these suffering souls. Join your prayers with hers, sending spiritual flowers to the hearts of all those trapped in pain and suffering.

✵

MOTHER OF WILD CREATURES

My friend and dear soul sister Harriett Crosby has no children of her own—
human, that is. The great loves of her life have been animals: foxes, bears, snakes,
wolves, dogs, chickens, and coyotes. When I think of Harriett, I think of the illustration on the card announcing her fiftieth birthday party: a happily beaming
woman, with a dog on one side, and a fox on the other side. An ardent environ-
mentalist, Harriett is always on call to take into her home wounded animals whose
lives are endangered. With tiny droppers of milk, she nurses them back to health.
Her animal stories are as touching to me as the stories of my friends' children. I
recall the poignant time when, like a mother whose child leaves home, she set two
foxes free—and how happily she rejoiced when one unexpectedly returned. When
my boys were little, Harriett used to come for dinner and awe them with stories of
her beloved honey bear. Now she is helping to nurture my oldest son and other
young people in their dreams to become environmentalists as well. In addition to
her work with several environmental organizations, Harriett is helping to create a
spiritual retreat for environmentalists and a haven for animals and organically
raised crops on her farm—Fox Haven—in rural Maryland.

The ancients had a goddess for Harriett's kind of love: she was Diana,
"Mother of Animals," or "Lady of Wild Creatures." At Ephesus, where she was
known by her older name of Artemis, she was worshipped as a figure thickly covered in breasts, symbolizing her role as nurturer of all the world's creatures. In one
statue, rows of egg-shaped breasts cover her chest, while beneath that, different
animals are carved into the rest of her body, forming a kind of female Noah's ark.
In pagan times, Diana's spirit was worshipped in a log or a cut tree branch. She
was venerated as the goddess of nature throughout the Roman Empire; even in
Europe throughout medieval times, Diana was worshipped as the lady of the wild
woodlands.[14]

To meditate on the Great Goddess in her role as the Mother of Animals, call
to mind the ancient image of Diana covered entirely in breasts and images of wild
creatures. Then, go deeply into the state of consciousness that gave rise to this
image: humanity's interdependence with the world of nature. If you are a mother,
for instance, imagine connecting to animals with as wide and deep a love as the
love you have for your children. Even if you are not a parent, think of the vulnerability of the birds, the deer, or the dogs who may be hurt or wounded from mod-

ern civilization's encroaching presence. Imagine your body as the body of the earth, sustaining and nurturing all creatures. Feel the ease with which animals and insects roam over the ground of your being, taking from you what they need to sustain themselves. Have an imaginary dialogue with an owl, a wolf, a heron, a whale, or a dolphin. Feel stirred by the sacred mystery they represent.

This is a meditation that can be carried on in your heart even after you have risen from your altar. Dare to be a Diana, an Artemis, a lady of the wildlands and the woods in your local neighborhood. Walk among the trees, sending love to the animals and creatures of the earth.

✹

Tapestry of Love

As described in this chapter, love is the work of a thousand tiny things. Yet often, we become so distracted by the tedium and boredom of our chores or our everyday grind that we forget the "bigger picture" we are creating through the labor of our lives and the care of our loved ones.

> *My will and my desire were turned by love,*
> *the love that moves the sun and the*
> *other stars.*
>
> Dante

One way to offset that is to imagine every task in your life as a stitch in a rare and exquisite tapestry. You may not be able to see it, but when you are washing dishes, gardening, driving the car pool, sitting in a school meeting, or having a difficult conversation with a stubborn teenager, imagine to yourself that you are taking part in a masterpiece of needlework that will ultimately result in something everlasting. Like a thousands-year-old rug, the work of love you are creating will long outlive you. Indeed, it will continue to exist in the generations and generations of those who take up the needle and thread of life and love, adding their own design to yours.

RECOMMENDED READING

Addiction to Perfection: The Still Unravished Bride by Marion Woodman (Inner City Books, 1988)

Alone of All Her Sex: The Myth and the Cult of the Virgin Mary by Marina Warner (Pocket Books, Simon & Schuster, 1976)

Cherishment: A Psychology of the Heart by Elisabeth Young-Bruehl and Faith Bethelard (Free Press, 2000)

Cultivating the Mind of Love: The Practice of Looking Deeply in the Mahayana Buddhist Tradition by Thich Nhat Hanh (Parallax Press, 1995)

The Devotional Poems of Mirabai, edited by A. J. Alston (Motilal Banarsidass, 1980)

The Divine Feminine: Exploring the Feminine Face of God Around the World by Andrew Harvey and Anne Baring (Conari Press, 1996)

A General Theory of Love by Thomas Lewis, M.D., Fari Amini, M.D., and Richard Lannon, M.D. (Random House, 2000)

The Hand of Poetry: Five Mystic Poets of Persia: Translations from the Poems of Sanai, Attar, Rumi, Saadi and Hafiz; Lectures on Persian Poetry, translated by Coleman Barks, edited by Hazrat Inayat Khan (Omega Publications, 1993)

Holy Mother: Being the Life of Sri Sarada Devi, Wife of Sri Ramakrishna and Helpmate in His Mission by Swami Nikhilananda (Ramakrishna-Vivekananda Center, 1982)

Kuan Yin: Myths and Prophecies of the Chinese Goddess of Compassion by Martin Palmer (HarperCollins, 1995)

The Return of the Mother by Andrew Harvey (Frog, Ltd., 1995)

Speak the Langauge of Healing by Susan Kuner, Carol Orsborn, et al. (Conari Press, 1999)

Testament of Youth by Vera Brittain, introduction by Carolyn G. Heilbrun (Wideview Books, 1981)

Women's Growth in Connection: Writings from the Stone Center by Judith Jordan, Alexandra G. Kaplan, Jean Baker Miller, Irene P. Stiver, Janet L. Surrey (The Guilford Press, 1991)

SUGGESTED MUSIC

Adagio for Strings by Samuel Barber, audio CD

Angel Love by Aeoliah, audio CD

"Ave Maria" by Jessye Norman, from *Amazing Grace*, audio CD

Devotional and Love Chants by Nusrat Fateh Ali Khan, audio CD

Lost Songs of the Silk Road by Ghazal, audio CD

Inner Harmony by Cecilia, audio CD

Inner Sanctum (Composed for Kuan Yin) by Aeoliah, audio CD

"Litany for Feast of All Souls" by Franz Schubert, *Favorite Schubert Songs*, sung by Bryn Terfel, pianist Malcolm Martineau, audio CD

Love Supreme by John Coltrane, audio CD

Path of the Heart by Rabbi David Zeller, audio CD

Robe of Love by Zuleikha, audio CD

Sao Vicente & Café Atlantico by Cesaria Evore, audio CDs

Through Eternity: Homage to Rumi, Persian Devotional Music by Dustan
Ensemble with Shahram Nazeri, audio CD

The Feminine Face of Magic

MAGIC: SAY THE WORD, AND IT CONJURES SUPERNATURAL REALMS OF enchantment where people fly, animals speak, and trees walk. Magic, in fact, is a rare, alchemical quality that bends the rules of everyday existence. Through its effects, our psychic senses are flung wide like windows and doors opening into alternate dimensions. Unlike the ordinary, day-to-day environment most of us inhabit, in the queendom of magic the unexpected, the irrational, and the wildly improbable exist as realities to be explored.

Imagine, for instance, seeing through the eyes of the child you once were. In this world of wonder, grown-ups are as huge as giants, an invisible friend keeps you company, and the house you live in is a cavernous cave containing pockets of dark and eerie places. Or, step into the mindset of an Australian aborigine or an ancient Greek pagan. Through their eyes, experience nature as alive and ensouled with intelligence, peopled not only with humans, but with talking trees, wise spirits, animal guardians, and invisible guides. If you can do this, then a spark of magic remains in your soul, just waiting to be fanned into a brighter flame.

> *Beside this picture I would like to place the spectacle of the starry heavens at night, for the only equivalent of the universe within is the universe without; and just as I reach this world through the medium of the body, so I reach that world through the medium of the psyche.*
>
> CARL JUNG

Of all the qualities, magic may be the one that I could least live without. For with magic not only is a person never bored, but they are also never alone. Magic confers upon a person the imaginative capacity to perceive and communicate with the unseen beings who crowd our physical world with their subtle presence. Spells are often associated with magic, and indeed a person under magic's spell lives in a universe pregnant with secrets and meaning; through the lens of magic, life is not just a successive series of responsibilities to be executed or problems to be solved, but a vision and a revelation to be uncovered. From the mandala-shaped astrological chart that reflects the patterns in the heavens at the exact moment of our birth, to the phantasmagoria of twilit images that inhabits our nightly dreamscape and the incantations of enchantresses and sorcerers, magical technologies intuit that there is an order and a design concealed within the chaos of our everyday lives. Magic is a quality that can help us to perceive and interpret that pattern, deepening our self-knowledge and connecting us to the purpose of our lives for which we were each intended.

On Moonlight:
Let my heart reflect Thy light
As the moon reflects the sun.

Hazrat Inayat Khan,
Nature Meditations

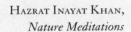

Problem is, for all of society's sophisticated technology, we are woefully ignorant when it comes to the time-honored art of magic. The astrologers, mediums, wizards, seers, and priestesses that were once an integral part of ancient cultures have for the most part vanished in our time, consigned to history books or slotted away in fantasy and science-fiction novels. And yet, sensing its lack in their lives, many make the occasional pilgrimage to a psychic or palmist. They are not so much seeking to get a glimpse of the future or to gain power over others, however, as they are searching for the missing element in their lives. Predictions, signs, and omens bewitch our ordinary lives, limning them with a ghostly touch of the numinous and the otherworldly. It is the long-gone world of wizards, enchantresses, and magi we yearn for. Indeed those who have been brought up in a secular culture, writes Thomas Moore in *The Re-Enchantment of Everyday Life,* "don't realize how much our lives have been impoverished by the lack of magic." Some may think the holy grail of modern life is youth, romance, money, or power. I happen to think it is magic.

While most equate magic with fortune-telling or the witchlike ability to manipulate people or events, authentic magic is about something much more mysterious and profound. We say that mediums have "second sight," that witches fly, or that the dead speak, for instance, as a way to convey the deeper truth that there exist many more dimensions of space, time, and reality than we are aware of. Even physicists have come to realize that reality is as riddled with alternate dimensions as rock is layered with veins of gold or other precious metals and minerals. Thus, like the key in fairy tales that unlocks the secret door in the heart of the castle, magic is that quality through which we can access those hidden realities enfolded within our everyday lives. As the seer is able to see in many directions, so magic allows us to traverse these landscapes: behind us into the long distant past and the realm of the ancestors; ahead, into possible futures and the unfoldment of our appointed fate; sideways, into the animal and nature kingdoms that surround us; below, into the depths of the underworld where exist the gods and goddesses that rule death and immortality; and above and beyond, into the transcendent heavens of saints and angelic beings. Like a wizard's wand, magic illuminates this hologram, bringing into focus all at once the multidimensionality of existence. Because magic functions as a kind of enhanced "seeing," it is associated with seers and visionaries: it opens, reveals, and brings to light all that which is obscured by the narrow perceptions of our limited ego consciousness. Magic can also be compared to a kind of spiritual cooking or mixing: like the alchemists of old who poured and measured liquids in their laboratories late at night, or the witches who mixed potions or spells in their cauldrons, magic is about intermixing the immaterial and intangible elements of spirit into the material world of physical reality. Practitioners within the pagan Wiccan tradition, for example, perform rituals that "raise the energy" or "call down the moon," as ways to evoke the invisible spirit worlds and transform attitudes that have become stuck or bogged down. Likewise, divination across the ages and across cultures has been practiced as a method to discern the will of those unseen beings who exist just behind the veil of physical appearances. Whether the Delphic oracle who channelled the wisdom of the god Apollo, or the African diviner who sought the guidance of the Orishas in the affairs of the tribe, the aim of positive magic is to harmonize the human realm with the Divine.

Atum replied:
"I will build the Zodiac—
a secret mechanism in the stars,
linked to unerring and inevitable fate.
The lives of men,
From birth to final destruction,
Shall be controlled
By the hidden workings of this mechanism."

And when the mechanism begins to work,
The keen-eyed goddess Destiny
Supervised and checked its movements.
Through this mechanism,
Destiny and Necessity are cemented together.
Destiny sows the seed.
Necessity compels the results.
In the wake of Destiny and Necessity
Comes order—
The interweaving of events in time.

FROM "The Zodiac and Destiny,"
FROM *The Hermetica:*
The Lost Wisdom of the Pharaohs

Thus, while magic is frequently discounted as impractical and unworldly by many, it could be said to be one of life's most practical arts. While mastering the skills of the everyday world is an important part of human development, there comes a time when every individual will be confronted with the intangible riddle of their existence, as well as their ultimate passage into the next world. If we have not gained some knowledge of ourselves and the invisible landscapes that lie beyond our ordinary perceptions, then death is likely to come as an unpleasant shock, and the life we have lived may seem like an undeciphered text.

But magic has its useful applications for daily life as well. In my own life, magic has acted as a sixth sense that has helped me to navigate the twists and turns of life's confusing pathways. I no doubt inherited this tendency from my mother who, perhaps because she was raised in a Latin culture in Buenos Aires, Argentina, by a Scottish mother with a strong mystical bent, was herself very sensitive to psychic phenomenon. I vividly remember the story she told me of the Spanish gardener who was also a "curandero," or healer, and who once, when she was a small girl, healed a cut on her finger within a matter of minutes by simply holding it within the palms of his hands. As a young wife apartment hunting with my father, my mother would often "read" the atmosphere of a place, determining whether or not its vibrations were peaceful or disturbed. Most important, my mother never denigrated my own psychic experiences; whether it was fairies in the garden or claims that I could fly, she always accepted that side of my nature.

Perhaps these positive early childhood experiences are the reason why, very early on, magic was an integral part of my connections with women. In my early twenties living in California, I studied the mantic arts, attending classes in tarot, palmistry, and visiting psychics and astrologers. I recall afternoons spent with girlfriends practicing different tarot card spreads and throwing the I Ching; upon the birth of each of my sons, I had an astrology chart cast, which I then shared among my friends for their interpretations. With two of my closest friends, Beaté and Chalice, I also began weaving the cycles of the moon into my daily life. Each month at the exact hour of the new moon, whether midday or midnight, we would trek into nature with our candles and veils. I remember one summer's night on a grass-covered hillside close to the ocean, when the three of us sat beneath the dark purple canopy of the midnight sky, evoking the Divine Mother, reciting prayers, and chanting. It was pure and timeless magic. Later, I joined together with a larger group of women for monthly new-moon ceremonies; the singing and silence of those holy communions still resonate after all these years.

Indeed, to set one's rituals according to the phases of the moon is a powerful and potent form of natural, healthy magic that has been used to schedule the holidays of many of the world's religious traditions for centuries. As the years have passed, my appreciation for the art of astrology—interpreting the alignment between the planets at the moment of a person's birth, and observing the influence of the ever-wheeling planetary cycles—has continued to evolve in new forms and expressions. After moving to Washington, D.C., I began studying astrology with Lynn Koiner—a colorful, magical soul sister whose rich imagination brought the cosmos of stars within and without sparklingly alive. Speaking the language of astrology with my closest friends is like sharing a special feminine secret that has drawn us closer together in what I sometimes think of as an informal "star sisterhood." Together with my friend Dana Gerhardt, I have continued to observe my monthly lunar practice, along with a virtual "mooncircle" of friends who meditate together at the new and full moons. As I mark the phases of the moon, so, too, do I celebrate the passage of the sun across the sky, celebrating the winter and summer solstices, and the spring and fall equinoxes. Often, my friends and I will join together for dinner, then participate in one of noted activist astrologer Caroline Casey's popular solstice or equinox community ceremonies of drumming, dancing, and predictions. In this way, my community of astrologer friends and I practice the magic that comes from weaving the patterns of our lives with the greater design in the heavens. "Atum implants each human soul in flesh by means of the gods who circle in heaven," says the Hermetica, a book of ancient Egyptian wisdom. "It is man's lot to live his life according to the fate determined for him by these circling celestial powers—and then to pass away and be resolved into the elements."[1]

One of the most powerful forms of magic I have worked with over the years is dreamwork. Under the guidance of a Jungian analyst, a wise older woman who acted as my guide, I spent nearly a decade learning to navigate the tricky waters of the unconscious. As one of my favorite books on this topic is titled, dreams are a "portal to the source," a gateway to the mythic dimensions within time and space. Through my dreams I have encountered unbelievable visionary vistas, Dante-esque landscapes inhabited by fantastical animals and numinous beings. At the same time, I have learned to decode the symbolism in dreams that at first glance seemed merely ordinary, yet contained extraordinary messages. Through dreamwork, I have time-travelled back into my childhood, gaining insight into psychological complexes and, on rare occasions, into past lifetimes. Most important, dreams have been a way to stay close to the winding river of my fate without being tempted off the path in the wrong

FOR THE DAY OF THE FULL MOON:
*Fill my heart with Thy light
so fully as the full moon.*

HAZRAT INAYAT KHAN,
Nature Meditations

direction. Indeed, those who seek psychic guidance in their lives can do no better than to turn to the dream oracle within their own psyches. Ask the way—and, I believe, our dreams will show us the path.

While magic in its many forms has graced my life and the lives of my friends, others I know have not been so charmed. Indeed, I have chosen to include a chapter on magic because, at least on the surface, it appears to be strikingly absent from modern women's lives. Often when I read magazines or watch television talk shows aimed at women, I am struck by the way their problems are reduced down to a single cause: lack of self-esteem. Women whose lives are too hectic, or who are depressed, or who suffer from bad marriages, eating disorders, or drug addiction are all told that the source of their distress is the absence of self-love. I do not disagree that low self-esteem caused by early childhood wounding can be a source of personal suffering—in fact, I have taken it very seriously in my own individual journey of discovery. Still, there is no ignoring the fact that most of us live in a culture that is stressful, tedious, and monotonous, that emphasizes material goals over spiritual ideals, and that has little awareness of the cycles of time.

RISING MOON:

Let my soul advance towards Thee
As the rising moon progresses towards
fullness.

HAZRAT INAYAT KHAN,
Nature Meditations

"Where's the magic?" we moan to a friend, or "The magic's gone out of my relationship, or my job, or my life," we say.

And indeed, they are right! For though we are led to believe that magic is an illusory quality, a kind of sham and glitzy trick, it is as necessary to our well-being as eating healthy food or exercising. Women need magic to keep them sane and centered in what really matters. They need the medicine of communal, seasonal rituals to help them shift from the profane to the sacred realm of nature. They need magic to help them reconnect to the ancient cycles and rhythmic ebbs and flows of energy taking place within their own female bodies. They need magic to help them reestablish the sacred bonds of sisterhood with other women—and to connect to the archetypal wise woman within themselves. They need magic to be whole and to learn to dream, imagine, and wonder as children again. And women need magic in order to feel companioned in their loneliness and their struggles by their invisible helpmates on the other side, the friendly animal and nature spirits that roam the earth, and their lineage of ancestors.

In the past, magic was an acceptable and natural part of a woman's life. It is difficult to imagine, for instance, that once upon a time women, as well as men, were revered practitioners of the mantic arts, functioning as priestesses, oracles, fortune-tellers, seers, shamans, and healers. Even though magic in some form or another is a part of many women's spiritual practice, like my own, it is still marked by a silent taboo. As astrologer Jean Lall says, there has been a tremendous "repression of magic" since the Renaissance. "Beginning with the Enlightenment, the Reformation, and the Counter-Reformation," says Lall, Western society "has attempted to distance itself from the magical and the mystical and the occult in favor of being more scientific and rational." Even despite the resurgence of interest in this country, magic is rarely treated with the same serious consideration as yoga, meditation, or prayer. Thus, like the other qualities I have explored in this book, women have their own unique history with regard to magic that each must disentangle for herself, a thread at a time, until she can reclaim it in her own right once again.

THE SYBIL

Sybil, "Cavern Dweller," a Latin form of Cybele, the Great Mother of Gods . . . Her oracular spirit occupied a succession of priestesses in the sacred cave at Cumae, near Lake Avernus, dedicated to Triple Hecate. The cave was famed as an entrance to the underworld. Sybils called up the dead there for necromantic interviews. . . . In the second century B.C. the . . . idol of Cybele was carried to Rome by order of the Cumaean sybils whose oracles guided imperial policy. Texts of the priestesses' sayings, the Sybilline Books, were so respected that both Christians and Jews spent many centuries rewriting these books and forging additions to them, to make it seem that the sybils foretold the coming of Christ and the Messiah. . . . Folk tradition maintained that after the Christian conquest of Europe, the sybils continued to occupy sacred caves in certain mountains that belonged to the Great Mother of the Gods. Many legends told of men who, like Tannhauser and Thomas Rhymer, entered such a cave and dwelt in "the Paradise of Queen Sybil."

Excerpted from The Woman's Encyclopedia
of Myths and Secrets *by*
Barbara Walker (HarperCollins, 1983)

MORGAN LE FAY AND MERLIN

Celtic death-goddess: Morgan the Fate or Fata Morgana . . . Morgans or "sea-women" could "draw down to their palaces of gold and crystal at the bottom of the sea or ponds, those who venture imprudently too near the water. . . ." Morgan sat at the head of the table in the Green Knight's castle, presiding over the death and resurrection of the rival year-gods as they beheaded one another in their proper seasons.

Gawain was obviously a solar hero, his strength waxing in the morning and waning in the afternoon; he was one of four brothers representing the four solar seasons. . . . Late romances deprived Morgan of her divinity and made her human, just as the Great Goddess Mari became a mortal Virgin Mary. Morgan became Arthur's sister, yet a "great clerk of necromancy," a prototypical witch. . . . Her name was applied to anything magical, miraculous, or misleading, as the Fata Morgana. An old word for witches' spells, glamor, *came from Glamorgan, the Goddess' sacred territory in Wales.*

Merlin, the Druidic wizard who was the wise-man of King Arthur's court, learned all his magic from the Goddess, in the guise of Morgan le Fay, or Viviane (She Who Lives), or the Lady of the Lake. At the end of his life she took him back into her magic cave and wrapped him in deathless sleep until his Second Coming. Here she was called Minue, or Fate, the same as the Moon-goddess Diana Nemorensis, or the Nemesis of the Greeks. Pagan Britons believed Merlin would return from his enchanted sleep to announce the coming of a new age of peace and fertility. . . . Merlin's secret cave was located either in the Breton fairy-wood of Broceliande, or in the British druidic shrine of Mount Ambrosius. Some said this was Chislehurst, a chalk cliff honeycombed with caves, long occupied by a college of druidesses. Merlin was associated with the druidic Goddess under many of her names: Morgan, Viviane, Nimue, Fairy Queen, Lady of the Lake—the Celtic Water—Goddess Muirgen, often called . . . the Good Priestess. Because Merlin was clearly associated with Goddess worship and the mass of Merlin literature was for centuries a vehicle for criticism of the church, in the sixteenth century the Council of Trent placed the Book of Merlin's Predictions on the Index of Prohibited Books.

Excerpted from The Woman's Encyclopedia
of Myths and Secrets *by*
Barbara Walker (HarperCollins, 1983)

Some say that women's disenfranchisement from their own magical powers began far back in time, even before Christianity, with the rise of a patriarchal priesthood that displaced the goddesses and her priestesses. The famed temple at Delphi, for example, was originally consecrated to the Earth Goddess; eventually, however, it became the seat of the solar hero Apollo. Especially with the rise of the monotheistic, "One God" traditions of Judaism, Christianity, and Islam throughout the civilized world, those pagan faiths that celebrated a multiplicity of gods and goddesses and the divinity within nature began their rapid decline. As they disappeared, so, too, did such once-traditional magical practices as communicating with the dead, dream incubation, spell-casting, herbal knowledge, healing, and moon worship.

It was during the famed witch hunts of the Middle Ages that magic became split off from religion and linked to both women and the devil. Because to have knowledge of magic was to have direct access to the Divine without an intermediary, it was seen, rightly, as a kind of power. Thus as patriarchy grew in strength, men retained their positions of spiritual authority, while women were stripped of the powers in which they had once shone. "Early in the Middle Ages almost anything women did could be described as witchcraft," writes historian Barbara Walker, "because their daily lives invoked the Goddess with a thousand small ceremonies as well as the larger ones connected with major holidays." As she quotes Martin of Braga, "For women to call upon Minerva when they spin, and to observe the day of Venus at weddings and to call upon her whenever they go out upon the public highway, what is that but worship of the devil?"[2]

Intuition is the treasure of a woman's psyche. It is like a divining instrument and like a crystal through which one can see with uncanny interior vision. It is like a wise old woman who is with you always, who tells you exactly what the matter is, tells you exactly whether to go left or right. It is a form of The One Who Knows, old La Que Sabe, the Wild Woman.

CLARISSA PINKOLA ESTÉS,
*Women Who Run
with the Wolves*

Indeed, any "unusual ability" in a woman during that dark time, writes Walker, could raise charges of witchcraft. "If crops failed, horses ran away, cattle sickened, wagons broke, women miscarried, or butter wouldn't come in the churn, a witch was always found to blame." Feminist Elizabeth Cady Stanton blamed the persecutions of women squarely on the Church, writing that "The spirit of the Church in its contempt for women, as shown in the Scriptures . . . and in the doctrines of asceticism, celibacy, and witchcraft, destroyed man's respect for woman and legalized the burning, drowning, and torturing of women."[3] Still, outside the official religion, Walker points out, women continued to "pass down their private family recipes and charms, curses and blessings, telling traditional tales of the past and foretelling the future from omens and signs."[4] Although the Enlightenment and the rise of skepticism and rational logic during the eighteenth century brought important advances in ideals of freedom and democracy, both religion as well as witchcraft began to fade. Though belief in magic was never thoroughly eradicated, it wasn't until the spiritual renaissance of the late sixties and early seventies that mysticism and enchantment flowered in Western culture once again.

Especially within the last thirty years, a growing number of women have begun to reclaim traditions of magic as an honorable and distinguished part of their everyday lives.

Whether as professional astrologers or psychics, in the informal women's meditation and ritual "circles" that have mushroomed across the country, or simply as everyday house rituals woven into the hours and days of the weeks and months of the ever-turning wheel of time, more and more women are bringing back into the present what was banished in the past. The following stories of women past and present are presented here as lanterns to help light the path of other women who wish to walk the path of magic. I offer here, too, several "keys to magic" to open wide the doorway of consciousness into a richer and fuller experience of the mystery of life.

SEEING PATTERNS

In terms of oracles, says my friend Dana, "one can read coffee grounds, the patterns of leaves, the overheard comments of strangers, almost anything, if your senses are open and your intuition is keen." Indeed, one of the basic principles of magic consists in seeing patterns of meaning in the events of our lives—the odd encounters, bizarre twists, and miraculous coincidences that Jung called "synchronicity."

If you want to bring magic into your life, take notice of such small occurrences as the friend who calls just at the moment you are thinking of her; the book that falls off the shelf or that opens to a particular page; or the sudden thought that pops into your head for no apparent reason. Notice the odd juxtaposition of events that sometimes occur. Once, years ago, when I was considering interviewing a best-selling author for a certain magazine, I suddenly had the idea to pick up the phone and call the editor, rather than write the usual query letter. Picking up the phone, I dialed, only to have the editor answer himself and tell me, in tones of amazement, that he had just walked out of an editorial meeting during which they had just discussed running a story on that very same author. Just as I was working on this particular section, a friend called to tell me the story of how, in need of borrowing money, she had been e-mailing a friend to ask for help. At the exact moment that she was typing out her request, her doorbell rang. Opening the door, a relative greeted her, handing her an envelope with some money and telling her that he had thought that she might need it.

Life is filled with many such magical moments. They may not seem to matter much, but, as Jungian analyst Robert H. Hopcke writes, a synchronistic event is a reminder of the important truth that "our lives have a coherence, a direction, a rea-

*son for being, and a beauty as well. Syncronicity reminds us how much a work of
art the stories of our lives can be."[5]*

PRIESTESSES OF THE ORACLE OF DELPHI

On an Attic vase painting dated 440 B.C., the High Priestess of Delphi is shown
seated on a round sphere atop a tripod. The woman appears youthful, slender, with dark curly hair that is partially covered by a veil. In one hand she holds a
sprig of laurel and in the other a flat dish. Her expression is calm but intent, her
body bent in studious reflection, as she peers into the surface of the divining dish
she holds up before her. A column divides the scene in half; on the other side
stands a man—the petitioner who has brought his question before the oracle
priestess. This evocative image shows the significance with which the ancient
Greek oracles were once regarded. At its height of fame, princes, kings, philosophers, and people from different countries and walks of life made the pilgrimage
to Delphi to receive guidance on matters of business, politics, war, and love. Even
cities sent emissaries to consult the famed Greek oracles.

The myths and legends that surround the origin of the Temple at Delphi
reveal much about the magic art of prophecy. To the early Greeks, earth was alive,
and spoke through oaks, doves, rivers, and streams. As
the Greek scholar Vincent Scully has written in *The
Earth, the Temple, and the Gods,* all important Greek
sanctuaries grew up around open altars because something about the geography of the place suggested the
presence of a divine being. At Delphi, located on the
steep mountain peaks of Mt. Parnassus at the cleft of
Castalia, that divine being was the Earth Goddess.
Thus, the Temple of Delphi was said to have been positioned at the "omphalos" or navel of the Earth Goddess's
body—in other words, at the very center of the earth, the womb of creation. The
temple site was marked by a sacred round stone called the omphalos, or womb;
beneath it, according to myth, lay coiled a mighty serpent, or python, also symbolic
of the underground power of the earth. For this reason, the original priestesses
were called "Pythonesses," from which the title "Pythia" was later derived.

To some scholars, the presence of the serpent links Delphi to the Snake Goddesses of Crete, one of the sites where a vibrant goddess culture once flourished.
But when the patriarchal gods began their ascendancy, the solar hero Apollo,
according to myth, arrived at Delphi, slayed the python where its decaying body

*Sender of true oracles
while I sleep send me your unerring skill
to read what is and will be.*

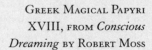

GREEK MAGICAL PAPYRI
XVIII, FROM *Conscious
Dreaming* BY ROBERT MOSS

remained below ground, and placed the Pythonesses under his control. Because the god could not be physically present before humans, he possessed the Pythian priestess as she inhaled the vapors emanating from the decaying python, speaking his words through her in the form of oracles. It was during this phase of the temple's existence that it rose to prominence throughout the classical world.

At first, the Pythia issued her oracles once a year, on the "seventh day of one month in the spring." As Delphi's reputation grew in popularity, however, she began to prophesy once a month. Two Pythias were employed on these days, with one held in reserve.[6] What was a day in the life of an oracle like? Three days before the day of her communication with the god Apollo, writes the esotericist Manly P. Hall, the priestess began a ceremony of purification. She bathed in the sacred waters of the Castalian well, and fasted, drinking only pure water piped into the temple for her use. Clothed in "sanctified raiment," she was then given a few leaves of the sacred bay tree to stimulate her visions.[7] Next, the priestess descended into an "adyton" or subterranean sanctuary where she took her place on a tripod. The inquirer, who had paid a fee, remained in an outer room, which was also below ground, and wrote down his question. Although the existence of a cleft emanating vapors has never been proven, legend has it that the Pythia next inhaled these fumes, entering into a trance during which she was possessed by the god Apollo. Scribes recorded her every utterance and movement during her possession; the predictions were typically confusing and unintelligible. The task of translating them fell to the temple philosophers, who then delivered them to the poets to be rendered into the lyrical odes for the querent and the general populace. Questions could also be posed that required simple "yes or no" responses; in this case, the oracle chose with her right hand from among black or white beans.

According to Hall, the Delphic oracles were originally young girls. Later, however, only women past the age of childbearing were allowed to fulfill the function of oracle. Hall reimagines the Delphic oracle in an illustration that is a vivid portrayal of the spiritual symbolism contained within the Delphic mysteries. The black and white drawing rendered by Hall is set in a high-ceilinged cave. Steeply descending stone steps lead to the center of the scene where a woman is seated with her eyes closed and hands folded on her knees. She sits upon a tall tripod inscribed with serpents and the face of Apollo. The tripod is set over a round open-

> *Dreams cannot protect us from the vicissitudes and illnesses and sad events of human existence. But they do give us a guiding line on how to cope with them, how to find a meaning in our life, how to fulfill our own destiny, how to follow our own star, so to speak, in order to realize the greater potential of life within us.*
>
> MARIE-LOUISE VON FRANZ, *The Way of the Dream: Conversations on Jungian Dream Interpretation with Marie-Louise von Franz* BY FRASER BOA

ing in the earth through which vapors are wafting upward, wreathing the priestess oracle in a fine smoke. Torches flicker in the background, and bearded priests
stand, heads lifted, hands poised over tablets, at the base of the tripod.

In this re-creation, Hall has attempted, he writes, to "follow as closely as possible the symbolism concealed within the allegory of the oracle. The Delphic mysteries used the oracle as their chief symbol, and it is the spiritual esoteric mystery
rather than the historical . . . aspect with which the student of symbolism is interested. While the spirit inhabiting the fumes which rose continuously from the fis-
sure entered into the body of the priestess, the tripod vibrated as though struck
severe . . . blows . . . which echoed through the cavern . . . and the rattling and
crashing did not cease until the spirit released its hold upon the Pythia. The three
legs of the tripod symbolize the three periods of time controlled by Apollo, namely
the past, the present, and the future. The space enclosed by the legs of the tripod
forms the sacred Pythagorean tetrahedron with the prophetess seated upon its
apex. As the priestess of Delphi is held aloft over the abyss of the oracle, supported
only by three slender legs ending in claws, so the spiritual nature of man is sus-
pended over the abyss of oblivion by three golden threads of Divine power. The
face of Apollo appears upon the tripod, and around the base are coiled serpents to
symbolize Python, whose decaying body lies beneath the Delphic shrine."[8]

What wisdom can the modern woman take from the story of the Priestess of
Delphi? Because Pythia is the spiritual name given to me nearly three decades ago
by my Sufi teacher Pir Vilayat, I have often contemplated the mystical significance
of the oracle, which is found throughout all religious traditions. Even in Judaism,
the Witch of Endor summoned the shade of Samuel to prophesy. In the African
tradition of the Yoruba, divining trays similar to the dish held by the Greek priestess are used to cast nuts or shells to read the will of the gods in the pattern they
form. In his fascinating book *The Eternal Drama: The Inner Meaning of Greek
Mythology* (Shambhala, 1994), Jungian analyst Edward Edinger writes that the
symbolism of the omphalos, or the stone that marks the womb of the earth, indicates that "by going to the center, one's questions can be answered." Thus, it could
be said that the Delphic oracle symbolizes our truest intuitions spoken by our
inner voice. At the same time, the image of the Temple of Delphi built over the
womb of the earth conveys the notion that wisdom also comes to us from the Earth
herself. When, like the Delphic priestess, we purify ourselves from the distractions
of the world, fasting and drinking only from the pure waters of the well of inspiration, then descend into the still place at the heart of the earth, we find the answer
to the questions that we have been seeking.

And what of the priestess's vapor-induced trance, her possession by a god, and her crazed utterances? Edinger writes that this is "a precise analogy of our consulting the images that arise from the unconscious." And indeed, our "inner oracle" doesn't always speak in the rational and logical language of the daylight world, but presents itself in chaotic images, scenes, and phrases that at first glance make no sense. Anyone who has awakened from a dream knows that feeling of confusion and bewilderment—as if one's soul had been cast as a character in a surreal Federico Fellini movie. Our daytime fantasies are the same—a wild and colorful "stream of consciousness" of images and scenarios that can leave us feeling embarrassed at the contents of our minds. That is precisely the reason why the oracles' message was never delivered directly to the querent, but underwent a process of interpretion, sifting through the grit and sand for the gold nuggets of real meaning. In ancient Greece, an entire religious class of experts and mantic priests, or "chresmologoi," sprang up as interpreters of the oracles. The same principle is at work in our own lives today when we take our inchoate impulses, nebulous intuitions, and nightly dreams to a therapist or wise friend for feedback, or when we sit down and consciously reflect in our journals or within ourselves upon their possible meaning. In this way, we are acting as interpreters for the oracle within. In studying the tradition of the Delphic priestess, I found the link between prophecy and the arts of poetry and philosophy revealing: It shows the way our own inner visions, fantasies, and revelations are the source of both creativity and also philosophical speculation on the meaning of life.

The principle of interpretation works in reverse, as well. Often I have gone to a therapist or visited an astrologer for a reading and received advice that didn't quite "ring true." Countless times friends have called in a panic over predictions or pronouncements from spiritual channels or psychics. One mother I know, for instance, was told by a psychic that she couldn't "see" my friend's daughter's life past the age of thirty—an irresponsible comment that has caused her endless anxiety and worry. Fate, however, is never cast in stone; to give authority over our destinies to so-called psychic experts is to cheat ourselves of unlived possibilities. Over the years, I have visited many psychics, palmists, and astrologers. Looking back, I found that I received the greatest benefit from those who were most gifted at giving me a sense of meaningfulness and purpose—that events in my life were unfolding for a reason, and that I was not alone, but guided by unseen forces. Whether the medium who communicated with my father after his passing, the astrologer who helped me to see the mythic pattern in my life, or my analyst who helped me to decode my dreams, it was the "big picture" that healed, not the practical predictions about money or love. When consulting psychics for advice, it's important to keep in mind that the psyche of the person before us may be clouded, leading to distortions and misjudgment. Indeed to misinterpret an oracle, writes Edinger, was to court grave danger. He cites the example of Croesus, who, when he consulted the oracle about his plans to invade Persia, received the response that "a great kingdom would be destroyed." Taking her words to mean success, Croesus launched his campaign—only to discover that the "great empire" to be destroyed was his own. This famous incident from the annals of history suggests that we should never surrender ourselves entirely to an outside source but must retain a measure of healthy skepticism and cynicism. Even in ancient Greece, overdependence among the populace on oracles led Euripides to pen these words: "The wisest men follow their own direction and listen to no prophet guiding them. None but the fools believe in oracles, forsaking their own judgement. Those who know, know that such men can only come to grief."[9]

Perhaps this is why the enduring motto of the Delphic oracle carved into her temple was to "Know thyself." In the end, the divining dish into which the oracle peers is the mirror of our own soul. The function of the Delphic priestess is to turn our attention within, where the true answers to life's dilemmas can be found, and to strengthen our faith in the voice of our own inner oracle. In coming to know ourselves this way, we draw close to the secrets of life and gain trust in following the destiny the gods have set forth for us to live—and which none but ourselves can fully divine or live out. In its essence, as the three legs of the tripod indicate, the Delphic oracle represents the authentic soul need for insight into the past, guidance for the present, and the all-too human desire to glimpse the future ahead. What matters most when consulting an oracle, whether inner or outer, it seems, is the intent to harmonize our lives with the greater intention of the Universe. This in itself is a powerful form of magic that can be transforming in its effects.

According to the ancient view, the moon stands on the border-line between the eternal, aethereal things and the ephemeral phenomean of the earthly, sublunar realm. Macrobius (an ancient writer) says: "The realm of the perishable begins with the moon and goes downwards. Souls coming into this region begin to be subject to the numbering of days and to time. . . . There is no doubt that the moon is the author and contriver of mortal bodies."

CARL JUNG,
Mysterium Coniunctionis

Modern-Day Diviner

Fifteen hundred years have passed since the Christian emperor Theodosius closed the Delphic oracle. In kitchens, living rooms, and offices across twenty-first-century America, however, women are taking up the feminine art of divination once again, listening for the voice of the god or the goddess or reading omens in the sky. One such example is my friend Jean Lall, a tall, soft-spoken woman in her late fifties with silver hair and penetrating hazel eyes. Her intellectual depth and serious demeanor might lead one to think that she is a professor or a researcher. Yet for the past twenty-six years, Lall has been a professional astrologer. How the cosmos influence human affairs and how the different deities work their various kinds of magic is her area of expertise. Raised in the Rocky Mountains of Colorado, Lall says that "like everyone else who was brought up in my time and place, I thought there was nothing to astrology. I came from a Methodist background, and my schooling was very straight." When she was a senior in college, however, Lall suddenly felt compelled to spend a year abroad and travelled to India on a Fulbright scholarship. "An instinct told me that I should try to get to the other side of the world. I had not studied any non-Western cultures, and I knew that it was something I had to do."

It was while working in India, recalls Lall, that she had her first encounter with astrology. "I met these very well-educated people who turned to astrologers to help their children find a mate. Then the astrologer would help select a date and time for the marriage. It turned my world upside down, and I saw things completely differently." Before her trip to India, Lall had intended to become a professor of English. Upon her return to America, however, she switched to the study of religion, attending Union Theological Seminary in New York City. Yet even that proved difficult, as her studies focused on Protestant theology. "I had been to the realm of the Great Mother," she says, "so I couldn't think inside of that box anymore with its abstraction and asceticism." Later, Lall moved to Washington, D.C., where, over the next five years, she worked for the Peace Corps and traveled to other countries. It was while living in Washington that Lall met and married her husband, Abner.

At that point in Lall's life, the spiritual dimension of life that had opened up for her in India began to intersect with the life she was living in the outer world. Drawn to study the works of Carl Jung, for instance, she discovered that Jung had had an interest in astrology, casting and studying the charts of his clients. Around the same time, her husband, who had been taking a yoga class, was approached by another student who offered to do his astrology chart. "He agreed, giving her his birth information. She drew up a chart and also wrote a long commentary about it—both of us were stunned by the insight she had into his nature." Suddenly, says Lall, there was "a collision of ideas" in her mind. She made the decision to enter into Jungian analysis and take up the study of dreams. At the same time, she found an astrology teacher and began to school herself in the science of the stars. For the next two years, Lall studied the two disciplines side by side, in a kind of tandem process.

Her inner work coincided with another life shift as well—the birth of her daughter. As a young woman, Lall says that she had been used to working long hours and, despite her developing interest in astrology and matters of the soul, had thought of herself as a professional woman. Motherhood, however, permanently altered her way of life. "I had been very identified with my job, and it was hard to give that up. I went into a depression, experiencing all the feelings and emotions that don't belong in the professional or productive world of careers." The night that her daughter was born, Lall had an epiphany. "I was in the hospital; I had given birth to her in the evening, and because I wasn't allowed to keep her with me, I was alone all night in the room. The next morning, I woke up very early, as light was just beginning to tinge the room, to a voice that said clearly, 'This is my body broken for you. So what else is new?' The words went through me like a flash of heat—though the phrase referred to the sacrifice of the body of Christ spoken during the mass, they were also a commentary about birth and labor. Every woman who has given birth knows that feeling of 'this is my body broken for you.' For the first time I realized that the religion I had been brought up in as designed and practiced by men is one step removed from a spiritual experience that is given by nature to women."

Her experience giving birth to her daughter, said Lall, helped her to understand why India had had such a significant impact on her consciousness. Since her sojourn in that country, she had been seeking a way to live her life "from the standpoint of the Divine Feminine—in the sense that spirit is here in this moment, in the body, and in the tasks of everyday life." In India, for instance, Lall had been deeply impressed by the way women would perform what she calls ritual housekeeping. "They would paint designs in rice flour around the perimeter of the room and around the threshold of the entry doors. There were so many rituals of that kind which served to weave the cosmos and daily life together." Her studies of astrology, as well, linked the mundane with the universal. "I had been brought up on the idea that God is the same today as yesterday and tomorrow. The only cycles that seemed to count were years, decades, centuries, and millenniums," says Lall. Yet once she began working with astrology, she says, a new world of time opened up. "Astrology shows how the macrocosm is operating while I am here on earth doing my gardening. Through the lens of astrology the whole cosmos is unfolding in the dance of cycles. Time becomes cyclical, and has color and flavors. It is punctuated by different qualities and elements, moving from fiery to airy to watery or earthy."

As all these experiences—motherhood, astrology, Eastern spirituality, and Jungian psychology—came together for Lall, her life was recreated along new lines. In 1975 she began her own astrology practice in Baltimore, Maryland, where she had moved with her husband and daughter. Immediately, she began to attract clients. Very quickly, however, Lall's work as an astrologer evolved into her own unique practice that combined astrology with Jungian archetypal theory and psychotherapy. "Often therapists would refer people to me. Clients would come to have their charts done, and then they would want to come back and see me again. Or, they would finish up therapy with somebody else, and then they would just want to work with their chart." Lall also began teaching astrology and archetypal studies. In 1986 she helped archetypal psychologist Thomas Moore establish the Institute for the Study of Imagination. Eventually she returned to school and received her master's degree from Lesley College in Archetypal Studies.

> *Sing Muses, of the moon*
> *with long wings*
> *from whose divine head*
> *sky-revealed lustre*
> *spirals down to earth and great*
> *adornment rises from her gleaming*
> *radiance.*
>
> HYMN TO SELENE, HOMERIC HYMN 32,
> TRANSLATED BY RONALD BASTO

Indeed, as Lall describes it, the work of the astrologer is the work of soul-making. Just as gardeners cultivate the seed of a rose into a flowering bush, so astrologers cultivate the soul-seed of their clients' God-given nature that they were stamped with at the moment of birth. Thus, her approach, she says, is aimed less at helping a person become more successful in business or love, and more toward deepening their knowledge of their God-given nature. The first step in this process, says Lall, may be the most profound: simply to study the image of one's own astrology chart—a mandala-shaped circle illustrated with symbols and signs that shows the patterns of the stars at the exact moment of birth—is in itself both healing and revealing. As Lall has written, "The chart gives the seed-form of our myth of creation and destiny; the formula for the alchemical experiment life is carrying on in us. It pictures the sacred hearth fire within and the guiding star overhead. We can carry it with us anywhere as our charter, the covenant between ourselves and the order of the universe, and as a portable altar and shrine. Once we have seen and been seen by it, it abides with us as a grace."[10] Just as there is an exchange of glances between two people on a street, so when a person reflects upon the images in their chart, there is a similar "meeting of the eyes"—only this time it is between oneself and the images within one's interior landscape. This process of imaginal reflection, explains Lall, is a kind of "psychic education" into a person's mythos.

What Lall means by this is that our psyches are peopled with an assortment of characters—some of whom we may know very well and others who are complete strangers. This diverse group of personalities may either get along well with one another or have nothing in common. This is pictured in the diagram of a person's chart in the way that the different planets "aspect" or interrelate to one another from their different placements around the astrological wheel. A planet in the serious and responsible sign of Capricorn, for instance, Lall explains, may not relate well to a planet in the more light-hearted, sociable sign of Gemini. And yet, as the chart reveals, each of these tendencies can be found within one person. Lall's work as an astrologer is to educate her client so that they avoid the mistake of projecting a disowned part of their personality onto another person. For example, she says, "You may think of your wife as a stick-in-the-mud. Or you may criticize your husband as careless and fickle. Yet as you begin to work with your astrology chart, you gradually begin to see that the characters that you are so upset with outside are inside as well. Once you realize that that part of a loved one or a friend that has bothered you so much is a part of your own makeup, then the relationship isn't so loaded and you can have a more conscious relationship with them."

Once a person begins to discover different aspects of themselves, then the real magic begins, as they discover new and unexplored dimensions within themselves. "If you are a Capricorn and you begin to study the Gemini aspect of yourself, then the mythological world of Gemini comes alive, and you begin to see possibilities that weren't there before," says Lall. "You cultivate the very thing that you had shunned; there is a weaving back and forth." This shift in perspective, she continues, gets us out of the modern mindset that seeks to fix things and moves us closer to a more magical worldview. "Jung said that life is not a problem to be solved; it's a mystery to be lived. So this approach brings a person closer to the mysterious, festive parts of life to be celebrated."

According to Lall, astrology is the Western world's most highly developed divination system. Not only does it help us to divine the subtle mythscape within ourselves, but it can be used as a technique to read the hidden order in the world without, or what she has called "the inner realm of nature," the "world of the gods, the Tao, the mundus imaginalis . . . the world of the dead and the ancestors, the matrix out of which everything is born . . ." Just as Greeks journeyed to Delphi to seek to know the will of the gods during a crisis, so the point of astrological divination, says Lall, is to weave together these two worlds, to "reconcile the human community with sacred order." Astrologers do this by "reading" conditions in the subtle world, she writes, then correlating them with the world of everyday existence.

She cites the example of the Magi, who by tracing the pattern of the stars in the sky, arrived at the right moment to worship Christ at his birth. Paraphrasing the Renaissance philosopher Marsilio Ficino, Lall says that "the Magus was like a farmer who cultivated the field, only he was a cultivator of the soul of the world. Just as the farmer for the sake of producing food to feed people tempers his field to the weather, so do the Wise Man and the Priestess temper the lower things of this world to the highest. In agriculture there is no point in planting wheat seeds during a snowstorm—it's just not going to happen!" In the same way, says Lall, astrologers practice a form of practical magic by adjusting individual lives to the psychic and spiritual weather patterns of the surrounding cosmos. As she quotes Chinese scholar Jin Hsu, "Divination is based on the belief that there are continuous, regulated changes operating throughout all levels of the universe, and that we must learn to know the cycles and tides of fortune if we are to achieve success."[11]

Ironically, the discipline of astrology has helped Lall to accept the nontraditional life path she has chosen for herself. "To have chosen the path of astrologer is to have stepped off the mainstream path. Many people won't even listen to me because I am an astrologer. But my chart has prepared me to accept the fact that I have the capacity to be alone—to think thoughts that nobody else is thinking, and to say things for which the ground hasn't yet been prepared. Like the biblical image of the stone that the builders rejected, which ultimately becomes the cornerstone of the temple, so I've had to create a profession out of what has been rejected by society—and still be professional. No matter what group I'm in—whether the Jungians or the astrologers—I'm a little bit unusual. But that is all right." And if self-acceptance isn't a potent form of magic, then I don't know what is.

KEYS TO BRINGING MAGIC INTO A WOMAN'S LIFE

✷

The exercises and meditations you will find here have less to do with popular notions of practicing magic—such as casting spells or performing incantations—as with living a magical life. Deep magic takes us into deep time. Through the imagination, the instrument of magic, the present moment expands into a universe still alive with the images and memories of long-ago ages, as well as invisible worlds and future landscapes still to come. In our dreams, we discover the companionship of a wise guide. Walking in nature or in communion with the moon, time becomes layered with cycles, tides, and phases. Discovering the pattern of the stars within our souls, we awaken to our appointed destiny. Taking metals, cloth, and stones, we infuse the material world with spiritual meaning. Thus, magic takes the merely ordinary and transforms it into an extraordinary, mysterious adventure. Not only do we discover intrinsic self-worth, but life itself becomes rich in value. Stepping onto the path of magic, we reclaim once again our roles as priestesses, oracles, astrologers, and wise women.

MOON MAGIC

La Luna, as the moon is sometimes called, is a cosmic well of feminine wisdom as deep and as old as time itself. Peering into her shimmering reflection set like a pearl against the velvet night sky, women see their souls reflected. The phases of the moon, a woman's monthly cycle, and the tides of the ocean are all linked together in an ancient and arcane rhythm of nature. Myths represent the moon's waxing, full, and waning faces as the triple-faced Moon Goddess who rules the three phases of a woman's life—the virgin maiden, the pregnant mother, and the wise crone. The timeless symbol of the crescent-shaped horn of the New Moon has been found carved into goddess figures and sacred vessels in archaeological sites around the world.

> *Lo! The level lake*
> *And the long glories of the winter moon.*
>
> ALFRED, LORD TENNYSON,
> "Morte d'Arthur"

At one time, the rhythms of daily life were set to the cosmic clock of the moon and the sun. While the sun marked the four quarterly seasons of winter, spring, summer, and fall, the moon was both "cause and measurer"[12] of time itself. The moon's twenty-eight-day cycle, the same as a woman's menstrual cycle, is the origin of our calendar month; our seven-day weeks are based on the quarterly lunar sabbaths marking the new, waxing, full, and waning moon phases. The religious festivals of many traditions, from Easter to Passover to Ramadan to the Chinese full-moon autumn festival, are still timed according to lunar cycles. In spiritual traditions, the moon has always been linked to the anima, the soul, the receptive, and the feminine principle of yin found within both men and women. Thus to the Sufi mystics, the moon symbolized the soul's inner receptivity toward the Divine; this is pictured as a crescent moon illuminated by a star. Because the moon disappeared from the sky each month for several days during the "dark of the moon," some faiths regarded the moon as the gateway between worlds, harboring the souls of the unborn awaiting birth, and the dead on their way to the afterlife. The "medial" nature of the moon as intercessor between this world and the spirit world, coupled with her rulership over the flux of daily life, has made her the natural ruler of mediums, psychics, witches, and oracles. According to the Homeric Hymn to Selene, magic was daughter of the moon, "She conceived and begot a daughter to Pandeia, Enchantress, magician, pre-eminent beauty among mortals." Indeed, writes Barbara Walker, the moon always governed magic, as "no sorcerer ever drew a circle of protection without observing the time of the moon."[13]

Moon Priestesses may no longer perform their rituals honoring the great mysteries around birth, growth, decay, death, and rebirth. And few are the farmers who still plant their crops by the light of a full moon. Still, a growing number of women today are practicing their own modern form of "moon magic," informally gathering on the new and full moons to pay tribute to the silver goddess who rules the night and all things secret and magical. Drawn together by our mutual love of the moon, my astrologer friend Dana Gerhardt and I, for instance, began a "soul sister" friendship exploring the moon's impact on our lives. Although we live on different coasts—Dana on the West Coast in Oregon, me on the East Coast in Washington, D.C.—we began a communication based on our feelings and observations around each new and full moon, exchanging thoughts on what the moon meant to us as contemporary women working and raising children. Our small mooncircle of two gradually widened into an informal E-newsletter we shared with friends, then blossomed into a "MoonCircles" website where women—and men—join together with rituals, meditations, and astrological reflections at the new and full moons.

Cultivating mindfulness of the moon's cycles can have great relevance for women. Dana, who worked for many years as an executive at a marketing firm, is especially sensitive to the way women's lives have been sundered from the sky and the stars, their bodies stressed by the off-kilter rhythms of modern life. Indeed, she has come to call moon practice "time medicine" because it is one way to help ease the physical and mental tension in a "24-7" world that functions by the principle faster and faster is better and better. Like Zen, moon practice is the simple path of reconnecting our personal rhythms to the broader rhythms of the natural world. The moon is nature's timepiece; it can help to reset our inner clocks as well.

To create a ritual life around the cycles of the moon is triply magic. First, each new and full moon functions as a kind of lunar sabbath. Each day can be set aside as sacred, in whatever form we may choose, whether by lighting a candle, taking a walk outside, or sitting in meditation. Adjusting our rhythms to the moon this way helps us to align our souls with the wider universe—even if it is simply a consciousness we hold in our hearts while commuting to work or making dinner. Moon mysticism, says Dana, is "a mysticism of rivers and weeds, not high church. It marks a wordless knowing, planted deep in our living cells."

Second, becoming mindful of the waxing and waning moon cycles is a key to learning the magic of timing. As Dana has written, the "New Moon is earth's monthly time for starting over," setting aside the past and beginning anew. "It sings with the joy of letting go to start afresh." As a full-time working mom coupled with an astrology practice, Dana has found that one of the best ways to honor the moon's fresh start is with "small domestic gestures. As a woman keeping a home, I have rituals of renewal that I synchronize with the rhythm of the moon. At every New Moon, I fertilize my roses. I put out a new sponge in the kitchen. I check the toothbrushes. I replenish the color in my hair. I visit my garden to see if anything new needs planting. I do these things in secret pleasure, enjoying my kinship with the New Moon."[14]

The full moon has its own feeling. Like the crescendo that punctuates an orchestral movement, or the pause between breaths, the mood at the full moon is one of still contemplation. It is a time to step back from pushing and trying; it is a time to let things be as they are. Then, as the moon wanes, says Dana, "it's time to slow down, move wisely, paring down effort to the essentials. When the moon wanes, life force draws underground, into the roots, into the earth. It's during these two waning weeks that the earth withdraws also, taking energy into herself, away from aboveground things. Especially in the fourth quarter, we should rest, contemplate, dream. Find yourself in the quiet details. Go inward. And take care."[15]

Third, to honor the cycles of the moon offers a built-in sacred moment "timed to the stars" to meet with our friends for a meditation circle. My sister Colleen and her friends make a point of hiking out into nature together each full moon; others choose to gather at the new moon. Just as the sun occupies a specific astrological sign during the twelve months of the year, so the moon passes through all the signs of the zodiac each month; the sign that a new or full moon is in provides a myth and a symbol around which to orient moon rituals. Because each sign is connected to a goddess, moon rituals are also a time to strengthen our links to our ancestral soul sisters: Diana, Kuan Yin, Aphrodite, Isis, Mary, and so on.

To take the first steps toward bringing moon magic into your life, purchase a good astrological calendar for the current year that marks the date and hour of the new and full moon of each month, along with the astrological sign that the moon is in. Then, circle those dates and make the intention to honor those days in a special way. Because the spiritual principle of the moon is that of receptivity—a "moving with" time, rather than forcing it to go your way—you may wish to build your moon practice slowly. Listening to the particular rhythms and moods of your own life, you will be better able to create a moon ritual that is a true mirror of your soul's needs. Though we each take care to note the exact hour of the new and full moon, for instance, Dana and I have discovered that, more often than not, we are rarely in a time or place where we are able to actually sit in silence at the moon's exact turn from waning to waxing crescent. So rather than force the moment, be organic, and let your ritual naturally arise at its own right time.

Crafting a special moon altar with seashells, goddess figures, or pictures, lighting candles and incense, playing beautiful music, and walking or sitting in nature, for instance, are some recommended ways of creating a sacred space within which to honor the new moon. Noting the element that the moon is in can "flavor" your ritual: If it is in a water sign, for example, take a candlelit bubble bath, or place a dish of water beside your bed before going to sleep, dip your fingers in it, and ask for a dream from the watery realms of your unconscious. If the moon is in a fire sign, you may wish to concentrate on the flame of a candle, imagining the hearth fire at the heart of the temple that glows within your heart as well. If air, concentrate on your breath, or go outside and let your spirit soar along with the zephyrs and the breezes; listen to the voices in the wind. If earth, plant a seed in the ground, walk barefoot in your garden, concentrate on grounding your energy, and embrace the earth with love.

She is the egg and the seed of the world. . . . She is darkness as well as light. Her cycles encompass all moods and all phases. She is queen of the Bright Night and of the Darkness, guide to the lost traveller and pathway to the underworld. She brings creativity and visions; she also brings sleep, darkness and death. . . . She is the home of the souls of the unborn and of the dead waiting for rebirth.

ANNE KENT RUSH,
Moon, Moon

Another way to work with the moon is to begin a journal, noting your own observations of life around the cycles of the moon: How are they different or the same? Take note of the rhythms of your day: Are they so harried that you forget to look up at the moon? Do you have time for your soul? Or, are they in rhythm with nature—a natural ebb and flow of busy, productive times intermixed with slow and dreamy times? Another form of moon magic is to become familiar with the moon in your own chart—if you know a reputable astrologer, you may want to find out what sign your moon is in, and how it is positioned in your chart with respect to the other planets. Your astrological chart's moon is the image of your very own "inner moon goddess." In addition, each person within the span of a lifetime goes through their own phases of the waning and waxing moon cycles that is marked by a particular psychological or spiritual stage of growth and unfoldment.

> *The magical tradition, when not corrupted, never concerns an interest in personal power, but rather the passage through three gateways leading to the capacity for perception of the world soul. The first gateway concerns remembering the ancestors, passing into living relation with the ancestors. The second gateway concerns passing into a living relation with archetypal beings, and the third gateway gives passage into the soul substance of the land. Rather than coming to personal power, through these activities humans become mediators between the ancestral and archetypal beings and the archetypal substance of the land. . . . The physical being of the planet is composed from numerous worlds that in the magical tradition are called the inner worlds. (From* Facing the World with Soul *by Robert Sardello)*

✷

SAILING TO THE ISLAND OF THE MOON

Here is a basic meditation to help you attune to the moon. First, settle before your altar in a meditative pose. Because the moon rules the changing face of nature, take note of the weather. Mark the season of the year and the time of the day. Become mindful of whether the sun is shining brightly or whether it is a gray and cloudy day. Observe whether the temperature is warm or cold, and whether the wind is still, breezy, or blowing about the treetops. As you become more conscious of the realm of nature, feel the animals creep out to greet you: the crawling insects, the chirping birds, and the rabbits, deer, and foxes. They, too, are always a part of any mooncircle.

After you have attuned to nature, spend a few moments calming your breath. Gradually, as your breath grows more even and smooth, feel the distractions of the outer world sift to the bottom of your psyche, like silt to the bottom of a glass of water. Let your mind become still, clear, and reflective. Let this feeling expand until your consciousness has become as vast and free and open as an ocean of unruffled water. As this expanse of water unfolds before your inner vision, imagine that you have set sail in a small boat across the ocean. The night is clear, and a full moon lights up the sky, transforming the waters below into a silver-hued mirror. The air is filled with a timeless and shimmering atmosphere of magical enchantment.

Imagine next that your boat is pulled along by the moon's rays until it arrives upon the shore of an island, where many other boats have arrived. Joining together with a group of women, you enter a marble temple that is open to the firmament of the sky, with stars shining in a dense canopy of twinkling lights. At the center stands a simple stone altar, with a single chalice at the center. Joining hands in a circle with your friends around this altar, each woman invokes the moon in her own way. A collective chorus of singing and chanting floats up into the sky, drawing down the moon's magic rays into the chalice, that then stream into the chalice within your heart and the hearts of all the women in the circle. As you do this, experience your whole body and imagination enlivened with the moon's light and the shared timeless knowledge of feminine wisdom.

At the conclusion of the meditation, return to your boat, then sail back across the ocean of crystal moonlight toward the shore of your everyday life. Looking back, you see that the island has vanished. Instead, you find the island of the moon in your heart, where it was all along: an ancient, collective, secret memory of a sacred place passed down through the centuries from woman to woman to woman . . . to woman . . . to woman.

✩

Dream Oracle:
Listening for the Voice of God

The idea that God speaks to us through our dreams is powerfully conveyed in the Old Testament story of Jacob and the ladder; in it, Jacob dreamed of a ladder reaching up into heaven, with angels ascending and descending. It is a beautiful metaphor of the way dreams are a bridge between worlds. In their prayers, students in the Sufi Order invoke "the spirit of guidance," who embodies the wisdom of all the illuminated souls. Thus, like winged messengers, our dreams take flight at night to the universal source of divine knowledge, returning like angels with advice to help guide us through the labyrinthine confusions of everyday life.

This was a well-known secret to the shamans of Paleolithic cultures, who turned to their dreams to get guidance on the next day's hunt. Both the Greeks and Egyptians made pilgrimages to sacred dream sanctuaries, where they sought visitation from a god in a dream to cure their illnesses through the practice of "dream incubation." The ancient Egytians, for instance, worshipped Serapis, the god of dreams, and built temples devoted to his worship. Professional dream interpreters known as "the learned men of the magic library" resided in these temples.[16] In Greece, dream interpretation was considered one of the "important signs of civilization" and dream incubation became a highly developed art. People travelled from around the world to visit the famous shrines dedicated to the god of healing, Aesculapius, where they underwent elaborate purification ceremonies before sleeping in the god's temple.

Imagine a place in America, for instance, like the grand limestone temple at Epidaurus, set beside the glittering Aegean Sea. In addition to a hotel for guests, there was a separate temple to Hygeia, the daughter of Aesculapius who was also a goddess of healing, a sacred well, and a library. Supplicants prepared for their dream ritual by abstaining from sex, following a special diet, and taking special baths. During the "hour of the sacred lamps," evening prayers were held; after the torches were extinguished, priests would move about the reclining devotees, offering words of encouragement.[17] Following the healing dream, the patient then discussed its meaning with one of the priests of the temple. So richly developed was the Greek art of dream divination that centuries later Islamic scholars cultivated their own dream literature and methods of incubation based on translations of Greek philosophers. The renowned seventh-century dream interpreter Ibn Sirin spent an entire day scrupulously questioning dreamers about their life conditions and other details before pronouncing his interpretation. The scholar Ibn Khaldun articulated his own dream philosophy, writing that "Dream vision is an awareness on the part of the rational soul in its spiritual essence, of glimpse(s) of the forms of events. . . . Through these glimpses the soul gains the knowledge of future events that it desires. . . ."[18]

Like buried treasure brought to light, these historical accounts show the great benefit that can come from attending to the voice of God through dreams. The technique of dream incubation—formulating a question to be answered in our dreams before falling asleep—tells us that within our psyches resides a wise oracle, a spirit of guidance, to whom we can turn for help. Though we may not have a temple to retreat to for dreamwork today, we can draw upon the wisdom of the past in crafting our own dream incubation ritual. The steps used by practitioners in ancient times—setting out upon a pilgrimage to a dream shrine, fasting and undergoing purification ceremonies, and the sacred atmosphere cultivated within the temple—reveal the importance of the attitude that we bring to dreamwork. By showing our unconscious the same respect we would give to a priest or a goddess, we create the conditions that allow our spirit guide to speak to us. Jungian analyst

The ego is only that field which is in my consciousness, but the psychic system is much vaster, it is the whole unconscious too, and we don't know how far that reaches. We can as little assume that the earth is in the centre of the solar system as that our ego is in the centre of the psyche.

CARL JUNG,
Seminar on Dream Analysis

and renowned dream expert Marie-Louise von Franz wrote that dreamwork was a living dialogue and that "When we listen to dreams, we change, and when dreams are heard, they change."[19] Indeed, dreams are a kind of ongoing conversation with our own soul. For this reason, when we work with our dreams over time, a gradual evolution in consciousness occurs as we are allowing our soul to do its work within us. It's as if the wisdom of nature within each of us is cooperating through our dreams in order to help find the healing solution to our life dilemmas. Night after night, our dream guide sends messages that show us where our life energy wants to go, centering us in what really matters and helping to solve the riddle of our existence. Night after night, our dream guide sends messages specifically tailored to the smallest and largest details of our everyday lives, proving that even in an age of mass globalization each individual is being lovingly cared for and watched over. Indeed, I know of no better method than dreamwork to get guidance on the eternal human questions: "Who am I?" and "Why was I born?" Yet if our spiritual senses are closed and we are not listening to our inner voices, God's messengers cannot deliver their message, and the oracle is turned away.

When initiating your own incubation ritual in order to consult the dream oracle within, you may wish to begin your preparation a day or two in advance. According to dream expert Gayle Delaney in her book *All About Dreams*, it is imperative to be free of drugs and alchohol so that the mind is alert. In addition, she recommends that you choose a night when you are not tired or overly anxious. Clear your evening, so that you have time to relax, meditate, listen to music, and spend time writing in your dream journal before bed. In your journal, describe the emotional tenor of your day, getting your thoughts and feelings on paper. Next, focus specifically on the issue for which you are seeking dream healing, what Delaney calls "incubation discussion." Ask yourself questions about various aspects of the situation that you are in—what are its causes; how you think it might be resolved; how would life be different if it were resolved; and what benefits you might be receiving from the situation as it is.

This is the raw material that will help you to shape what Delaney calls your "incubation phrase." In other words, this is the question that you are addressing to your dream oracle. As the Islamic philosopher Ibn Khaldun said, "The dream words produce a preparedness in the soul for a dream vision."[20] Simply finding the right way to frame a question is powerful magic: by asking the question that needs to be asked, we are at the same time calling upon the unseen spirit of guidance, evoking its presence, summoning the answer forth from the cosmos. After finding the right phrase, I recommend writing it down on a piece of paper, folding it up, and putting it on your altar. You may even wish to leave it there for several more days, allowing the question to take root in your mind. Or, that evening, sit before your altar and, question in hand, spend some time in meditation. (You may wish to include the contemplation on the messenger goddess Iris on page 178 to help connect to the inner guide.) Then, before finally falling asleep, place the piece of paper beneath your pillow. As you drift into sleep, keep coming back to your question as you would a mantra or a prayer. In my own dream incubation practice, after framing the question, I submit myself entirely to the wisdom of God, letting go of all my attempts at trying to fix or solve things with my ego and trusting in the unseen forces to lead me in the right direction. Often, I repeat the phrase from a Sufi prayer by Hazrat Ihayat Khan: "Use us (me) for the purpose that Thy wisdom chooseth and guide us on the path of thine own goodness."

Then, of course, give yourself over entirely to the magic world of sleep and dreams. These are the hours when your dreammaker takes over, weaving new insights and perspectives to present to you. Enriched by the collective wisdom of the collective imagination, as well as by the storehouse of your accumulated life wisdom, your dreammaker is capable of poetic and ingenious insights. As Delaney writes, "Our inner self sees our life and problems more clearly, more objectively, and from a far broader perspective than we usually do while awake."[21] Jungian analyst Sylvia Brinton Perera likens the dream process to the Celtic design motifs that "interweave, interlace, and spiral, forming intricate patterns that can illuminate our relationships in the outer world as well as in physical, emotional, and spiritual dimensions." Like an enchanted needle in a fairy tale, dreams weave meaning out of the chaos of life, both embroidering a mythic narrative of the soul's journey, spinning wise counsel for everyday life, and creating a beautiful work of art in the process.[22]

Indeed, dream annals are filled with stories of the way dreams have saved lives, predicted the future, shed psychological insight, and even been responsible for some of the world's greatest literature and scientific inventions. Perera tells the story, for instance, of the woman who was interred in a concentration camp during World War II who dreamed one night that she was eating wonderfully nourishing food prepared by her mother. When she awoke, she felt so full from her "dream meal" that she passed up the thicker soup the guards unexpectedly were serving. As it turned out, the soup was filled with ground glass; the Nazis were hoping to kill the inmates before the Allies arrived.[23] I love the story of Elias Howe, whose lockstitch sewing machine was invented with the help of a dream. Unable to get the needle to work because he had placed the eye in the middle of the shank, he dreamed one night of being captured and surrounded by painted warriors. "Suddenly he noticed that near the heads of the spears which his guards carried, there were eye-shaped holes! He had solved the secret! What he needed was a needle with an eye near the point!"[24] Writers are frequently inspired by their dreams. Novelist Isabel Allende dreamed the conclusion to her book, *House of the Spirits*, and Stephen King has drawn on dream images from nightmares as settings for his horror novels.

In my own life, dreams have become my trusted guide—both counselor and healer, inspirator and companionable consoler. Uncertain over whether to edit Pir Vilayat's teachings into a book, for instance, I was guided by a dream in which a woman named "Palma"—the letter P is the first initial of my name, and "alma" is Spanish for soul—commanded in a loud voice, "This is your soul speaking!"

> The dream world is the real world.
>
> SENECA INDIAN HEALER,
> FROM *Conscious Dreaming*
> BY ROBERT MOSS

When penning my story on the soul of Washington, D.C., I dreamed of touring the city with one of Washington and Jefferson's "lost brothers." Even this chapter is the result of a dream: having decided to omit it, I dreamed of discussing the book with my editor and publisher, who mentioned how much they "especially enjoyed the chapter on magic." Numerous times, my dreams have guided me in raising my children. Once, when I was busy and preoccupied with work, I had a vivid dream of one of my sons crying in pain. As it turned out, he had been having a difficult time in school with friends and studies, and needed my attention.

The final step in the dream incubation process is to record the dreams of the previous night. It is best to do this the first thing in the morning, when the details are still fresh in your mind. Indeed, when incubating a dream, plan to do it on a night when you know that you won't have to jump out of bed right away and can awaken slowly. As you emerge from sleep's depths, try to stay close to your dream, going over and over it again in your mind. Steep yourself in its atmosphere; memorize every detail, rehearsing it as you would a play or a favorite scene from a book. Then, write it down, making no judgments. Often I notice that after I have requested a dream, I have an initial sense of disappointment as my critical mind takes over. Oh, I might think to myself, "It's nothing but a dream about the grocery store," or "What meaning can it possibly have that I'm chewing a big wad of gum?" After writing down the dream and playing with its possible meanings, however, a light begins to dawn. Very often this is because our dreams respond in unexpected and surprising ways that can startle our conscious minds and upset our usual way of thinking. As Delaney writes, "The dreams may redefine your problem, translating it from the way you consciously see it into the way your inner self sees it. . . . The dreams may present alternatives to your dilemma that you've not considered."[25] When going over my dream about chewing gum with my friend Sylvia, for instance, we determined that it referred to the feeling I had of having "bitten off more than I could chew," taking on too much work without "spitting some out," or finishing up old projects first.

Indeed, dream interpretation is a wonderful ritual to share with a soul sister. I have a delightful circle of friends with whom I share my dreams and whom I help, in turn. Just recently, a close friend called with a disturbing dream. In it, she had been diagnosed with breast cancer in both breasts. Because dreams can often predict illnesses, we both felt that she should do a "reality check" and make an appointment for a mammogram immediately. Yet because more often than not our dreams speak in metaphors, like song or poetry, we began to examine the symbolic meaning of her dream. This friend, who is a writer, felt that her dream was sending her a "carpe diem" message urging her to get to work on a book she had been putting off. When I pointed out that breasts were a symbol of feminine nurturing, and that cancer was a disease caused by cells growing out of control, she had a "lightbulb" moment of recognition that her burgeoning domestic responsibilities had been draining her of creative energy. Her dream was a dramatic warning from her psyche that her tendency to give too much of herself to her friends and family was endangering her life as a writer. Whenever we understand a dream properly, writes Marie-Louise von Franz, "we feel . . . the supernatural nourishment we need inside, which comes from the unconscious . . . when it hits the mark . . . one feels 'Now I know where I am going. Now I can go on.' Something becomes peaceful and satisfied within one."[26]

If, after requesting a dream, you either don't receive one, or you have a dream that you don't understand, try not to become impatient and dismiss the process. Sometimes I have found that if I don't have a dream about a problem, it's because the issue simply isn't as important as I thought it was. Or, if the dream remains indecipherable, I sit with it as I might sit with a Zen koan, savoring the mystery until it reveals itself slowly over time. Jung said that we should take our dreams from the night and turn them over and over, like a stone in our hands, during the day. If our dream seems to be pointing us in a certain direction, yet we still feel unsure about the dream's message, after some reflection go ahead and make your decision while at the same time affirming your intention to do the right thing. Dreamwork, in fact, does not require the same aggressive and ambitious stance that we might bring to achieving our goals in the world. Rather, dream incubation is a gentle opening to the wise spirit of guidance within; like a rare and precious flower, our inner oracle reveals herself to us through our sensitive attendance to her well-being. She is a helpful soul sister who is on our side and who is the essence of our destiny. The following meditation can help strengthen the dream guide within us.

Iris, the Rainbow-Messenger Goddess

Can you remember the first time you saw a rainbow? How, through the innocent eyes of childhood, you felt stirred to wonder by the sight of an effervescent band of translucent colors arcing across the sky? You probably experienced what humans since the beginning of time have felt—touched by a message of beauty, hope, and inspiration emanating from a more heavenly world.

As the Greek goddess of the rainbow, Iris was considered the swift-footed "Messenger of Light." She personified the luminous bridge that stretched between heaven and earth; her function was to bear messages from the gods and goddesses who lay beyond the many-hued veils of appearance to humankind. She has been described as "A symbol of the relationship between heaven and earth and gods and mortals—a form of divine speech."[27]

As message-bearer, Iris symbolizes that within each of us that desires direct communication with the Divine. Like her, we each have the capacity to travel to the land of the gods and goddesses, to receive a message, and to translate this "divine speech" into a form of guidance inspiring our everyday lives.

To attune to the goddess Iris, imagine that you are sitting on a mountaintop. A storm has passed, and the sun has burst through the dark clouds, lighting up the sky. Suddenly, a magnificent rainbow appears in the freshly washed, blue sky. Because of your vantage point high up, you can see the rainbow in its entirety, stretching from horizon to horizon. On the current of your breath, imagine that you are a winged spirit able to traverse this rainbow. Travelling quickly along this bridge of light, you go beyond it until you reach a beautiful temple. Once there, you meet with a wise being who embodies for you the spirit of wisdom and all-knowing intelligence. You may sit together in silence, or there may be an exchange of words. At the end of this communion, your guide hands you an envelope that contains a special message—an answer to your heart's deepest yearning. After giving thanks for this message, you depart homeward along the rainbow bridge. Once back on earth, on the mountaintop, transcribe the message you have received. Perhaps the wisdom inside will take the form of a poem, a journal entry, or even a drawing. Whatever the message con-

The magic of a face.

Thomas Carew, *Epitaph on the Lady S——*

*tains, honor it in your heart as a keepsake of your visit to the other side. Don't allow
the radiant beauty of your rainbow message to fade. Instead, keep it alive by imagining that it is enlivening and inspiring your connections to others with a sparkling
rainbow spirit of hope.*

✧

TALISMANS AND AMULETS

A talisman or an amulet is a stone, ring, or small round medal engraved with figures or characters from a particular religious or spiritual tradition that carries with
it magical powers to protect, heal, charm, or bring good fortune to the wearer.
Egyptian amulets, for instance, bore the emblem of the ankh, symbol of the key of
life; the scarab, or sacred beetle; or the all-seeing "eye" of the god Horus. Various
religious medals bear images of Buddhist deities, or Christian saints, such as Mary
or St. Christopher. Certain precious stones carry symbolic meaning, such as the
amethyst, which was worn by bishops and, according to Pliny, "protects against
enchantment if it is engraved with figures of the Sun and Moon . . ."[28]

These small objects are a lovely way to grace your life and your loved ones
with a touch of magic. I have been given holy medals, and collect them as well, as
gifts to pass on to friends and family. A St. Christopher
medal given to me by my mother, for instance, hung over
the dashboard in my car for years, and has been worn by
each of my sons for protection while travelling. My gold
Mary medal given to me by my friend Tatiana more than
twenty years ago is now with my friend Ann, to give her
comfort as she helps her son through an illness, and has
also spent years with each of my children. Before her son
went on a round-the-world trip, my friend Barbara
chose a special Buddhist medal of a specific deity, wrote down a protective sacred
phrase on a piece of paper for him to invoke in case of danger, then enclosed the two
in a small pouch, which she gave to him to carry on his travels.

To bring magic into your life, begin a collection of old pieces of fabric, small
stones, beads, and medals; keep them on your altar, and hold them in your hands
while meditating; or wear them or carry them with you for a period of time to
magnetize them with good, loving intentions. Then, at the right moment, fold
them up along with a special phrase or prayer, and pass them along to that special
friend who needs a bit of magic to get them through life.

*Magic is not just a procedure; it's a way of
life. The magus lives every minute of every
day magically.*

THOMAS MOORE,
*The Re-Enchantment
of Everyday Life*

The Magic in Nature

"Magical arts offer a way of living so intimately with the ways of nature that its magic becomes our magic," writes Thomas Moore in *The Re-Enactment of Everyday Life*. And indeed, for many of my friends, nature is the living medium which speaks to them of the sacred. My friend Harriet, who is as close to her foxes and dogs as mothers are close to their children, has had remarkable experiences communicating with the spirits of wild animals. In a shamaniclike experience, she once entered the body of a leopard and felt its fierce strength bounding and running along the ground. And though she has been awed by the great cathedrals of Europe, the monasteries of India, Tibet, and Nepal, and the temples of Egypt, Harriet says that nothing has compared to the reverence she has felt for God's divinity in nature, "walking through the redwood cathedral of the ancient forest in Northern California, lying on a bed of moss watching a mother eagle teach her baby how to fly, or kayaking down the Eau Claire River seeing deer, eagle, loon, and king fishers."

Nature's mythical, magical ability to enchant the soul was conveyed in a dream I once had. In it, a woman was driving me through the Hopi Indian mesa in Arizona, showing me their thousand-year-old sacred sites. As we rounded the edge of the plateau, a voice said, "These are the religious symbols of the future." All around me, as far as I could see, stretched enormous cliff faces covered in animal and plant designs in brilliant colors. Indeed, to the awakened heart, nature is a living teacher, a book of revelation as rich with wisdom as the Bible or the Koran. "The mystic," wrote Hazrat Inayat Khan in his beautiful essay on nature, "recognizes this manifestation as a written book; he tries to read these characters and enjoys what they reveal to him. To the mystic it is not only the waxing and waning of the moon, it has some other significance for him; it is not only the rising and setting of the sun, it tells him something else; it is not only the positions of the stars, but their actions and their influence relate something to the heart of the mystic . . . the lion with its wrath, the elephant with its grandeur, the horse

*For I dipped into the future, far as human
   eye could see,
Saw the Vision of the world, and all the
   wonder that could be: . . .*

ALFRED LORD TENNYSON,
Ulysses

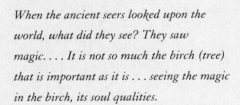

*When the ancient seers looked upon the
world, what did they see? They saw
magic. . . . It is not so much the birch (tree)
that is important as it is . . . seeing the magic
in the birch, its soul qualities.*

ROBERT SARDELLO,
Facing the World with Soul

with its grace . . . tell the mystic something. He begins to see the meaning of the
wrath of the lion and of the modesty of the deer; he listens to the words that come
to his ears through the singing of the birds, for to him it is not a wordless song."[29]

The idea that nature is alive and speaks to us is at the heart of all the pagan
faiths. Whether in the Mid East, America, Europe, or Mexico, the churches, synagogues, and mosques of mainstream religious traditions have been built on top of
holy sites once dedicated to the gods, goddesses, and spirits that once honored the
divine forces in nature. This tells us that nature is the living source of religion.
Thus, when it comes to bringing magic into our lives, there is no more powerful
spell or incantation than relearning the old ways of our ancestors who spoke the
language of nature—who heard voices in the wind, took their direction from
the stars, and were protected from danger by trees and
animals.

How can the modern woman bring magic into her
life through the medium of nature? To begin with, it
helps to walk in nature with all one's senses opened
wide. Often, I find myself going out for my daily walk
so absorbed by personal problems or work that, at first, I
don't even notice the landscape around me. It requires
great consciousness to simply bring one's mind back to
the outside world—the halo effect of afternoon light as
it slants through the trees, the cry of a bird as it wheels in
the sky above, the smell and feel of wet wind and rain.
After becoming attuned to nature this way, another
practice is to begin to communicate with the elemental
nature spirits who inhabit the trees, streams, rocks, and
bushes that surround us. Even if we live in the city, we
can re-imagine the landscape as it once was, summoning
the spirits of the land that still exist. In many pagan
faiths, every important river and hill was associated
with a god or goddess. In the Celtic tradition, fairies, leprechauns, and elemental
spirits were thought to live beneath rocks, in tree hollows, and below ground. In
the Zoroastrian tradition of the Magi, angels and archangels were associated with
the different elements of fire, air, earth, and water.

Through the vehicle of your imagination—the magic wand of all wizards
and enchantresses—as you walk or sit outside, imagine yourself talking with the
myriads of unseen beings who populate nature. As you sit beside a stream or river,
imagine the water spirit who lives there. Gently coax the gnome who lives within

*Make no little plans; they have no magic
to stir men's blood.*

ATTRIBUTED TO
DANIEL HUDSON BURNHAM

*The inner—what is it?
If not intensified sky,
Hurled through with birds and deep
With the winds of homecoming*

RAINER MARIA RILKE, from *The
Enlightened Heart*, edited by
Stephen Mitchell

the large oak tree in your yard. Indeed, magic traditions tell us that invisible cities lie hidden within nature; as you become aware of them, they reveal more and more of their mysterious realities to you. Perhaps you hear a word of hope in the song of a bird; perhaps you sense a feeling of friendship reaching out to you from the meadow of flowers; or perhaps you glimpse the aura of the archangel of the sun radiating about you on a hot summer afternoon. If you can remember what it was like to be a child, no doubt you can remember what it was like to wordlessly communicate with nature's surrounding presence.

To him who in the love of Nature holds Communion with her visible forms, she speaks a various language.

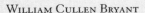

WILLIAM CULLEN BRYANT

In the past, shamans and wizards drew their power from a specially charged spot in nature. Merlin, for instance, was called the "wild man of the woods." Morgan le Fay, the priestess-goddess who taught Merlin his magic, was called the "Lady of the Lake." At the end of Merlin's life, le Fay took him to her magic cave where he fell into the enchanted sleep from which he has yet to awaken. Shamans were said to draw their power from a special secluded spot or tree. Likewise, we can draw magic into our lives by cultivating a place of enchantment all our own. There is a certain large boulder along the Potomac River where I sometimes hike, for instance, where I can climb off the path and sit secluded from sight behind a screen of trees. Nestled into the crevice between rock and tree, I can look out over the river toward the horizon and watch the blue herons as they come out to perch silently along the banks. As dusk falls, people vanish, the stars begin to come out, and the crickets and frogs begin their evening symphony. In the silence I become as old and motionless as the rock I am sitting on; like the shamans, wizards, priestesses, and enchantresses of ages past, I am joined to an ancestral lineage stretching back into the mists of time.

It is from such moments as these that deep magic arises, infusing our lives with sacredness and meaning, returning us to the arms of the ever-renewing mystery of the Universe within which we live, move, and have our being.

RECOMMENDED READING

All About Dreams: Everything You Need to Know About Why We Have Them, What They Mean, and How to Put Them to Work for You by Gayle Delaney, Ph.D. (HarperSanFrancisco, 1998)

The Book of Divination by Ann Fiery (Chronicle Books, 1999)

Celebrate the Solstice: Honoring the Earth's Seasonal Rhythms through Festival and Ceremony by Richard Heinberg (Quest Books, 1993)

Conscious Dreaming: A Spiritual Path for Everyday Life by Robert Moss
(Crown, 1997)

Drawing Down the Moon by Margot Adler (Beacon Press, 1979)

The Eternal Drama: The Inner Meaning of Greek Mythology by Edward F.
Edinger (Shambhala, 1994)

The Goddess in Your Stars: The Original Feminine Meanings of the Sun Signs
by Geraldine Thorsten (Simon & Schuster, 1989)

The Hermetica: The Lost Wisdom of the Pharaohs by Timothy Freke and
Peter Gandy (Tarcher/Putnam, 1997)

The I Ching or *Book of Changes* by Wilhelm/Baynes (Princeton University
Press, 1950)

Making the Gods Work for You: The Astrological Language of the Psyche by
Caroline Casey (Three Rivers Press, 1999)

Mysteries of the Dark Moon: The Healing Power of the Dark Goddess by
Demetra George (HarperCollins, 1992)

Oracles and Divination, edited by Michael Loewe and Carmen Blacker
(Shambhala, 1981)

*Our Dreaming Mind: A Sweeping Exploration of the Role That Dreams Have
Played in Politics, Art, Religion, and Psychology, from Ancient Civilizations to
the Present Day* by Robert L. Van de Castle, Ph.D. (Random House, 1994)

The Penguin Dictionary of Symbols by Jean Chevalier and Alain Gheerbrant,
translated by John Buchanan-Brown (Penguin, 1994)

*The Secret Teachings of All Ages, An Encyclopedic Outline of Masonic, Her-
metic, Qabbalistic and Rosicrucian Symbolical Philosophy* by Manly P. Hall
(The Philosophical Research Society, Inc., 1962)

The Spiral Dance: A Rebirth of the Ancient Religion of the Great Goddess by
Starhawk (Harper & Row, 1979)

There Are No Accidents: Syncronicity and the Stories of Our Lives by Robert H.
Hopcke (Riverhead Books, 1997)

Wisdom of the Heart: Working with Women's Dreams by Karen Signell
(Fromm International, 1998)

Witches, Nurses, and Midwives: History of Women Healers by Barbara Ehren-
reich and Deirdre English (Feminist Press, 1973)

A Witch's Book of Dreams by Karri Allrich (Lwellyn, 2001)

The Woman's Encyclopedia of Myths and Secrets by Barbara G. Walker
(HarperSanFrancisco, 1983)

Woman's Mysteries: Ancient & Modern by M. Esther Harding (Harper &
Row, 1976)

SUGGESTED MUSIC LIST

Ancient Voices by Ah Nee Mah, audio CD

Athos: A Journey to the Holy Mountain by Stephan Micus, audio CD

Avalon Rising by Avalon Rising, audio CD

The Book of Secrets by Lorenna McKennitt, audio CD

Dance the Spiral Dance by Ubaka Hill, audio CD

Moon Dancing by Amber Wolf with Kay Gardner, cassette

Moonsongs by Celestial Winds, audio CD

Mythodea by Vangelis, audio CD

Parallel Dreams by Lorenna McKennitt, audio CD

The Planets by Gustav Holtz, audio CD

Shapeshifters by Ubaka Hill

Singing the Wheel of the Year by Ruth Barrett

Through the Darkness: Chants by Beverly Frederick, audio CD (includes chants by Starhawk)

Under a Violet Moon by Blackmore's Night, audio CD

CHAPTER SIX

The Way of the Soul Sister

WHAT IS A "SOUL SISTER"? QUITE SIMPLY, A SOUL SISTER IS A WOMAN friend who tends to the needs of our souls. A soul sister keeps her eye on what really matters, even when we may not be centered on that ourselves. She is that person who recognizes the simple truth that while material security and professional success have their place in life, they cannot satisfy all our needs. Instead, a soul sister recognizes a different kind of happiness the Greeks called "eudaemonia," or the contentment that comes from keeping faith with one's higher calling or individual destiny. The meaning of life, said Jung, "is not exhaustively explained by one's business life, nor is the deeper desire of the human heart answered by a bank account." Thus, soul sisters are those who are loyal to the innermost essence, the deepest heart's desire, of their friends. By maintaining a fidelity and trust to the better part of their friend's nature, they help nurture it into existence.

> *The secret of a friend should be kept as one's own secret; the fault of a friend one should hide as one's own fault.*
>
> HAZRAT INAYAT KHAN

FIND TIME FOR "THE ULTIMATE THINGS"

> *The distinguishing hallmark that defines a soul-sister connection is the space two women make between them for the deeper side of life. This may take as simple a*

form as taking long walks together in nature. Or it may happen while sharing a meal, allowing each other to give voice to the emotional narratives running just beneath the surface of their everyday lives. Soul sisters create a safe place between them wherein each can share their most intimate encounters with God during prayer or meditation, as well as the dark nights of the soul—the doubts and despairs—each may undergo along the way. Soul sisters give full permission to hear each other's dreams, visions, and intuitions without harsh criticism. Soul sisters share with each other the thoughts of other poets, mystics, and thinkers who inspire them that will, in turn, inspire the friendship to greater heights and depths. Finally, soul sisters share the wine of friendship as a gift poured from the cup of the ultimate Friend, the divine Beloved. And soul sisters always, always find time to laugh at the wild, unpredictable, and joyful nature of life.

One of the complaints I hear women voice today goes something along these lines: "I have a loving husband, wonderful children, a good job, and a beautiful house. But I'm not happy." Stricken with guilt that they should feel unhappiness in the midst of such abundance, they try to push down their growing depression and sadness, ignoring the fact that it is the inner poverty of their souls that is causing them distress. A woman can have everything, even a religious life. Yet if there is a discrepancy between the needs of her inner self and her outer life, then she is going to suffer. A charming home and fulfilling career are benefits to any woman. But if there is no room in it for her soul— if her individual creative voice has no space in which to sing, dance, write, or to do whatever it is that she feels called to do—then she is unable to find satisfaction in her surroundings. Indeed, women miss the point when they pin the blame for their malaise on either the spiritual or material end of the spectrum. What heals is not more or less of one or the other—it is bringing the two into alignment, so that the life they are living on the outside is in accord with who they are on the inside. A businesswoman may have the imaginative heart of a musician, for instance, or a housewife may have the courageous spirit of a lawyer. Integrity comes when we are true to the truth of our own nature.

It is my strong conviction that we are each born, as Jungian thinker James Hillman has written, "called." Each person comes into this world, I believe, with a

If we can remember that we are here to sister one another, not to mother or be mothered, the possibility of another kind of relationship is opened to us. The turn from mothers to sisters is, as Freud saw, like the turn from goddesses to human women, the transition from a sacred to a profane relationship. Between sisters there is the possibility of a genuinely mutual, reciprocal relationship; each is giver and receiver.

CHRISTINE DOWNING,
Psyche's Sisters

spiritual mandate, and the realization of that mandate is the soul's aim. Only a rare few, however, are privileged to know the secret of their reason for being from birth. Though we may have hints and gleanings when we are young, our life purpose only becomes visible over the course of time, forged through life's trials and errors. As the heroine in the classic fairy tale must spin fine cloth from sheaves of wheat in order to win her freedom or the hand of the prince, so, too, must we each sort and sift through the childhood memories, social and cultural influences, dreams, emotional conflicts, and major life events that have gone into making our lives, spinning from them the fine cloth of our own particular destiny.

There is great meaning in the image of the Moira, or Three Fates, for women. Pictured with their spindles at the spinning wheel, they are the feminine forces dispensing threads of destiny. Together they weave beautiful designs in the shape of human lives, then cut the thread of life when the pattern is complete. We learn from them that fate is an ongoing creative process of interweaving bits and pieces of many colors, shapes, and textures into a complex, whole, and beautiful image. We learn from the Fates that this is not a solitary task, but one undertaken with the companionship and involvement of others. Whether quilting, sewing, weaving, embroidering, or knitting, needlework is an activity that sums up the process of soul work through which women arrive at their unique life destiny.

This, of course, is the work of many years. That is why we all need a soul sister—someone who, metaphorically speaking, can sit beside us at the spinning wheels of our lives—talking, laughing, crying, feeling—weaving, in the process, commonsense wisdom out of who we are and why we are here. This process between soul friends is what feminist thinker Christine Downing calls "the mutuality of soulmaking," the "reciprocal and equal love for one another's psychic development."[1] Though the metaphor of spinning may seem a stationary task, soul sistering is an evolutionary process. Says my longtime acquaintance Jan Clanton Collins, a Jungian analyst and professor of anthropology, "Friends are steadfast companions on the spiritual pilgrimage. They are a grace that makes the journey worthwhile. Just to know that they are in the world and that we are not alone gives us courage to go on." Delving into Celtic wisdom, Irish Catholic

> *A friend is called a guardian of love or, as some would have it, a guardian of the spirit itself. Since it is fitting that my friend be a guardian of our mutual love or the guardian of my own spirit so as to preserve all its secrets in faithful silence, let him, as far as he can, cure and endure such defects as he may observe in it; let him rejoice with his friend in his joys, and weep with him in his sorrows, and feel as his own all that his friend experiences.*
>
> AELRED OF RIEVAULX,
> "Spiritual Friendship,"
> FROM *The Education of the Heart*

scholar John O'Donohue has called this kind of profound kinship *anam cara*, or soul friend. Part of the role of one's anam cara, he says, "is to see for you in places where you're blind. There is a secret destiny in every friendship that awakens the hidden possibilities asleep in people's hearts. Thus part of the magic of anam cara is that the human psyche is given to each individual, but it remains relatively unborn—friendships help you to birth yourself." Collins concurs, saying one of the markers of a genuine soul friendship is the "sense of looking into a mirror that reflects something of our soul back to us." For though such bonds may include the usual gossip and events of daily life, they are centered on the search for deeper meaning.[2]

The endearing elegance of female friendship.

SAMUEL JOHNSON

Friendship is love without his wings!

LORD BYRON

For centuries, women's love has helped sustain society, forming a vital emotional ecostructure that has nurtured children, husbands, lovers, and even professional relationships in the workplace. But who cares for the souls of women? Who loves women as they love others? Among the unsung forms of love left blank on the pages of the history books is the kind of deep affection that has existed between women friends. We have not, as Carolyn Heilbrun has written, dared to say as men have done, "I love my friend."[3] Most of the great stories of friendship in history, she points out, have been about men. "If one sets out to read the annals of friendship . . . one finds oneself reading, in Plato, Aristotle, Epicurus, Plutarch, Erasmus, Montaigne, Johnson, Rousseau . . . of male friendships. If the friendships of women are considered at all . . . they intrude into the male account as a token woman is reluctantly included in a male community."[4]

Today, however, women are forging the same kinds of legendary friendships as the celebrated Biblical partnership of Jonathan and David. Like my friend Lis Akhtarzandi, they are being examples of courage to one another. Like Murshida Taj Glantz and Bishop Dixon, they are upholding new standards of religious faith that honor the feminine face of God and women's ways of being. Like artists Dale Loy and Elise Wiarda, they are inspiring one another in artistic and creative collaborations. Like Susan Kuner and Carol Orsborn, they are reimagining feminine forms of healing; or like Ruth Berlin and Abby Rosen, they are seeking to serve the world through divine love and compassion. And like the mooncircles collaboration between Dana and me, women are infusing magic into their lives, drawing down energy from ancient sources of wisdom in the sky. Whether meeting together in sacred prayer circles, informally for potluck suppers, over dinner and a glass of wine, on hikes in nature, in book clubs and mother's groups, or pondering astrology charts or tarot card spreads, women are coming together as soul sisters who lend unconditional support to one another's spiritual and life quests. Such friendships are equal in strength and endurance to the bonds of marriage and parenthood. Perhaps, in some cases, even more so.

Indeed, my life without my friends would be unimaginable. I could not have been a mother, I could not have been a writer, I could not have been a seeker on the spiritual path, without the wonder-working power of my friends' cherished sweetness, generosity of spirit, and unconditionally loving support. Too, as the historic accounts in this book attest, I have felt sistered by those women who have lived before me. Their stories of spiritual and artistic triumph against overwhelming odds give wings to my soul and inspire me with hope. They are my muses and my angels. Last, I cannot imagine a life without the myths of the Divine Feminine and the images of the Great Goddess. Like an underground fountain, they nurture my soul with their stories and adventures that yield forth the treasures of wisdom and insight into life's mysteries.

> *The perfection of friendship, in which lies all spiritual perfection, comes when the soul is so developed that there is no one whom it cannot bear. When it has reached this state, it has certainly passed into the ranks of those initiates whose names are written in the spiritual records.*
>
> Hazrat Inayat Khan

The miracle is, I am not alone in feeling this way. My friends feel the same about their friends, their friends feel the same about others, and we all feel the same about our visible and invisible soul sisters who have gone before us. Like a golden band, the bonds among women form a shining spiral of soul sisterhood encircling the globe with love and compassion.

Soul Sister Stories

Women who aspire to cultivate a "soul sister" friendship with another woman can find a model in the thirty-year-long friendship between sixty-two-year-old Episcopalean Suffragan Bishop Jane Holmes Dixon and sixty-three-year-old NPR radio host Diane Rehm. At a Sacred Circles conference for women held in the Fall of 1999 at the National Cathedral in Washington, D.C., an audience of more than a thousand women listened raptly as the two told the story of how their friendship first began. As Dixon told the story that evening, the two first met at their local parish of St. Patrick's in Washington, D.C. At the time, says Dixon, they were "young women, young mothers, young wives, and great cooks." Dixon had already been a member of the parish. So when Rehm walked into the parish kitchen for the first time, says Dixon, "we checked each other out to be sure who was who and what was what." Little did they know, she said, that thirty years later they would be standing together on stage telling the story of their friendship.

The two did not "catch on immediately," Diane Rehm recalled in her talk that evening, and the "process of checking each other out went on for a while," she said. Through their mutual friendship with five other women, however, the two grew to know each other. They cooked together, shared some wine, and, said Rehm, "little by little we began talking about ourselves—but it came very slowly." Then, said Rehm, she faced the frightening spectre of having to undergo a hysterectomy—a procedure that her husband was firmly against because he did not trust her doctor. As it turned out, however, the same doctor had performed a hysterectomy on Dixon two years earlier. The day before her operation, said Rehm, "I was so upset I was beside myself. So I went outside and I talked with Jane beside her car and began to weep with fear. Jane got out of her car and put her arms around me and said, 'Do you want me to be there for you when you come out of anesthesia?' and I said, 'yes.'" That incident initiated a new level of intimacy between the two women. After Rehm's successful operation, they began sharing their mutual joys and frustrations around their children and husbands on a daily basis.

> *In working with a spiritual friend we learn to love in an open-ended way—to love and be loved unconditionally. We're not used to this kind of love. It's what we all want but what we all have difficulty getting.*
>
>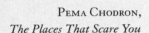
>
> PEMA CHODRON,
> *The Places That Scare You*

As stay-at-home moms, their friendship took a new twist when, their children growing older, Rehm enrolled in a college course she laughingly called "Feminism 101" to help guide her in choosing a career. Inspired by her course, she volunteered at the local NPR radio station, WAMU—the first step in her long and successful career as a nationally known radio talk-show host with more than 700,000 daily listeners. Not long after Rehm took up her newfound profession, Dixon enrolled in the same course—but experienced a dramatically different outcome. As Rehm retold the episode, Dixon called her one day and said, "Ms. Rehm, do you promise you will not laugh if I tell you what I want to do? I want to be a priest." To which Rehm responded warmly, "Darling girl—you go for it." As I have told the story earlier in the book, it was a decision that culminated in Dixon's election as the Suffragan Bishop of the Episcopal Diocese in Washington, D.C.— only the second woman to be elevated to the office of bishop in the Episcopal Church in this country, and the third worldwide.

For the past twenty years, the foundation of Rehm and Dixon's extraordinary friendship has rested on the 7:00 A.M. telephone conversation they share at the start of each day. Though it is a ritual each describes as sacred as prayer or meditation, it originated in a bitter dispute. When Dixon first entered seminary, she explained to her audience, she became less available to Rehm. As a busy mother and wife, she would go to bed early, then awaken at 3:00 A.M. to study—the only time that she could find the solitude necessary for her studies. Thus, when Rehm called late one evening, Dixon responded angrily that she didn't want her friend interrupting her sleep that way. But Rehm also felt angry, as, she said, her dear friend "was no longer available to me whenever I wanted her to be. It took some adjustment because . . . suddenly she was no longer my supportive angel giving me encouraging words every day." The rift caused a falling out, and the two didn't speak for more than a month. It was only when they decided to see a therapist together that they began to see how precious their relationship was to each other. The therapist helped them to see that the disagreement they had suffered through was proof of the strength of their feelings for each other.

It was then that the two women worked out their habit of speaking to each other the first thing each morning. Said a tearful Dixon to her friend Rehm that evening before a hushed audience, "I say my prayers before she calls on the phone, and that conversation is an extension of that conversation with God: to have that human touch, that human voice, that incarnate presence say to me, 'Jane Dixon, you're all right. And you can do it.' I love you for that, I love you for that." The kind of spiritually based friendship that she shares with Rehm, says Dixon, allows her to have conversations about the things that matter the most—the "ultimate things," as theologian Paul Tillich would say.

Both Rehm and Dixon say they learn from each other, and acknowledge their friendship as a valuable source of self-knowledge. Rehm, for instance, credits Dixon's faith with helping her in her career as a radio talk-show host who must often contend with hostile callers. While thirty years ago she might have "hollered or fussed right back," Rehm said Dixon's training as a minister has taught her how to be open to what different people have to say, and to try to present reasoned comments rather than arguments, to help people think things through. "I have learned that . . . in listening you become an opening for that other person," said Rehm. Because of her friend, said Rehm, she can "learn from others in ways I never would have done without her." Likewise, Dixon said one of Rehm's gifts to her has been to teach her how to become a "fighter." Their deep faith and trust in each other made it possible for her to overcome her hesitance to confront another per-

> The relationship with our spiritual friend inspires us to step out fearlessly and start exploring the phenomenal world.
>
> PEMA CHODRON,
> *The Places That Scare You*

son, and, encouraged by Rehm's own feisty outspokenness, to speak her true feelings to her friend. This helped her in her work as a priest in a male institution. "I've got a loud mouth," said Dixon that evening in her address, "but I don't like conflict. Yet there are times when you just have to speak up for yourself. The Episcopal Church is still very much a man's world and it's been important for me to be able to stand up for myself. If it hadn't been for Diane, I wouldn't have developed that ability to be able to believe in myself and to get good at telling others what I will or will not do."

He who realizes the relation of friendship between one soul and another—the tenderness, delicacy, and sacredness of this relationship—he is living, and in this way he will one day communicate with God.

HAZRAT INAYAT KHAN

Today the two women are both grandmothers. They still talk on the telephone every day, and share feelings about their husbands, children, grandchildren, professions, and their inner spiritual lives. They worry over who will die first, as each would like the other to be present at their funerals. Listening to them talk, however, I have a feeling that their relationship will continue long past death, opening into new worlds and new forms. As Rehm said that evening, "I commend friendship to you in the deepest, closest way, because it really is life-changing."

TRUST IN THE SECRET OF TIME TO SHAPE YOUR FRIENDSHIP

Often, when looking for a true soul sister, we imagine that such a bond can only be found with someone with whom we can talk about God, pray, or meditate. While that is an integral aspect of a soul-sister relationship, it is important not to omit the sacredness found in the daily lives we lead as women. Something magic transpires, for instance, with that woman with whom we have shared significant life passages, and whom we have known over the course of many years. I have rarely been able to see the five friends I grew up with, for instance. But when my friend Virginia sent me a photo of her three grown daughters—the same age as my sons—I felt deeply touched. And when she wrote to me during the course of her husband's illness, I suffered with her. And when our mutual friend Cheryl wrote to me to share details of Virginia's husband's funeral, we grieved together in a circle of friends. So trust in the secret wisdom of time—the weddings and promotions, the successes and failures, the deaths and births—as an alchemy that deepens a friend into a true soul sister.

The story of Jane Dixon and Diane Rehm shows how it is possible to begin a friendship in the middle of adulthood, with all the responsibilities of children, husbands, and careers. The story of my good friend Nancy Kadian and her friend

Charlotte (not her real name), however, reveals the way a soul sister is sometimes someone we may have known since childhood. Nancy is a psychotherapist who is also a Sufi meditation teacher and the mother of two sons; Charlotte is a school counselor and the mother of four. Nancy's extroverted, outgoing nature is in direct contrast to Charlotte's more reserved and serious personality. The two first met when they were thirteen years old in middle school. While Charlotte tended to be a loner, Nancy was popular and had a wide circle of friends. As young as they were, they each recall their first encounter.

> *The use of friendship for a selfish purpose is like mixing bitter poison with the sweet rose-syrup.*
>
> HAZRAT INAYAT KHAN

"I had a very instantaneous and intense connection to Nan when we first met. For me it was like falling in love," recalls Charlotte. "I had three brothers but no sisters and mostly male cousins. So while I knew girls, I didn't have the same bond with them as I did with boys. But it was different when I met Nan. I lived inside myself, but with Nan I could let myself out and have more fun. Sometimes I felt that what was in me could come out through her."

Laughs Nancy in response, "She makes me feel like Lucy. I always feel like I have some scheme for her. Yet when we first met, I recognized that Charlotte had a depth to her that I had not experienced with anyone else I had been friends with before. There was an immediate trust; I knew I could tell her anything and that she would never tell anyone else or laugh at anything I said. From the beginning, we could see into the depths of each other." Both Nancy and Charlotte felt as if their connection predated their actual encounter. Says Nancy, "It's as if we came into life knowing each other—as if destiny chose us for each other."

And though the two shared the usual teen girl talk about makeup and dating, from the outset a strong spiritual undertone marked their friendship. At fourteen, they would pray together at the underground grotto in the Bronx, a series of caves that is a sanctuary for Mary, with flickering candles and statues of different saints. When the two girls grew to young womanhood, however, their lives veered in separate directions. Charlotte married, had a child, then divorced and remarried a minister, with whom she had three more children. Nancy married, had three sons, and became initiated by Pir Vilayat Inayat Khan into the Sufi Order.

When it was discovered that Nancy's oldest son had irreversible brain damage, Charlotte, whose husband's work in inner-city ministries was taking them to different cities around the country, felt isolated from her close childhood friend. "I remember feeling after Nan's son Colbi was born that I didn't know how to be there for her. She was in a different life with the Sufi community that I wasn't a part of. For a period of about four years I felt as if I might have lost our friendship.

While I knew intellectually what was happening, I didn't know what was happening to her emotionally." As Nancy recalls that painful period of time in her life, "I had to be so tough and strong that I couldn't appear to need people. I could never express any pain or grief, so people felt excluded from that process. I had two other little boys who needed a mother, so I didn't have the luxury of feeling my feelings." It wasn't until her son and her father both died within a short period of time that Nancy felt as if she could "let down and let it all go."

It wasn't long after the death of her son that Nancy's marriage began falling apart. "When I got divorced, through the grace of God, Charlotte moved to a town just two hours away. I used to get in the car all the time and hightail it to her house." For the first time in their adult life, says Charlotte, "We were able to just be together." This time, they not only reconnected with each other, but with each other's children as well. They began celebrating holidays like Easter and Thanksgiving together. "Charlotte's family sees her as very conservative, so I get to be Auntie Mame," says Nancy. At the same time, says Charlotte, Nancy brings out the fun, light-hearted side of her, just as she did when they were young. She also appreciates the way Nancy sees the more passionate side of her nature that she has been unable to share with others.

> *We cannot tell the precise moment when friendship is formed. As in filling a vessel drop by drop, there is at last a drop which makes it run over; so in a series of kindnesses there is at last one which makes the heart run over.*
>
> JAMES BOSWELL

Nancy and Charlotte's friendship illustrates the way many women nurture each other's sexuality in a way that goes counter to most stereotypes. "There is no question," says Nancy, "that we encourage, support, and celebrate each other's passion. Men only know what you're like with them. But your best friend gets to know what you're like with all the rest of the men you've been with!" This aspect of their friendship was especially important to Nancy when she began dating again, confiding in her friend her experiences as a single woman. "Just telling Charlotte gave me a feeling of safety. Sharing an experience with her was grounding because by saying it out loud to her I could tell if I was going out on a limb." When Nancy began a steady relationship with a mutual old friend from high school, the two friends felt like they were "sixteen again," giggling and sharing secrets. Then Charlotte, who was still married, fell deeply in love with a man she felt was her soul mate. The experience was life-changing, dramatically impacting her marriage and her family. Separating from her husband, Charlotte, who was beside herself with joy over her newfound relationship, felt a kind of passion and happiness she had never known before. But her love affair was not destined to last;

her partner, Warren, had a sudden and unexpected heart attack and from one minute to the next her life was changed forever. "Never in my entire life," says Nancy, "have I felt such grief in a person. It was truly profound. There were times when I knew she didn't want to live anymore."

"I wouldn't have lived without Nan after Warren died," recalls Charlotte. "There's no doubt in my mind about that. Sometimes, when I'm still feeling blue, I often think about the way she would reassure me that I would not always feel so badly. It was a very difficult situation, because this was a relationship that was not known to very many people, so there was no place I could go for comfort. Nan was the only one I could grieve with because she was the only one who knew the depth of how I had felt. Everyday I had to go to work and present a professional façade. I'd be in my office in a building with thousands of kids, and I had to function, and I would call her weeping and crying, unsure how I was going to hold it together. Nan was my lifeline in terms of maintaining my sanity. It was more than nurturing someone—it was holding me up when I couldn't do it for myself. It wasn't even like she was breathing life into me—she was breathing for me."

What is the odds so long as the fire of soul is kindled at the taper of conviviality, and the wing of friendship never moults a feather!

Charles Dickens,
The Old Curiosity Shop

Friends are born, not made.

Henry Brooks Adams

As she began to emerge from her heartfelt depression, an important part of Charlotte's healing process included reconnecting to spirituality. With Warren's death, she had begun having very deep mystical experiences around death and immortality that she shared in turn with Nancy. And although until then the two friends had followed divergent spiritual paths, says Charlotte, "they'd been leading to the same point; more and more we found we shared the same spiritual perspective." Although Charlotte had participated in some Sufi workshops with her friend, her interest wasn't in belonging to an organization, says Nancy, as much as it lay in exploring the Sufi perspective that the spiritual relationship with God is one of lover and beloved—a notion that helped Charlotte transform the grief she felt over her lost love into a deepened relationship with the Divine. "Slowly, it began to feel as if we'd come full circle—from the time we were young, sharing crushes on boyfriends, to the depths of spirituality, and the very core of our inner beings," says Nancy. "We talk about God all the time now. I can talk to Charlotte about God the way I can't with anybody else. It's so private and intimate, it would be embarrassing with someone who didn't know me the way she does."

Like a long and fruitful marriage that has weathered many ups and downs, Charlotte says that over the thirty-eight years of their friendship "we've lost marriages and children and parents and dreams. Even though there have been many fun times, those are the moments that have solidified our relationship." Indeed, each time they've gone through something together, adds Nancy, "it's drawn us closer together. Now we have no doubt that the other would be there—no question of the fact that we can count on each other." Echoing the views of many women, their friendship, says Charlotte, revolves more around their identities as individual women than around the roles they're engaged in at work and at home. In many ways, they say they have come to rely on each other even more than a husband, becoming the repository of each other's life secrets. "Our friendship has a wonderful feeling of permission—we never feel that we're draining the other person," says Nancy.

And after all these years, romance and mystery remains a part of their friendship, they say. "We still love each other and there is still an element of surprise in our relationship," says Nancy. What is most meaningful to her, says Charlotte, is the way that she and Nancy can share all sides of themselves with each other, whether through "deep and soul-searching conversations, a heart-wrenching discussion about something very painful, or lying on the floor and listening to our knees popping and looking for gray hairs! I still feel exactly the way I've always felt with Nan since I was a child—we are still these two totally idealistic, love-will-conquer-all romantics."

> *Friendship is a sheltering tree....*
>
> SAMUEL TAYLOR COLERIDGE,
> "Youth and Age"

> *Time, which strengthens friendship,
> weakens love.*
>
> JEAN DE LA BRUYÈRE

Judith and I developed friendships that have literally been life-sustaining with each other and with other women who have shared our work. We have shared meals and wine. We have laughed and cried together. We have assisted or witnessed major transitions in each other's lives: marriages, births, the publication of books, divorces, commitment ceremonies, moves across the country and around the world. We have been there for each other over the years. When we begin to speak the truths that come from the deepest places in ourselves, we know that there are others who can "hear us into speech."

CAROL CHRIST, *Rebirth of the Goddess*

FINDING A SOUL SISTER

My friend Sylvia recently called to share a dream with me. In it, a caravan of cars was passing her by, filled with women laughing and talking on their way to a large gathering. The winding procession of cars was led by a woman with whom she had once enjoyed a long friendship. When we talked about the dream, Sylvia shared that she had just been to a fiftieth birthday party for one of her old friends. The experience, reflected by the symbolism in her dream, had stirred within her a nostalgia to spend time with her women friends, whom she felt were passing her by and leaving her behind. As we continued to talk, it became clear that she had been sacrificing her personal life in favor of her family and work—and that the dream was telling her to join up with a caravan of soul sisters before it was too late.

For memory has painted this perfect day
With colors that never fade,
And we find at the end of a perfect day
The soul of a friend we've made.

CARRIE JACOBS-BOND

While many women are blessed to have a soul sister in their lives, just as many lack a friendship with someone with whom they can share their deepest selves. They may have acquaintances or even longtime friends, but still not have found that special someone to talk about the things of "ultimate value," as Bishop Dixon mentioned—the meaning of life, the purpose of one's own individual life, one's feelings around other love relationships, and a woman's everchanging and evolving relationship to the Divine.

How can women find a soul sister? To begin with, I think any search must begin with an intention. Just like dream incubation begins with a process of soul searching, so, too, does the quest for a true friend begin with an honest survey of one's own life. While friendship is a process that facilitates awareness, we must have a certain measure of self-knowledge ourselves before we can engage at a certain depth with another person. Thus, a person seeking a friend might start out by first drawing a character map of themselves. They might sketch out the basic framework of their life, noting such basic conditions as whether or not they are married and meeting the demands of children and a husband, or whether they are a single parent, or whether they have an all-consuming career. Next, a woman should identify where she falls on the age continuum: is she young and just setting out on life's adventure, is she midstream and somewhat settled down, or is she entering the elder years of her life?

Asking ourselves these questions helps us to know from the outset what kind of friendship we are interested in building. As trust and truth are the foundations for any lasting friendship, a woman must be able to be honest about the kind of commitment she is capable of. In my own life, for example, I am not the kind of friend who likes to spend a lot of time hanging out. Going to a matinee or out to lunch midweek is a real treat, but one that I enjoy only rarely. As a writer, I require a lot of solitude for my work. There have been times when my children have placed enormous demands on me emotionally, and I have had little energy left over for my closest women friends. Blessedly, however, my strongest friendships are with women who, whether parents or not, are more like me—independent-minded, busy pursuing their own creative projects, and involved in a nexis of rich interrelationships with other people and interests. So what works for me, works for them.

At the same time, perhaps you are a woman with greater intimacy needs. Perhaps you need to be able to see someone on a frequent basis, or the friendship won't work for you. The age and place at which you are in life, of course, may also determine the time that is available to you. Typically, age brings with it increased responsibilities, while youth has more time for play. Often, the telephone is a girlfriend's best ally. Diane Rehm and Jane Dixon say that sometimes several months might elapse during which they are each too busy to get together in person. Still, they keep their friendship current and dynamic by talking on the phone each day. E-mail, too, can help facilitate communication, as I have found with all my long-distance friends. One reason I have focused so much on the issue of time with regard to friendships is because I find that for most contemporary women, time is the overriding influence in their lives. Most have too little of it to go around. It is important to keep this in mind when making a friend, for if her friendship is important enough to you, you may have to sacrifice some of your own ideas around how much time you would like to spend together. One of the best things I enjoy about my friendships, for example, is the way we give each other lots of tolerance, understanding, and forgiveness around the issue of time.

Once you have mapped out a sketch of what kind of friend you are capable of being to others, then formulate an image of the kind of friend that you would like to attract into your life. Paint a picture of her attributes: Is she politically involved, spiritually developed, strong-minded, funny, loving, or gentle? Is she an outdoors person, an artist, or a get-together-over-dinner type of girlfriend? Is she more thoughtful and serious, or is she extroverted and fun-loving? Next, determine if there is some specific area that you would like to focus on with a friend. It's

Only solitary men know the full joys of friendship. Others have their family; but to a solitary and an exile his friends are everything.

WILLA CATHER,
Shadows on the Rock

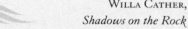

often said that male friendships are centered on activities, while women mostly like to relate and talk, but I have found that women share activities and interests just as much as men do. My friends Harriett and Jan, for instance, bonded over years of hiking and river rafting in exotic places, while my friend Lis and I love nothing better than to talk intensely for hours in a crowded restaurant over a glass of wine. Note the kinds of things that you want to be able to talk about with a friend: perhaps you are a writer, and would like the company of other writers; perhaps you are politically active and want to be able to talk politics with a close friend; perhaps you need to share the journey of motherhood with another mother.

A friend is one to whom one may pour out all the contents of one's heart, chaff and grain together, knowing that the gentlest of hands will take and sift it, keep what is worth keeping and with a breath of kindness blow the rest away.

ARABIAN PROVERB

There are other ways to go about the search for a soul friend. In addition to setting an intention and making a descriptive list of characteristics, you may also want to be spontaneous and let life surprise you. Ultimately, every human being is a mysterious creature whose quirks, talents, depths, and idiosyncracies could never be fully captured or imagined in advance. Before I moved to Washington, D.C., for example, all of my closest women friends were Sufis, or on some other spiritual path. Thrown back on my own for the first time in my adult life, I was lonely and uncertain how to meet new people. When I decided to open myself up to friends who were not as formally involved in spirituality as I had been, I was delighted to meet and make friends with a number of women whose lives had been quite different from mine, yet with whom, years later, I share a deep and abiding relationship. Difference, as well as sameness, can sometimes be a refreshing component in a friendship. After spending a day alone in my study with my books and my computer, for instance, it is a welcome relief to spend time with my friends Lis or Janet hearing about their struggles in the business world. In fact, one of the aspects of my own circle of friends I enjoy most is the wide diversity of women I have come to know, ranging from CEOs to environmental activists, astrologers, healers, artists, writers, editors, and mothers. I think of my various circles of friends as interlocking spheres, each with their own unique interests, joined at the center by a soulful depth that then radiates back out again. "Friendship is like love," said Bishop Dixon in her lectures, "the more you have the better it gets. You don't have to limit yourself to just one friend. Our friends have other friends, too. But each one has a special component to it." Indeed, agreed Rehm, "My friendship with Jane has allowed me to grow and have other dear friends. In other words, friendship is habituating. You get into the habit of reaching out and being

a friend and you realize that what you get back is so incredibly rich—whether the
friendship is thirty or five years old."

The qualities that have shaped the chapters and stories in this book are yet
another way to help you find a soul sister. Like stepping stones, they can lead you
out of the solitude of yourself and into a profound kinship with a life companion.
But first, the path that leads to friendship with another woman begins by connecting to one's own inner friend—the *soror mystica*, or mys-
tical sister. Like all archetypes, writes Christine Downing,
"the Sister" both appears in projected form and also as
an inner aspect. "Sorting through the meaning of sisterhood in our lives requires attending to all three modes:
that of the literal sister(s), the surrogate sisters, and the
sister within, the archetype," writes Downing.[5] Often
when women complain of loneliness, in fact, it as much
out of a yearning for contact with this neglected part of their psyche, as it is longing for friendship with a woman in their outer life. As I told a friend once who felt
a lack of feminine intimacy in her life, "I think you must be lonely for yourself."

The bond with our inner sister can lead to healthier, more balanced friendships in the outside world, as well. Too often, women make the mistake of over-
burdening a relationship with expectations. They may see a friend as someone
who can answer all their needs. This is especially a pitfall with friendships that
have a spiritual component; a person may be prone to see a newfound friend as
someone all-good and compassionate, rather than as an ordinary and flawed
human being. The presence of the archetypal sister is a source of help that comes
from within. She is the symbol of an interior resource of "energies and perspectives, complementary to our everyday version of ourself, that we can draw upon in
situations of need."[6] Finally, knowing our inner sister cultivates a capacity for
depth, solitude, magic, and reflection—qualities that are intrinsic to the tasks of
soul work and soul sistering.

> *I had three chairs in my house: one for
> solitude, one for friendship, one for society.*
>
> HENRY DAVID
> THOREAU, *Walden*

✵

MEDITATION ON THE SOROR MYSTICA,
THE INNER SOUL SISTER

Among the stories recounted about the great Hindu saint Sri Sarada Devi, I found
great meaning in the anecdote about her vision of the beautiful, "dark-skinned"
woman who appeared as her sister at her bedside during the illness she suffered en

route to be with her husband, Ramakrishna. Devi's vision companion was her spiritual soulmate—her "soror mystica," or mystical sister who appeared to her at a crucial juncture in her destiny.

We cannot hope to have a genuine relationship with another until we have begun to deepen our intimacy with the soul sister within. This is the "invisible companion" who goes through life at our side, the magical travelling friend who appears at moments of crisis, offering comfort and guidance. Jung gives three accounts in religious tradition of the friend who appears on the path: Jesus who appeared to the disciples on the road to Emmaus in the Bible, Krishna who appeared to Arjuna in the Bhagavad Gita, and Khidr who appeared to Moses in the Koran. In the mystical tradition of Sufism in Islam, the scholar Henri Corbin describes Khidr as the "invisible spiritual master, reserved for those who are called to a direct unmediated relationship with the divine world . . ."[7] This is based on a famous passage in the Koran, where Khidr appears to Moses as his guide who reveals to him

This person of light . . . before you is called . . . the suprasensory Guide.

NAJM KOBRA,
*The Man of Light in
Iranian Sufism*

the "secret, mystical truth." According to spiritual legends, Khidr is described as the source of life, "the Eternal Youth" who has drunk the water of immortality. For this reason he is associated with nature's greenness, and is known as "the green man" because wherever Khidr appears, flowers blossom and a garden springs to life.[8]

In one account, an initiate who is facing the spiritual quest is urged to "put on the sandals of Khidr" as a way to surmount the difficulties he will encounter along the way. Another tradition refers to the disciples who receive the "mantle of Khidr." This symbolizes how a spiritual state of consciousness is tranferred from Khidr to his disciple. In one of the most beautiful passages of spiritual literature, Corbin writes of Khidr that his "mission consists in enabling you to attain to the 'Khidr of your being,' for it is this inner depth in this 'prophet of your being,' that springs the Water of Life. . . . In the voice of a Khidr every Spiritual hears the inspiration of his own Holy Spirit, just as every prophet perceives the spirit of his own prophecy in the form of an Angel Gabriel."[9]

Who is the invisible companion who accompanies us, if not our soul? Whose voice speaks to us in moments of quiet, if not the voice of our soul? We are each born twinned, one part human, one part divine sibling. Our immortal double is she who lives on after our physical bodies pass away. She is the keeper of the record of our life, and the holder of the secret of our fate. To begin a dialogue with her is to begin a dialogue with our true and eternal Self. For both men and women, she is "Sister Soul." As Khidr appeared to Moses, as Krishna spoke to Arjuna at the beginning of battle, and as Jesus appeared to his disciples immediately following his death, our soul travels the road of life alongside us, watching over us like a spiritual helpmate. "The inner brother or sister," writes Downing, "honors our humanness, helps without asking too much or giving too much."

Over the course of my life I have had many encounters with my inner soul sister, most often in the form of a reassuring and loving presence, quiet voice, or strong intuition. Two incidents, however, stand out vividly in my memory. The first occurred when I was just eighteen years old. During my first year in college I had become pregnant by my boyfriend. At that time, abortion was illegal and difficult to obtain. Like any young teenager, I was frightened to death to tell my parents, especially my strict, Catholic father, for fear of his reaction. Telling my parents instead that I was dropping out of college, I went to live with some college friends in Washington, D.C., in a group house just off of Dupont Circle. At the time, I was confused and uncertain as to what to do. My boyfriend urged me to have an abortion. Other friends encouraged me to keep the baby. While I wanted to have the child, I had no idea how I would care for it as a single mother. Meanwhile, I had no money to even arrange for an abortion. I began to feel as if I had no way out. One humid summer's day, as I was walking back from my fast-food job, feeling like the loneliest person in the world, an emotion of intense happiness washed over me. Suddenly, I felt the presence of someone, and looking slightly up and to my left, I had a brief but stunning vision of a beautiful, laughing young woman. It was as if she were dancing and singing with joy all at once; she didn't say anything, but her whole being conveyed to me the message that everything would be all right. And, eventually, things did work out. When my boyfriend made arrangements for me to have a safe, but secret abortion, at a local hospital, I made the decision to go forward with it. And although I have always born a deep sadness inside myself over that event, I have never forgotten the appearance of my beautiful soul sister in my moment of genuine need.

> *. . . For thou art with me . . . all the days of my life.*
>
> PSALM 23:4,6

The second time I encountered my inner sister occurred many years later, when I found myself unable to sell any articles or book proposals. Feeling as if my writing career was at an end, I dreamed one night that I was literally "hanging by my nails" over a steep precipice—so steep, in fact, that it was as if I were hanging on the edge of the world and, if I dropped, I would fall into the depths of infinite space. Looking below me, all I could see was emptiness, save for one small piece of ground where I was supposed to land. As I hung in space pondering my dilemma, a woman suddenly appeared above me—the very same woman I had seen so many years before. She was still young, and lovely, and smiling with joy. Now, she was laughing at my fear. Without saying a word, she began gently prying my fingers loose . . . until I dropped, landing squarely on the ground. When I awoke, it was with a deep feeling of peace and well being that, once again, things would turn out all right. Not long after that dream, assignments began pouring in once more.

My vision and dream illustrate the principle behind Khidr's transference of a spiritual state to his disciples through the mantle placed about their shoulders. In the same way, my soul sister transferred to me the divine joy and enthusiasm for life I needed at those difficult times. Like a "soul trans- fusion," she infused me with energy and vitality, resur- recting my dashed hopes. Some may feel as if they are a stranger to their inner soul sister. But if we take a moment to reflect, we may recognize certain moments when we have felt her presence nearby. The soror mys- tica is the source of that unmistakable feeling of deep inner knowing, for instance, that comes over us when we suddenly know the right thing to do, or acceptance for why something is the way that it is. She is our better half, embodying a natural and ancient intelligence as old as time and as wise as night who is yet eternally young and sweetly innocent. The inner soul sister wraps her arms about us when we are tired from life, and com- forts us when our heads are bowed down late at night with worry.

. . . every being in the physical universe has its counterpart in the heavenly Earth, inhabited by the descendants of a mystical Adam and Eve.

HENRY CORBIN,
*The Man of Light in
Iranian Sufism*

A woman can cultivate her connection to her guardian companion through creative imagination and a kind of inner dialogue and conversation. Often when I am stressed, I simply imagine her presence beside me. When I am confused and disoriented, I may close my eyes and imagine that she is thinking and speaking for me from a much clearer, steadier place. Indeed, if you can imagine the kind of ideal woman you would like to be, that picture may be an image of your soul sister. My friend Debra, for instance, dreamed recently of Xena, the Warrior Princess— tall, fearless, and courageously strong. This modern-day goddess was a vivid rep- resentation of the quality of Debra's innermost feminine being.

To draw nearer to the soul sister within, call to mind the quality that you feel most defines you, whether courage or beauty, wisdom or truth. Closing your eyes, imagine that this quality is beginning to assume a shape, like a body that is crystal- lizing around a seed of light. Perhaps this woman is a wizard, like Morgan le Fay.

Maybe she is a moon priestess. Or, your soul sister could appear in the form of a healer who soothes the wounded and the distraught. In his book, Pir Vilayat Inayat Khan describes the vision of a sage from a Gnostic text. In it, the sage was walking in a landscape of light; surrounding him were vague forms he could barely make out. "Then, just off in the mist, the form of a magnificent face seemed to emerge. Gradually assuming a whole form, it then seemed as though a person was approaching him, while at the same time he was walking toward that person. . . . Suddenly, it struck him that the being resembled himself. Finally, in a moment of sublime illumination, he realized that the being facing him was his soul, his celestial counterpart."[10]

> *In reality this Face is your own face and this sun is the sun of the Spirit.*
>
> NAJM KOBRA,
> *The Man of Light in Iranian Sufism*

Indeed, our celestial counterpart is who we are evolving to be. Without a vision of this being, we cannot hope to become that person. Because we have had to develop certain aspects of ourselves in order to survive the battle of life, writes Pir Vilayat, we think of ourselves as defiled. Yet in truth, he continues, "our self-image is nothing in comparison to what we really are. Our original, celestial nature is immaculate, genuine, and completely lacking in any guile or artifice."[11] Just realizing this can help our original nature to blossom forth into life, bringing us closer to the loving heart of our soul sister.

HOW THE QUALITIES CREATE AND KEEP A SOUL SISTER FRIENDSHIP

✦

The divine qualities that I have written about in this book emerge from the stories of our lives like diamonds from coal. So too, however, is the art of friendship refined by such qualities as faith, beauty, and magic. If we let them, these qualities can help us grow beyond the isolation of our individual lives to join with another on the journey of life. They can also be forged within the crucible of friendship: the courage it takes to make a new friend, for example, is in turn the boon we receive from the relationship itself. So let these qualities be your guide in friendship; following them, they lead to deeper bonds and truer lives.

✻

COURAGE

After a presentation I recently gave at a Maryland writers' conference, a tall and striking blonde woman approached me from the audience. She introduced herself with a heartfelt smile, shook my hand, then offered to be my intern. Taken aback, I agreed, touched by her warmth and outgoing nature. The conference had taken place in Baltimore, about an hour from where I live. As we chatted, however, it turned out that Suzanne lived just minutes away from my house, with her husband and three children. Not long after that, Suzanne and I embarked on an adventure together, touring historic sites and interviewing different people for an article I was researching. I valued her insights and perspectives, while she became inspired to begin her own writing career. Later, she confided in me that she had prayed before the conference that she would meet a friend with whom she could share her inner spiritual life. Through that initial encounter, we began a friendship that is beginning to blossom into something rich.

Suzanne's initiative was an example of the way courage plays a role in shaping friendships. We may pine for a friend, but if we do not risk stepping outside the safe boundaries of our lives, we will not find her. Friends rarely drop from the sky onto our doorstep, but are encountered in the busy matrix of everyday life. When I think back on the beginnings of all my friendships, most were the result of an involvement in various interests and activities. The first friend I made outside my small high school growing up was sparked when I enrolled in a summer-school course in history in a town nearby. Santa and I took one look at each other and found ourselves embroiled in an intense exchange of ideas. I met my Sufi friends after following my heart

> *But if the while I think on thee, dear friend,*
> *All losses are restored and sorrows end.*
>
>
> SHAKESPEARE,
> Sonnet 30, l.13

and going off to a meditation camp in the middle of the Arizona desert. Still other friendships were formed through my passion for Jungian dream studies and astrology; I forged more connections through writers' groups and political involvement.

So for the person seeking a soul friendship, the first step might be to begin by gathering your courage, putting aside your fears and hesitations, and following your heart's desires. Before setting out, ask yourself: What are my ideals? What is it that I wish to study or accomplish with my life? What are my creative passions, and what are the political causes I believe in? Follow the lead provided by the answers to these questions, and not only will you begin to live the life you dreamed of for yourself, you might also find a soulful companion along the way.

Finally, make courage a part of your friendship. While men engage in friendships that include risk and adventure, women are more likely to orient their friendships around a mutual exchange of emotional feelings and experiences. Yet the sisterhood of women might be strengthened were they to dare more often to be bold and brave, undertaking adventures in the outer world of power and accomplishment.

FAITH

Once you have sparked a connection with a newfound friend, the next phase of relationship begins. Like any romance with a significant other, as time passes, friendships lose their original shimmer of attraction. They become less exciting; intimacy may deepen, but so does a certain comfortable familiarity. As much as you love your friend, you may become bored and restless. The excitement wears off, and interest may wane. More than likely, your friendship may be strained as the reality of life intrudes into the close circle of your intimacy—the sudden loss of a loved one, financial difficulties, a turbulent romantic relationship, or the time constraints of a demanding career or home life.

In these ways and in many others, our faith in friendship is tested. If the friendship is one that is worth keeping, however, our task is to remain faithful to our friend. Just as in marriage, friendship is about weathering both the good and the bad, the exciting and the banal realities of everyday life. As many women have attested throughout this book, hardships often strengthen the ties between soul friends. To pass through something together—to help one another survive the loss of a great love, endure the loneliness of lack of love or the physical suffering caused by illness—is the greatest form of spiritual initiation: We emerge transformed, as does the friendship. Faith is the quality that makes such an initiation possible; it is an alchemy that turns the dross of everyday life into something golden, precious, and durable.

But there is yet another dimension to the quality of faith within friendship:

> *The only reward of virtue is virtue; the only way to have a friend is to be one.*
>
>
>
> RALPH WALDO EMERSON,
> *On Love and Friendship*

the faith we maintain in one another's dreams and aspirations. This has been the greatest gift to me from my soul sisters, all of whom never once stopped believing in me as a writer and as a mother. They have given me money to help pay bills, sent books to inspire me, lavished flowers on me when I finished a project, and raised a toast in celebration when a child graduated or an article was published. They are each one of them shining examples of the power of faith in friendship. Helping to midwife the soul of a friend is the true work of any soul-sister friendship.

☼

BEAUTY

What would a friendship between women be without the quality of beauty? Like the three graces who attended Aphrodite, the goddess of beauty, soul sisters bring joy, flowering, and brilliance to one another's lives. I think of the spirit of beauty as the color, shape, and scent of a lovely flower; in the same way, so, too, does beauty perfume our friendships, painting them in the bright and lovely hues of the feminine spirit. Friendships between women are in themselves an embodiment of the quality of beauty. I have watched women share meals together, walk and talk together, and work to-

> *A friend is a person with whom I may be sincere. Before him, I may think aloud.*
>
> RALPH WALDO EMERSON,
> *On Love and Friendship*

gether. Inevitably, I am struck by the mood of charm that emanates from their companionship. As the mother of three sons, I have often observed the way the presence of my women friends in my house has changed the atmosphere.

Thus, while faith is the quality that may sustain a relationship over time, beauty is the quality that infuses friendships with something uniquely secret and special to women. Beauty rites date far back in time; for aeons, women have been coloring one another's hair, finding new ways to soften their skin, and adorning one another in bracelets and robes. Soul sisters today can bring delight into their friendships through the time-honored beauty ritual of relaxing at a spa together. They can take time out from their pressured lives to engage in the feminine pursuit of talking about hair, clothes, perfume, makeup, creams, and potions. They can beautify one another's lives through small gifts such as bath oils, a frivolously unnecessary but pretty piece of jewelry or scarf, a lovely piece of music, or a book of poetry, or by arranging a special day trip to the museum. These gestures, however small or large, bring a touch of grace to life. They remind us of the pleasure that arises from beauty. And they can remind us that the Goddess's creation is something beautiful to be reveled in.

Because a soul-sister friendship brings depth to whatever subject it touches, friends can deepen their relationships by witnessing the particular beauty possessed by each individual woman. Indeed, no woman, when seen through the Goddess's eyes, is without beauty, just as no child lacks beauty in its mother's sight. Especially in an era when feminine styles of physical beauty have become reduced to the shape of nineteen-year-old stick-thin models, women can celebrate one another's unique shapes, sizes, hairstyles, and approaches to adornment—or lack of it. When through meditation and prayer we are able to train our perspective to see beyond the physical and into the nonmaterial, we can see the beauty of our friends' souls shining through their faces—we glimpse what Pir Vilayat has called their "divine countenance." Then we see our friend as the reflection of the handiwork of the Divine Artist.

The quality of beauty can inspire two soul friends as they pursue their creative work, acting as muses as they toil to create works of art. I have greatly appreciated, for instance, the influence of several women editors on my writing. I recall sitting with Joan Connell, my editor at *Religion News Service*, for instance, as she carefully worked with me to craft each sentence and paragraph into a perfect newspaper column. I recall, too, magazine editors such as Anne Simpkinson at *Common Boundary* and Stephanie von Hirschberg at *New Woman,* as we excitedly planned and executed feature articles on such esoteric topics as dreams and spirituality. Last, sensitizing our souls to beauty, friends on the spiritual path can help one another see the beauty in the world around them—in their friends' children, in one another's husbands and lovers, and in one another's social causes. For as soul sisters, women's real "beauty work" is to join together to bring about a more beautiful, just, fair, and pleasing world.

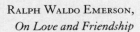

> *A friend may well be reckoned the
> masterpiece of nature.*
>
> RALPH WALDO EMERSON,
> *On Love and Friendship*

LOVE

When you have found a soul sister whose friendship you treasure, whether someone you have known all your life or someone you have just met, it is important to recognize that you have embarked upon a relationship as significant as marriage or parenthood. Though society rarely teaches us to envision it that way, friendship is among the greatest forms of love. It was written of the English social reformer Sir Thomas More, author of *Utopia,* for instance, that he seemed "born and destined" for friendship as "no one is more openhearted in making friends or more tenacious in keeping them. . . . In a word, whoever desires a perfect example of true friendship, will seek it nowhere to better purpose than in More." Thus, as the great men in history realized, friendship is an opportunity to develop breadth of character and depth of heart—a chance to learn to love graciously, generously, unreservedly, and open-heartedly.

Women's friendships, of course, are a wholly unique expression of love. They are about the feelings that exist between two people, yet they are more than that, as they provide a kind of vessel wherein women forge the truths of their feelings for the other people in their lives. When you discover a soul friend in another woman, you will have found a partner in love in more ways than one. You will have found an ally who will help you figure out the meaning and significance of your relationships with your parents, your husband, either lover or lesbian lover, siblings, and children. You will have found someone who will help you discern how to handle these other relationships—whether to get angry, nurture them, argue with them, or patiently understand them.

What is a friend? A single soul dwelling in two bodies.

Aristotle, from
*Diogene Laertius: Lives of
Eminent Philosophers*

*What though youth gave love and roses,
Age still leaves us friends and wine.*

Thomas More,
"Spring and Autumn"

I think of women's kinships as pottery kilns, where two together shape the rough clay of emotion into humankind's most valuable and prized vessels: human community. As cooking vessels are regarded as one of civilizations greatest inventions, designed by women to cook food to feed loved ones, so women's friendships are, too, vessels of love that sustain and nurture the soul lives of those around them. Yet in the process of creating and sustaining relationships with others, a remarkably rare and different kind of love grows up between two soul sisters. A phrase women use repeatedly to describe their friendships is "permission-giving"—women friends, in other words, often enjoy a kind of blank slate of acceptance, nonjudgmental attitudes and tolerance with their women friends that might never be accepted by any other person with whom they are involved. Women speak the truths of their souls to one another in ways that might break other relationships. Thus, it is women, Carolyn Heilbrun wrote in her essay on friendship, "who have long understood and embodied the one quality essential to friendship: intimacy, the openness of the loving gesture."

This kind of intimacy, however, cannot bloom without implicit trust. Thus, if you have found a woman with whom you wish to share the secrets of your heart, it is important that you hear her confessions in a sacred way, and that, likewise, she hears yours in equal confidence. The question of gossip often arises with women friends: we have all been guilty, at one time or another, of passing on the secret of a friend when we were told "not to tell *anyone*." As I have grown older, I have come to understand that it isn't so much a matter of whether a friend breaks a trust, but with whom they share my secret. If my friend tells my secret to someone who bears me ill will or doesn't like me, then that is a betrayal. But if she shares my secret with another woman who has my best interest at heart, and if she shares through a desire to better understand me as a friend, then, I think, that is a broken confidence that can be understood and forgiven.

MAGIC

Magic is the life spirit of every soul-sister friendship. For if by magic, we mean the presence of the invisible and the unseen, the enchantment of the spirit worlds that interweave and interpenetrate the daily world we inhabit, then magic is the key that frees the genie of the soul trapped in material existence. Soul sisters bring magic into their lives through participating in rituals together; like a jazz riff, they play off one another's creative spirituality, making up dances, prayers, blessings, and giving one another talismans and holy keepsakes.

Indeed, magic is the medium through which we keep the soul alive and happy within us. Soul sisters I have known have been adepts at magic. Through the magic carpet of their imagination, they enter into alternative realities together. Musing and meditating, contemplating and reflecting, they openly communicate with angels, spirit guides, dream teachers, and otherworldly beings, sharing their past life encounters and mystical experiences with their closest friends. Soul sisters meet the gods and goddesses in their lives and one another, tracing the lineaments of myth in the seemingly ordinary occurrences of their everyday lives. Indeed, nothing comes close to an evening spent spellbound by the stories of women's inner lives.

So if you have found a soul sister, remember that magic is a key component to your friendship. Dare to share with her your innermost spiritual experiences.

Without friends no one would choose to live, though he had all other goods.

ARISTOTLE, *Metaphysics*

Allow her to see into your soul, and to glimpse the visions you have seen. If you have dreamed of her, then tell her your dream. If you have had an insight or an intuition regarding her, share that, too. And, in turn, be a witness to your friends' soul searchings in invisible worlds. In this way we fulfill the religious impulse to move beyond surface appearances and to participate in the *real* story that lies hidden from sight—only waiting to become manifest through the medium of friendship.

PRAYER FOR THE GROWTH OF FRIENDSHIP

By Bishop Jane Holmes Dixon

> *"Most gracious God whom we know in many ways and by many names, we give you thanks for the privilege of being in relationships. For we believe that you have created us just for that. As the great poet James Johnson wrote, you created us because you were lonely, and you brought us into being to be in relationship with you and with one another. We thank you for the relationships you have given us and for those that are to come. We do this knowing that our relationships are based on you, and because you love us in all our frailty, knowing that we disappoint you as well as bring you great joy. You never turn your backs on us. Help that to be the standard for each of us in our friendships—that we never turn our backs on one another. That we strive with everything that is in us to be loving, generous, and kind. And let us laugh together! We thank thee for many gifts and ask for these things in your holy name." Amen.*

SUGGESTED READING

Being Bodies: Buddhist Women on the Paradox of Enlightenment, edited by Lenore Friedman and Susan Moon (Shambhala, 1997)

A Circle of Stones: Woman's Journey to Herself by Judith Duerk (LuraMedia, 1989)

The Feminine Face of God by Sherry Ruth Anderson and Patricia Hopkins (Bantam Books, 1991)

Four Centuries of Jewish Women's Spirituality by Ellen Umansky and Dianne Ashton (Beacon Press, 1992)

Girlfriends for Life: Friendships Worth Keeping Forever by Carmen Renee Berry and Tamara Traeder (White Canyon Press, 1999)

Girlfriends: Invisible Bonds, Enduring Ties by Carmen Renee Berry and Tamara Traeder (White Canyon Press, 1995)

A God Who Looks Like Me: Discovering a Woman-Affirming Spirituality by
Patricia Lynn Reilly (Ballantine Books, 1995)

*The Healing Wisdom of Africa: Finding Life Purpose Through Nature, Ritual,
and Community* by Malidome Patrice Some, L. M. Some (Tarcher/Put-
nam, 1999)

*Living in the Lap of the Goddess: The Feminist Spirituality Movement in Amer-
ica* by Cynthia Eller (Beacon Press, 1994)

Psyche's Sisters: Re-imagining the Meaning of Sisterhood by Christine Downing (Continuum, 1990)

The Sacred Hoop: Recovering the Feminine in American Indian Traditions by
Paula Gunn Allen (Beacon Press, 1986)

When the Drummers Were Women: A Spiritual History of Rhythm by Layne
Redmond (Three Rivers Press, 1997)

A Woman's Journey to God: Finding the Feminine Path by Joan Borysenko
(Riverhead Books, 1999)

Women's Bodies, Women's Wisdom by Christiane Northrup, M.D. (Bantam
Books, 2001)

*Women Who Run with the Wolves: Myths and Stories of the Wild Woman
Archetype* by Clarissa Pinkola Estés (Ballantine Books, 1992)

SUGGESTED MUSIC LIST

Ancient Mother, On Wings of Song and Robbie Gass, audio CD

"Bowl of Soul" by Circle of Soul, *Circle Songs*, audio CD

Devi by Chloe Goodchild, audio CD

Gifted, Women of the World by Various Artists, audio CD

Goddess Chant by Shawna Carol

Portrait of the Goddess by Celeste Alayne, audio CD

Songs of Sanctuary by Adiemus, audio CD

Voice of the Feminine Spirit by Cecilia, audio CD

Women's Yoga Chants by Various Artists, audio CD

Womyn with Wings & Womyn in Circle by Carien Wijnen & Friends,
accapella Goddess and Circle chants, audio CD

EPILOGUE

Reflections on the Ultimate Quality of Peace

AT THE FOOT OF CAPITOL HILL IN WASHINGTON, D.C., A TRIO OF sculpted goddesses called the Peace Monument poignantly conveys the age-old grief caused by war. Clio, the Greek muse of history, stands solemnly, her head bowed; huddled beside her is the allegorical figure of America, her hand over her face, weeping bitterly on Clio's shoulder. On the eastern side of the Peace Monument stands another woman. Though part of her right arm is missing, it is said that she once held aloft the olive branch of peace.

The feminine face of the Peace Monument is a woman's story set in stone. For just as these goddesses capture humankind's sorrow over war, so, too, have many women since September 11, 2001 wrestled within themselves about peace and war. Joining a chain of women stretching far back in time, they have asked, as they have asked for centuries, why humankind end-lessly repeats the tragic cycle of violence and retribution. Once again, they have mourned lives needlessly sacrificed to bitter political and religious rivalries. And once again, much as their soul sisters before them have done in the past, women—each in their own unique way, whether as healers or teachers, activists or artists—have taken up the time-honored quest for peace. For if the life we are living is a

> *The term Satyagraha was coined by me. . . .*
> *Its root meaning is "holding on to truth,"*
> *hence "force of righteousness." I have also*
> *called it love force or soul force. . . .*
>
> MAHATMA GANDHI,
> DEFENSE AGAINST CHARGE
> OF SEDITION, 1922

spiritual journey, then the road we travel as pilgrims leads inevitably toward the ultimate goal of peace.

Yet it seems, sadly, that we appreciate peace only in its absence. Millions, for instance, mourned the simple ordinariness that had marked the day before the September 11 tragedies. Overnight, peace became as fleeting as the ruby and emerald leaves that, in the days after, floated through the air to the ground. Indeed, because lasting peace in any form, inner or outer, is so rare, it could be said to be the divine orient of the human condition, the vision that draws us onward along our evolutionary path. It is the highest ideal of all noble causes, the great opus humanity is continually striving to complete. It is the grail of knights, the island in the pearl mist, the castle shimmering in the air. Knowledge of it lingers in our consciousness like perfumed incense from a long-ago age—each of us, it seems, is born with a memory of a paradise lost, a vanished era of innocent happiness we seek to reclaim in our own time. Because there is no abiding peace on earth, it is how we imagine heaven: a peaceable kingdom unmarred by anger, murder, revenge, or hatred, and where the lion lies down with the lamb.

> *Inner peace is found by facing life squarely, solving its problems, and delving as far beneath its surface as possible to discover its verities and realities. . . . Inner peace comes through working for the good of all. . . . No one can find inner peace except by working, not in a self-centered way, but for the whole human family.*
>
> PEACE PILGRIM

MEDITATION ON THE VISION OF PEACE

There can be no peace in the outer world unless greater numbers of people become inspired to make it a reality. Yet without an intimate experience of the serenity of peace, or without a vision of the radiant face of peace, we lack an ideal to beckon us forward in our quest. Because form follows thought, if we cannot imagine it, we cannot make peace on earth come true. For this reason, meditation, prayer, and visualization, while not the final step, are essential in beginning and maintaining the lifelong work of peace.

To meditate on peace, find a quiet place to spend a few moments in contemplation. To help focus your concentration, light a candle and incense; then, say a prayer, repeat a sacred phrase, or play a piece of sacred music. Imagine that, as you do this, the spirits of peace are drawing close to you. You may wish to repeat the Hebrew phrase "shalom" for peace, the Arabic word "ya salaam," or the Hindu phrase "shanti." Or, simply repeat the word "peace" silently on the inhalation and exhalation of your breath.

To go even more deeply into your meditation on peace, imagine a stormy lake with ruffled waves. Then, imagine that the lake is beginning to calm. Slowly, the wind dies down, and the surface of the lake, like the surface of your heart and mind, becomes as clear as a lucid diamond. Even the sky above the lake is cloudless. The trees on the shore stand motionless. A holy presence permeates this scene; your soul drinks it in like a heavenly draught of nectar. The sun begins to dip in the sky, sinking lower and lower into the horizon, and the stillness of dusk deepens.

Then, as the sun sinks below the horizon, something magical transpires: The twilight air above the lake begins to shimmer with expectancy, as if invisible curtains are about to part. Suddenly, a visionary landscape appears above the lake, hovering in the air. As your heart thrills at the sight, you recognize it as a place that you have glimpsed during a few rare and fleeting moments: it is Avalon, Camelot, Shangri-la, the heavenly city of Jerusalem—that mystical heaven where all creatures, human and animal, coexist in loving harmony. Music fills the air and beauty is everywhere—in the faces of the people, in the shape of the buildings, and in the absence of malice or envy. Angels and other evolved beings walk the streets, mingling in joyful companionship with their fellow humans. You see the Buddha, Christ, Mary, St. Francis, St. Claire, and others. Many are busy making art, singing, writing, or playing. Transported, you, too, participate in the life of this luminous city of peace; a visiting pilgrim, your soul drinks from the sacred well of serenity.

Ever so gently, the vision begins to fade from sight. The wind picks up, rustling the branches of the trees, whipping up the surface of the lake. The darkness of night falls, drawing a veil across the golden abode of peace. Slowly, you return to your life as it was. Still, you are different. Within your heart is a small and precious seed, a star of peace and light that you will follow for the rest of your life—a vision of the heaven that might one day become a reality on earth.

So all-encompassing is the quality of peace that it could be said to be the very definition of what is sacred. The word itself emanates a feeling we equate with the ideals upheld by religion and spirituality. "Religion is the vision of something which stands beyond . . . the passing flux of immediate things"; wrote the philosopher Alfred North Whitehead, ". . . something whose possession is the final good, and yet is beyond all reach; something which is the ultimate ideal, and the hopeless quest."[1]

Indeed, no more "ultimate ideal" or "hopeless quest" exists than peace. The peace that surpasses the fray of everyday life is embodied in the beings of the great mystics, saints, and prophets: to imagine oneself in the presence of Jesus, Buddha, Mary, Mohammed, Moses, or Kuan Yin, for instance, is to feel immersed within a timeless space of profound transcendence. Likewise, the glow of an angel, an emerald forest glen, the starry cosmos, or the sacred chants of monks and nuns all convey a message to a world mired in suffering that despite the impossibility of peace, it yet exists, if only we will take up the search.

For like the grit of sand in the oyster shell that transforms into a pearl, it is the painful divisiveness and heartfelt suffering of everyday life that propels the spiritual search. Like the young Gautama Buddha, whose shock at discovering illness, old age, and death caused him to embark upon a journey for that which is eternal, the turbulence of life itself is the spur that cultivates desire for both inner and outer peace. I vividly remember the time when, as a young girl struggling to keep my sanity in a family riven by my father's alchoholism, I first discovered the ageless wisdom in the contemplative writings of the Christian mystic Thomas Merton, *The Tibetan Book of the Dead*, and the Sufi poets. These discoveries were like a raft that served to keep me afloat during the emotional storms of my youth, transporting my soul toward safe harbor on the inner shores of consciousness.

For others as for myself, the yearning for just a drop of miraculous balm to quiet the troubled waters of daily life is universal. Loved ones hope to heal the bitter quarrels that sunder them from one another. Busy people maneuver to snatch a moment of calm. Those who are poor long for the peace of a full stomach and physical security. Individuals in war-torn countries pray they will live out their lives. Thus, we walk in the footsteps of the great mystics because, ultimately, we seek the peace their messages promise. Torn apart from within by warring emotions, or traumatized by the violence that scars everyday life, practitioners seek to build an interior refuge wherein they can find a measure of tranquillity. God is love, beauty, and truth, say the great teachers, but beyond that, God is sublime peace, too. In this sense, peace is the ultimate quality, containing within it all other qualities as the color white contains within it the colors of the spectrum.

Despite the powerful example set by spiritual figures and the abundance of religious teachings accumulated over the centuries, peace remains as unattainable

---

In this world, children will not be taught epics about men who are honored for being violent or fairy tales about children who are lost in frightful woods where women are malevolent witches. They will be taught new myths, epics, and stories in which human beings are good; men are peaceful; and the power of creativity and love—symbolized by the sacred Chalice, the holy vessel of life—is the governing principle.

FROM THE CONCLUSION
OF *The Chalice and the
Blade* BY RIANE EISLER

All things pertaining to spiritual progress in life depend upon peace.

HAZRAT INAYAT KHAN

and profoundly desirable as ever. I have experienced sublime peaks of transcendent calm in meditations. Yet such experiences have not prevented me from the unease and uncertainty of life. As the Sufi teacher Pir Vilayat Inayat Khan has frequently said, it is relatively easy for a great master to maintain his high state of consciousness while on retreat or in a cave—but far harder to do so juggling the everyday demands of family and work. Humankind, it seems, has much to learn about the arts of peacemaking. Many longtime religious practitioners and meditators who have experienced the blissful depths of inner peace, for instance, have found it difficult if not impossible to translate that into their outer lives. Likewise, political activists have stumbled in their efforts to negotiate peaceful conditions, blocked by their inner psychological shadows of intolerance and hatred.

But these very inconsistencies reveal an important clue in the great work of peace: peace cannot only be found inwardly, or fought for outwardly—it is a disciplined struggle that must continually be engaged on several fronts. Psychologically, we each must do battle with the inner "shadow" that would subvert our growth; while the spiritual path requires warriorlike discipline. Outwardly, we are called upon to fight the wrongs of injustice and oppression. Thus, like all the other qualities, peace includes within it its own opposite—tension, change, and dissatisfaction. Acceptance of that fact of life is what begins the path of peacework. To accept that conflict is a natural part of life—and to find enlightened ways to deal with that—is what some say prevents the outbreak of petty arguments, war, or violence. For while we may all be one in the spirit, we exist in a dimension of reality that teems with passionately fractious differences. So peace is not something that is singular and static. Rather, it is a work in progress that takes place in the give-and-take dialogue between the different parts of oneself, between oneself and another, between rivals, and among nations, faiths, and ethnicities. Peace in action is exemplified in the lives of the legendary nonviolent peacemakers. Jesus, Mahatma Gandhi, Martin Luther King, and Nelson Mandela all are extraordinary examples of men who put truth to work in the name of peace and justice—not from the distance of a cave, but directly in the heart of everyday life. The impact of inner peace brought to bear on conditions in the outer world in a nonviolent but engaged fashion is what Gandhi called "satyagraha," or "soul force."

Although the bright stars of the peace movement have mostly been men, it is largely men who have started and fought wars, while women have stood helplessly alongside history's bloody battlefields. Like Penelope spinning at her wheel patiently

Her ways are ways of pleasantness, and all her paths are peace.

PROVERBS 3:17

awaiting the return of her husband Odysseus from the Trojan War, women have been the ones to bear the brunt of emotional damage caused by the wounds of war. "I do not see my life as separate from history," writes Susan Griffin in *A Chorus of Stones*. "In my mind my family secrets mingle with the secrets of statesmen and bombers. Nor is my life divided from the lives of others. I, who am a woman, have my father's face. And he, I suspect, had his mother's face."

The feminine experience of enduring centuries of waiting, healing, nurturing, and sustaining family and community ties has resulted in what many thinkers have come to realize is a valuable contribution to the tasks of sustaining peace.

> *Peace is not a knowledge; peace is not a power, peace is not a happiness; yet peace is all these. Besides, peace is productive of happiness, peace inspires one with knowledge of the seen and unseen, and in peace is to be found the Divine Presence.*
>
> HAZRAT INAYAT KHAN

Women's collective experience overseeing squabbling children, negotiating family differences, nursing physical and emotional wounds, and tending friendships has resulted in a stockpile of wisdom that can be applied on a large world scale. "For generations," remarked U.N. Secretary-General Kofi Annan in October 2000 to the Security Council, "women have served as peace educators, both in their families and in their societies. They have proved instrumental in building bridges rather than walls."

The notion of women as peacemakers is not just political correctness run amok, write Swanee Hunt and Cristina Posa in their article "Women Waging Peace," in the May/June 2001 issue of *Foreign Policy*. Rather, they write, "Social science research supports the stereotype of women as generally more collaborative than men and thus more inclined toward consensus and compromise." Pointing out that women are at the center of nongovernmental organizations (NGOs) and popular grassroots movements, Hunt and Posa argue that international peace negotiators should include more women in their ranks. "While most men come to the negotiating table directly from the war room and battlefield, women usually arrive straight out of civil activism and—take a deep breath—family care." A popular E-mail sent to me by almost every woman I know circulating after the attacks humorously makes the same point: "Uniting all the warring tribes of Afghanistan in a new government? Oh, please . . . we've planned the seating arrangements for in-laws and extended families at Thanksgiving dinners for years . . . we understand tribal warfare."

START A GRASSROOTS WOMEN'S CIRCLE OF PEACE

As friendship is a template of peace in action, women who are interested in finding ways to bring peace into the world can strengthen their cause by starting a women's circle of peace. They can practice meditations aimed at deepening peace within and visualizing peace in the world without. They can study the lives of women peacemakers. A peace circle is a wonderful place for women to support one another in the time-honored tasks of everyday diplomacy: raising children, and mediating disputes and conflicts in the family and workplace. Women can join the personal with the political by choosing a social cause to support, whether working for the rights of women worldwide, drawing attention to the plight of refugees, or advocating for the homeless. Participants can balance spiritual work with political action by writing letters, circulating petitions, or making a formal group visit to local representatives.

And finally, let the power of music strengthen the circle's mission. Ysaye Barnwell, who has been a vocalist with the African-American female a capella quintet Sweet Honey in the Rock, has taught workshops at Omega Institute throughout the United States and in several other countries integrating creative arts with community and social activism. Music, she says, is a beautiful metaphor for how we live our lives in relationship to others and for the values upon which we build community.

Drawing on the African tradition in which music is a cooperative activity, Ysaye teaches musical techniques that help cultivate listening. For example, she leads participants in polyrhythmic exercises in order to show how different rhythms fit together to make something larger—a musical expression of the way community, too, has the potential to be polyrhythmic, noncompetitive, and cooperative. Through such exercises, she says, "People begin to realize that in order to be in a relationship, they must constantly make minute modifications in how they respond to a person, rhythm, or organization. Music, like relationship, is figuring out the give and take—like a musical call and response."

In her workshops, Ysaye also teaches participants about the importance of "movement songs" in building community. The Civil Rights movement of the sixties, for instance, says Ysaye, "was rooted in music that was used to galvanize people at mass meetings. A huge body of music was created that was used during marches and demonstrations." Songs such as "Eyes on the Prize," and "We Shall Overcome," says Ysaye, who grew up in the black church in New York, were derived from spirituals originally created by slaves who sang about freedom.

> *Peace is not an absence of war, it is a virtue, a state of mind, a disposition for benevolence, confidence, justice.*
>
> BENEDICT SPINOZA,
> THEOLOGICAL-POLITICAL
> TREATISE

As more women tell their stories and take their place on the stage of history, a growing number are emerging as peace heroines in their own right: There is Burmese pro-democracy movement leader Aung San Suu Kyi; the Mothers of the Plaza de Mayo, the mothers of the disappeared during Argentina's "dirty war"; Madame Irene Laure, a fighter in the French resistance who initiated reconciliation with the Germans after World War II; and American Civil Rights leader Rosa Parks, among others. And, of course, there are the ordinary stories of women who day after day weave the thread of peace into the fabric of daily life.

Like my friend Susan Roberts, a therapist and school counselor, they are practicing peacemaking in the public sphere. Like so many these days, Susan had felt a need to do something to enhance the cause of peace—especially in a city that had been a terrorist target. In addition to helping to organize a vigil and counselling students, she invited another longtime friend of mine, the storyteller and dancer Zuleikha, to perform at an international school in Washington, D.C., where she worked. As I sat among the students that afternoon, I revelled in the cultural differences of the students who surrounded me, as well as in their playful, youthful spirit. As Zuleikha, exotically dressed in an Indian costume with bells on her ankles, danced stories and myths taken from the world's treasure chest of myths and traditions, I felt a spirit of universality arise out of the rich mosaic of that scene. Here was what the goddess movement upheld as the pluralism and inclusivity of humankind—a joyous and dynamic event that revealed the variety innate within the human condition.

In Zuleikha's final piece, she donned a bell-shaped white robe and whirled soundlessly like the dervishes of the ancient Sufi tradition. Watching her whirl as I simultaneously watched my friend "Miss Roberts" calm the middle-school students from acting out, I sensed the presence of something larger. Peace in the balanced, energetic movements of a dancer. Peace in the kids who misbehaved and the teacher who lovingly corrected them. There was tension in the room, but there was also a subtle harmonizing of parts, a coming together of fragments into a magical whole—the hidden pattern of peace taking shape, a hint of what might one day come to pass in humankind's next stage of evolutionary unfoldment.

Following her performance, Zuleikha and I decided to visit Arlington National Cemetery. Wandering along the paths set among the tombstones that marked the graves of soldiers who fought in wars, we visited the memorial to women who had fought as soldiers. There we happened upon a woman setting up a table for a party. She was preparing to celebrate her retirement from more than

> *A musician must make music, an artist must paint, a poet must write, if he is to be ultimately at peace with himself. What a man can be, he must be.*
>
>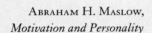
>
> ABRAHAM H. MASLOW,
> *Motivation and Personality*

twenty years of service in the U.S. Army, she told us proudly. I felt proud of that woman's military success, too, despite my own inclination toward nonviolence. As my friend and peace educator Corinne McLaughlin reminded me, we would not even be having a discussion on peace if it were not for those who fought and died during World War II. "Sometimes the sacrifice of life is necessary in order to prevent the enslavement of the human spirit," she said. "The Nazis had to be stopped and that required tremendous sacrifice and courage." Yet another activist friend, Ruth Berlin, pointed out that the warrior is "as necessary as the compassionate heart. For without the warrior we could be overtaken by evil." But balance, too, is necessary, said Ruth, as "the masculine hero in both sexes offers us the ability to strategize, while the feminine provides us with the empathy necessary to understand the other's experience and begin the process of negotiation."

> *To everything there is a season, and a time to every purpose under the heaven. . . . A time to love, and a time to hate; a time of war, and a time of peace.*
>
> ECCLESIASTES 3:1–8

The work of attaining peace, it seems, is a constantly evolving mystery. Perhaps what matters most is intention—that whatever action taken in the name of peace and justice be for those purposes and no other. The following insights of women who have worked for peace, both in the past and in the present, can be our guides. Their experiences both on the inner frontiers of consciousness and in the outer world of politics and community can inspire other women who wish to become courageous peacemakers in the world.

Modern-Day
✿
Women Peacemakers

It has been said that God is a verb. But as the following impassioned women show, peace, too, is a verb. The experience of my good friend Corinne McLaughlin—an activist who was on the board of the Institute for Multitrack Diplomacy and who has helped craft legislation for a proposed U.S. Department of Peace—on the morning of September 11, 2001, is emblematic of her life work bringing spiritual principles to bear on politics.

As coauthor with her husband, Gordon Davidson, of *Spiritual Politics* (Ballantine Books, 1994), and as codirector of the Center for Visionary Leadership in Washington, D.C., Corinne found herself that day in a cab on the way to the United Nations to participate in the International Day of Peace. It was to be the opening day of the U.N. General Assembly. As they drove from their hotel through the streets, they began hearing news on the radio of the first attack on the World Trade Center. Just as they were about to disembark at the UN, the radio announced the second attack. Hurrying inside, they rushed to the meditation garden where Secretary-General Kofi Annan was to ring the peace bell, symbolically ringing in the General Assembly. But Annan never arrived; gathering together with a group of spiritually oriented people, said Corinne, they decided to do a "meditative circumambulation of the peace garden, visualizing light and protection for the U.N. and asking for the highest good." Following their meditation, they were soon evacuated from the building. Returning to a friend's hotel room, they decided that the best thing they could contribute was to meditate on peace.

"I aligned with my soul and with the masters and saints. The message that I got was that it was not time yet to ring the peace bell—we cannot ring a bell of peace until there is unity and justice in the world," recalls Corinne. "The symbolism was so powerful, but I also felt that, as horrible as this was, it might bring us together. Despite the surrounding chaos, I emerged from my meditation with a feeling of hope." At the same time, says Corinne, she realized "how personally I felt the attack as an American, and that we needed to do some deep national soul searching." Action followed Corinne's insight. Following her return to Washington, D.C., Corinne and her husband, Gordon, invited participants to gather with them at their center to pray and meditate, focusing on the highest good as the outcome of the tragedy. In addition, they facilitated citizen dialogues at their center, where people could air their fears and concerns, as well as explore what the event meant for Americans and the world. Corinne's skills in conflict resolution helped her contain the wide difference of opinions that were aired during those meetings.

> *Ah! When shall all men's good be each man's rule, and universal peace lie like a shaft of light across the land . . . ?*
>
> ALFRED LORD TENNYSON,
> *The Golden Year*

Corinne's quest to integrate spiritual principles into politics had its origins during her youth when, inspired by her traditional Christian upbringing, she became responsive to the suffering in the world, from "the Vietnam war to racism, poverty and the environment," she says. During the sixties, she began studying Eastern perspectives, visiting the different spiritual teachers available on the West coast during that time. It was while living at Findhorn, a spiritual community in Scotland, that Corinne found her path, the "ageless wisdom of East and West, the golden thread that connects the inner teachings of all the world religions." The Findhorn community's emphasis on finding God within helped her establish a daily meditation that she has now practiced for more than thirty years.

Yet unlike many spiritual seekers during that time, it became increasingly important to Corinne to connect meditative states of inner peace with working for peace in the outer world. "You can't be effective spiritually until you find a path of service," she says. Yet, she says, inner concentration does have a powerful effect on the material world. "Energy follows thought. Thus our own thoughts affect the world— something that even scientists are beginning to prove." At the same time, says Corinne, many seekers have fooled themselves into thinking that they can't be active in the political arena if they feel any anger or conflict within themselves. But waiting for perfection is not the answer as, she says, "we avoid responsibility by endless work on ourselves. Often this is another form of self-centeredness, or even fear of taking a stand." Indeed, says Corinne, she has often noticed that indignation often motivates people to have courage and take action in redressing wrongs. The important key in working with anger, however, she says, is to harness its energy and transform it into positive action. Likewise, it is important not to personalize one's anger through hating the enemy but to try instead to deepen one's understanding as, she explains, "The spiritual work is to transform the dehumanizing of the enemy."

Another like-minded woman pioneer in the quest for peace is Angel Kyodo Williams, author of *Being Black: Zen and the Art of Living With Fearlessness and Grace.* An African-American priest in the Soto Zen and Peacemaker orders, Angel is the founder of the urban-PEACE organization in New York City, which seeks to bring spiritually informed peace to urban environments. Angel's commitment to diversity began in her youth, when, growing up in a multicultural neighborhood in Queens, her best friends were Moroccan and Cuban. Now thirty-two, Angel took up the study of Buddhism at the young age of twenty-one, when, following the death of her grandfather, she learned meditation at the San Francisco Zen Center. When she realized that even American Buddhist practitioners—mostly white and middle class—couldn't see "beyond her color," she became launched on the unusual path as both Buddhist activist and peacemaker bridging differences and challenging prejudices.

"What's available in Buddhist and spiritual practice is desperately needed by mainstream culture," says Williams, who lives in Brooklyn, New York. "You have to have mechanisms to bring teachings to people wherever they are." Like the concept of the pure-white lotus flower that grows out of the mud, says Williams, "the

Lord, make me an instrument of Your peace. Where there is hatred let me sow love; where there is injury, pardon; where there is doubt, faith; where there is despair, hope; where there is darkness, light; and where there is sadness, joy. O divine Master, grant that I may not so much seek to be consoled as to console; to be understood as to understand; to be loved as to love. For it is in giving that we receive; it is in pardoning that we are pardoned; and it is in dying that we are born to eternal life.

PRAYER OF ST.
FRANCIS OF ASSISI

best environment in which we can challenge ourselves to make peace is in an urban environment because it is so diverse and chaotic." Urban environments present an unprecedented opportunity to see if spirituality really works, says Williams with passionate conviction, as it's a challenge "to talk about peace and compassion with someone who looks utterly alien to you."

Angel Kyodo Williams's activist passion belies stereotypical images of Buddhist calm and repose. Indeed, she is outspoken about shattering spiritual expectations that stand in the way of preventing genuine peace work. Explaining her "different take" on peacemaking, she tells the story of her web designer, who first designed the site in the color blue. "He said it was because when he thought of peace he thought of blue and calm. I disagreed, explaining to him that the Zen-like juxtaposition of words—urban and peace—represents a force that is hot and aggressive." To Williams, the "old laidback image of peace just doesn't work anymore. Peace is dynamic—the environment is constantly changing, and if the notion of peace doesn't change with the environment then it's useless. I find incredible value in sesshins—but the real sesshin is here, in the city, because this is where we have to rub up against each other. You're just not doing the work if all you're doing is sitting on your cushion."

> *Blessed are the peacemakers, for they shall be called the children of God.*
>
> Mathew 5:3–11

> *Peacemaker: One who makes or brings about peace; one who reconciles opponents.*
>
> From the *Shorter Oxford English Dictionary*

As for the connection between inner and outer peace, Angel, like Corinne, advises that people shouldn't wait to find perfect harmony within themselves before taking action. "It's all now. You're living in chaos and your life is hell and you don't have a clue about what you're doing. But your intention is to make peace and to do something. I'd much rather have an unenlightened person busting their ass than someone with all their practice and knowledge clinging to their state and doing nothing. Spiritual practice has to be engaged."

As both Corinne and Angel make clear, the concept of balance—balance between inner and outer, between spiritual idealism and the limitations of the real world—is pivotal in twenty-first-century peacemaking. Indeed, says clinical and political psychologist Diane Perlman, a longtime colleague who has studied the psychological dimension of gender politics and nuclearism, it has often struck her that almost all social ills are rooted in imbalance. Imagine, for instance, she says, the image of the Chinese yin yang symbol drawn with the white half of the circle predominating over the dark, and without the contrasting "dots"—a vivid picture of extreme lack of balance. Citing the work of Riane Eisler in *The Chalice and the*

Blade, Diane points to those "partnership" societies who have achieved a gender balance both between men and women in the public sphere, as well as between masculine and feminine energies, as more peaceful.

In the eyes of many, the peace movement has lacked balance, seeming to tilt too far in the direction of "do nothing" passivity without providing a compelling alternative. Coining a new phrase, "metaforce," Diane describes the balanced actions of a contemporary peacemaker as combining bloodless forms of force—educational, political, psychological, economic, spiritual, and moral— toward achieving the aim of peace. "It combines the force of the more active and heroic dimension with the loving, nonviolent spirit of eros or connectedness," she says, "transcending the dualities of the politics of left and right, the male and female gender."

Balance within; balance without: As more women take their seat at the negotiating table and occupy positions of political influence alongside men, perhaps the gender imbalance in the world will be righted and the feminine qualities of tolerance, forgiveness, and inclusion will be rightfully placed alongside the masculine qualities of aggression, warriorship, and physical bravery. Similarly, as individuals learn the difficult art of balancing inner spiritual knowledge with compassionate action in the world, perhaps the world will one day know peace—the ultimate ideal of humanity.

> *If we take one side, we cannot fulfill our task of reconciliation in order to bring about peace.*
>
> THICH NHAT HANH,
> *On Being Peace*

RECOMMENDED READING

All Her Paths Are Peace: Women Pioneers in Peacemaking by Michael Henderson, foreword by the Dalai Lama (Kumarian Press, 1994)

The Art of War by Sun Tzu, translation by Thomas Cleary (Shambhala Books, 1988)

Being Peace by Thich Nhat Hanh (Parallax Press, 1987)

The Chalice and the Blade by Riane Eisler (Harper & Row, 1987)

A Chorus of Stones: The Private Life of War by Susan Griffin (Anchor Books, 1992)

Conscious Evolution: Awakening the Power of Our Social Potential by Barbara Marx Hubbard (New World Library, 1998)

A Desperate Passion: An Autobiography by Helen Caldicott (W.W. Norton & Company, 1996)

Faith in the Valley: Lessons for Women on the Journey Toward Peace by Iyanla Vanzant (Simon & Schuster, 1996)

A Force More Powerful: A Century of Nonviolent Conflict by Peter Ackerman
and Jack Duvall (St. Martin's Press, 2000)

The Forgiveness Factor: Stories of Hope in a World of Conflict by Michael
Henderson (Grosvenor Books, 1996)

Peace Pilgrim: Her Life and Work in Her Own Words, compiled by the friends
of Peace Pilgrim (An Ocean Tree Book, 1983)

*A Peace Reader: Essential Readings on War, Justice, Non-violence, and World
Order,* Revised Edition, edited by Joseph Fahey and Richard Armstrong
(Paulist Press, 1992)

Spiritual Politics: Changing the World from the Inside Out by Corinne
McLaughlin and Gordon Davidson (Ballantine Books, 1994)

Women at the Peace Table: Making a Difference, United Nations Development Fund for Women (New York UNIFEM, 2000)

Being Black: Zen and the Art of Living with Fearlessness and Grace by Angel
Kyodo Williams (Viking, 2000)

SUGGESTED MUSIC

Meditations on Inner Peace

Ancient Voices by Michael Vetter, audio CD

Angeli, sung by Ensemble P.A.N.

Buddhist Chants & Peace Music by Jim Long Uem and Chinese Buddhist
Chanting Group

Hearing Solar Winds by David Hykes and the Harmonic Choir, audio CD

Inner Vistas, Tibetan bowls, audio CD

Sacred Treasures, all volumes, a collection of Russian Choral masterpieces
including Rachmaninoff's and Tchaikovsky's sacred works, audio CDs

Sea Peace by Georgia Kelly, audio CD

Working for Peace in the World

"City Called Heaven" by Jessye Norman, from *Amazing Grace*, audio CD

"Dream in an Open Place" by Vangelis, *Voices*, audio CD

Freedom Song, Sweet Honey in the Rock, audio CD

"Imagine" written by John Lennon, performed by The Beatles

Sacred Ground, Sweet Honey in the Rock, audio CD

Still on the Journey, Sweet Honey in the Rock, audio CD

*Voices of the Civil Rights Movement: Black American Freedom Songs
1960–1966,* audio CDs

Soul Sister Circles

WITHIN THE LAST DECADE, A NEW FORM OF NONHIERARCHICAL, ECUMENICAL spiritual community has arisen: sacred circles. Prayer circles, healing circles, wisdom circles, social change circles, dream circles, storytelling circles, and especially women's circles have flourished, nurtured by books and conferences centered on this grassroots phenomenon. In a world characterized by rapid change and uncertainty, a sacred circle can provide a much-needed anchor of calm and repose. Indeed, write the authors of *Wisdom Circles*, our predominant feeling of "lack of community" may actually stem from "too many commitments too shallowly made." Thus a sacred circle can be a place for the soul to expand and breathe freely.

Soul sisters, of course, are a kind of contemplative kinship based on equality, respect, and a love of the spiritual quest that lends itself naturally to a women's circle. Those women who would like to cultivate female friendships with greater depth and commitment to social transformation may find many of the concepts in this book a useful starting point for beginning a regular soul-sister circle. Each one of the chapters in this book provides a road map of inner and outer exploration. Women could initiate a soul-sister circle by beginning with the book's introduction and studying the developing field of women's spirituality, the Divine Feminine, and the ancient traditions of the goddess. From there, the circle could go on to devote a period of time to the divine qualities that I have chosen to write about through the lens of feminist spirituality: courage, faith, beauty, love, magic, and peace. The books, music, and meditation listed in each chapter, as well as the stories of historical, mythological, and modern-day women, provide the material for dialogue, meditation, ritual, and ways to help improve the human condition. Drawing inspiration from the chapter on "The Way of the Soul Sister," circles can spend time as well consciously cultivating the time-honored art of women's friendships as an emotional "ecosystem" that nurtures women, their loved ones, and society.

Before beginning your own soul-sister group it may be helpful to study many of the current books on sacred circles for ideas on how to decide the circle's purpose, share coleadership, express intimate feelings, create rituals, and maintain a committed schedule. Because the very essence of a sacred circle is nonauthoritarian, however, remember to keep alive the spirit of spontaneity. I have participated in many women's meditations, circles, and spiritual gatherings over the years. The older I get, the more I find that I equally appreciate the simple tradition of hosting a group of women for a potluck dinner, then enjoying the rich conversation that invariably unfolds, wandering naturally over a wide range of topics from books, breast cancer, and politics to children, pets, men, makeup, exercise, and the environment.

In addition to the boxed tips, I offer here a list of books to get you started on your circle, as well as websites based on some of the women's organizations mentioned throughout this book. May the circle you create be like the first small circle cast by a pebble into the water—rippling outward into ever wider circles of care and community throughout the world.

Here are some tips that will help point the way to starting your own Soul Sister Circle.

1. Declare it in your being that you wish to form a circle—energy follows thought. Write a statement of intent, then share this in the form of an invitation with those you think may be interested. Let the feedback you receive be the inspiration that shapes the spirit of your circle.
2. Limit the number of members to six to keep things intimate. Consider your circle a sacred space where spiritual friendship may blossom.
3. Together, compose a basic ritual that will help to structure each circle. This may be as simple as lighting a candle, sharing silence, opening a dialogue, and then closing the circle. Or it may be as complex as designing rituals, exploring various spiritual practices, or journal writing.

4. The spirit of the circle is egalitarian and nonhierarchical. Understand that there is a facilitator, not a leader, whose responsibility can be rotated on a weekly basis. Give everyone an equal amount of time. Cultivate respect for the various religious, political, and philosophical perspectives each woman may bring to the circle.

5. Meet weekly. Maintain commitment to building the soul of the circle over time. At the same time, be flexible with regard to the stresses and demands placed on women by everyday life.

6. Remember that you are there to offer support, not therapy. Friendship is not about being an "expert" but about extending empathy, love, and respect to those companions who walk beside us along the spiritual journey.

SUGGESTED READING

Calling the Circle: The First and Future Culture by Christina Baldwin (Bantam Books, 1994)

The Millionth Circle: How to Change Ourselves and the World, The Essential Guide to Women's Circles by Jean Shinoda Bolen (Conari Press, 1999)

Sacred Circles: A Guide to Creating Your Own Women's Spirituality Group by Robin Deen Carnes and Sally Craig (HarperSanFrancisco, 1998)

Ritualizing Women: Patterns of Spirituality by Leslie Northrup (The Pilgrim Press, 1997)

Wisdom Circles: A Guide to Self-Discovery and Community Building in Small Groups by Charles Garfield, Cindy Spring, and Sedonia Cahill (Hyperion, 1998)

A Woman's Book of Rituals and Celebrations by Barbara Adinger (New World Library, 1992)

The Woman Source Catalog and Review: Tools for Connecting to the Community of Women, edited by Ilene Rosoff (Celestial Arts, 1995)

Women Circling the Earth: A Guide to Fostering Community, Healing, and Empowerment by Beverly Engel (Health Communications, Inc., 2000)

The Women's Retreat Book by Jennifer Louden (HarperSanFrancisco, 1997)

WEBSITES*

The Association for Women's Rights in Development, promoting the rights of women worldwide: www.awid.org

The Catherine Collective, supporting the values of the Divine Feminine: www.catherinecollective.com

The Center for Visionary Leadership, linking spiritual principles with politics: www.visionarylead.org

Femaid, helping women in poverty around the world: www.femaid.com

The Hunt Alternatives at the John F. Kennedy School of Government, recognizing the role of women in preventing violent conflict: www.womenwagingpeace.org

Ladyslipper, a catalog of women's music: www.ladyslipper.org

Mooncircles, offering rituals and wisdom based on the lunar cycles: www.mooncircles.com

Music for the Soul: www.wisdomschild.com

Sufi Order website: www.sufiorder.org

Urban Peace Center, promoting spiritual principles in urban environments: www.urbanpeace.org

The website for the women's organization working to reduce gun violence: www.millionmommarch.com

A website that provides links to other women's spirituality sites: www.voiceofwomen.com

Wisdom Circle Newsletter, providing information on sacred circles: www.wisdomcircle.org

Women for Women International, providing financial assistance and friendship to women in wartorn countries: www.womenforwomen.org

Women's International League for Peace and Freedom: www.peacewomen.org

Zuleikha's website: www.storydancer.com

*While the author has made every effort to provide accurate telephone numbers and Internet addresses at the time of publication, neither the publisher nor the author assumes any responsibility for errors, or for changes that occur after publication.

Notes

INTRODUCTION

1. Carol P. Christ, *Rebirth of the Goddess: Finding Meaning in Feminist Spirituality*, Routledge, 1997.
2. Ibid.
3. Gerda Lerner, *The Creation of Feminist Consciousness, from the Middle Ages to Eighteen-seventy*, Oxford University Press, 1993.
4. Christine Downing, *Psyche's Sisters: Reimagining the Meaning of Sisterhood*, Continuum, 1990.
5. Pir Vilayat Inayat Khan, *Awakening: A Sufi Experience*, Tarcher/Putnam, 1999.

CHAPTER ONE: THE FEMININE FACE OF COURAGE

1. Judith V. Jordan, "Courage in Connection: Conflict, Compassion, Creativity," *Work in Progress*, a publication series based on the work of the Stone Center for Developmental Services and Studies of Wellsley College, #45, 1990.
2. Isak Dinesen, *Out of Africa*, Vintage Books, 1985.
3. Isak Dinesen, "On Mottoes of My Life," an essay from *Daguerrotypes and Other Essays*, University of Chicago Press, 1979.
4. Gerda Lerner, *The Creation of Feminist Consciousness from the Middle Ages to Eighteen-seventy*, Oxford University Press, 1993.
5. Ibid.
6. Ibid.
7. Ibid.

8. Christine Lunardini, Ph.D., *What Every American Should Know About Women's History: 200 Events That Shaped Our Destiny*, Adams Media Corporation, 1997.

9. Jean Overton Fuller, *Noor-un-nisa Inayat Khan (Madeleine)*, East West Publications, 1971.

10. Ibid.

11. Ibid.

12. Judith V. Jordan, "Courage in Connection: Conflict, Compassion, Creativity," *Work in Progress*, a publication series based on the work of the Stone Center for Developmental Services and Studies of Wellsley College, #45, 1990.

13. Eleanor Roosevelt, *You Learn by Living: 11 Keys for a More Fulfilling Life* (John Knox, 1983)

CHAPTER TWO: THE FEMININE FACE OF FAITH

1. Carol Christ, *Rebirth of the Goddess: Finding Meaning in Feminist Spirituality*, Routledge, 1997.

2. Edward Whitmont, *Return of the Goddess*, Crossroads Publishing Co., 1992.

3. Mansur Johnson, editor, *Tales*, told by Hazrat Inayat Khan, Sufi Order Publications, 1980.

4. Margaret Smith, *Rabi'a the Mystic and Her Fellow Saints in Islam*, Cambridge University Press, 1928.

5. Ibid.

6. Annemarie Schimmel, *My Soul Is a Woman: The Feminine in Islam*, Continuum, 1997.

7. Margaret Smith, *Rabi'a the Mystic and Her Fellow Saints in Islam*, Cambridge University PressSwami Ghananda and Sir John Stewart-Wallace, 1928.

8. Ibid.

9. Swami Ghananda and Sir John Stewart-Wallace, editorial advisors, *Women Saints East and West*, Vedanta Press, 1955.

10. Annemarie Schimmel, *My Soul Is a Woman: The Feminine in Islam*, Continuum, 1997.

11. Margaret Smith, *Rabi'a the Mystic and Her Follow Saints in Islam*, Cambridge University Press, 1928.

12. Ibid.

13. Pauline Schmitt Pantel, editor, *A History of Women: From Ancient Goddesses to Christian Saints*, Harvard University Press, 1992.

14. C. G. Jung and Carl Kerenyi, *Essays on a Science of Mythology: The Myth of the Divine Child and the Mysteries of Eleusis*, Bollingen Series, Princeton, 1973.

CHAPTER THREE: THE FEMININE FACE OF BEAUTY

1. Apostolos N. Athanassakis, trans., "To Aphrodite," in *The Homeric Hymns*, Johns Hopkins University Press, 1976.

2. Ginette Paris, *Pagan Meditations: Aphrodite, Hestia, Artemis*, Spring Publications, 1986.

3. Anne Higonnet, "Women, Images, and Representation," *A History of Women: Toward a Cultural Identity in the Twentieth Century*, Harvard University Press, 1994.

4. *Larry King Live*, January 22, 2001.

5. *The Washington Post*, Feb. 2, 2001.

6. Pythia Peay, "An Interview with Marion Woodman," *The San Francisco Jung Institute Journal*, Volume Eleven, Number One, 1992.

7. Simone Weil, *Waiting for God*, G. P. Putnam's Sons, 1951.

8. Barbara G. Walker, *The Woman's Encyclopedia of Myths and Secrets*, HarperCollins, 1983.

9. Thomas Moore, *The Re-Enchantment of Everyday Life*, HarperCollins, 1996.

10. Christine Downing, *Psyche's Sisters: Reimagining the Meaning of Sisterhood*, Continuum Publishing Company, 1990.

11. Ginette Paris, *Pagan Meditations: Aphrodite, Hestia, Artemis*, Spring Publications, 1983.

12. Ferdinand Protzman, *The Washington Post*, May 11, 1996.

13. Mary E. Giles, editor, *The Feminist Mystic: And Other Essays on Women and Spiritualiy,* Crossroad, 1982.

14. Material in this section adapted from the article "Making the Invisible Visible," by Pythia Peay, *Common Boundary*, November/December 1990.

15. Simone Weil, *Waiting for God*, Harper & Row, 1973.

16. Ibid.

17. Ibid.

18. Pir Vilayat Inayat Khan, *Awakening: A Sufi Experience*, Tarcher/Putnam, 1999.

CHAPTER FOUR: THE FEMININE FACE OF LOVE

1. Robert Bly, *The Kabir Book: Forty-Four of the Ecstatic Poems of Kabir*, Beacon Press, 1993.

2. Elisabeth Young-Bruehl and Faith Bethelard, *Cherishment: A Psychology of the Heart*, Free Press, 2000.

3. Pythia Peay, "An Interview with Marion Woodman," *The San Francisco Jung Library Journal*, Volume, Eleven, Number One, 1992.

4. Carolyn Heilbrun, from the Introduction to *Testament of Friendship*, by Vera Brittain, Wideview Books, 1981.

5. Ibid.

6. "The Kagaba of South America," Andrew Harvey and Anne Baring, editors, from *The Divine Feminine*, Conari Press, 1996.

7. Swami Nikhilananda, *Holy Mother: Being the Life of Sri Sarada Devi, Wife of Sri Ramakrishna and Helpmate in His Mission*, Ramakrishna-Vivekananda Center, 1962.

8. Estella Lauter, *Women as Mythmakers, Poetry and Visual Art by Twentieth-Century Women*, Indiana University Press, 1984.

9. Swami Nikhilananda, *Holy Mother: Being the Life of Sri Sarada Devi, Wife of Sri Ramakrishna and Helpmate in His Mission*, Ramakrishna-Vivekananda Center, 1962.

10. Swami Ghananda and Sir John Stewart-Wallace, C. B., editors, *Women Saints East and West*, Vedanta Press, 1979.

11. Ibid.

12. Meinrad Craighead, *The Mother's Songs: Images of God the Mother*, Paulist Press, 1986.
13. Meinrad Craighead, *The Litany of the Great River,* Paulist Press, 1990.
14. Ibid.
15. Barbara G. Walker, *The Women's Encyclopedia of Myths & Secrets*, HarperCollins, 1983.

CHAPTER FIVE: THE FEMININE FACE OF MAGIC

1. Timothy Freke and Peter Gandy, *The Hermetica: The Lost Wisdom of the Pharaohs*, Tarcher/Putnam, 1999.
2. Barbara G. Walker, *The Women's Encyclopedia of Myths and Secrets*, HarperCollins, 1983.
3. Ibid.
4. Ibid.
5. Robert H. Hopcke, *There Are No Accidents: Synchronicity and the Stories of Our Lives*, Riverhead Books, 1997.
6. Michael Loewe and Carmen Blacker, editors, *Oracles and Divination*, Shambhala, 1981.
7. Manly P. Hall, *The Secret Teachings of All Ages: An Encyclopedic Outline of Masonic, Hermetic, Qabbalistic and Rosicrucian Symbolical Philosophy*, The Philosophical Research Society, 1962.
8. Ibid.
9. Euripides, *Iphigenia in Tauris.*
10. Jean Lall, "Dark Matter, Bright Stars, Toward a Theory of Astrological Depth Psychology," master's thesis, Lesley College Graduate School, 1987.
11. Lall, "Counselling in the Chinese Temple: A Psychological Study of Divination by Chien Drawing," in William P. Lebra, ed., *Culture-Bound Syndromes, Ethnopsychiatry, and Alternate Therapies*, Honolulu: The University Press of Hawaii, 1976.
12. Barbara G. Walker, *The Women's Encyclopedia of Myths and Secrets*, HarperCollins, 1983.
13. Ibid.
14. Dana Gerhardt, *Moon Teachings*, mooncircles.com, March 2000.
15. Gerhardt, *Moon Teachings*, mooncircles.com, August 2000.
16. Robert L. Van de Castle, *Our Dreaming Mind*, Ballantine, 1994.
17. Ibid.
18. Michael Loewe and Carmen Blacker, editors, *Oracles and Divination*, Shambhala, 1981.
19. Fraser Boa and Marie-Louise von Franz, *The Way of the Dream: Conversations on Jungian Dream Interpretation with Marie-Louise von Franz*, Shambhala, 1992.
20. Michael Loewe and Carmen Blacker, editors, *Oracles and Divination*, Shambhala, 1981.
21. Gayle Delaney, *All About Dreams: Everything You Need to Know About Why We Have Them, What They Mean, and How to Put Them to Work for You*, HarperSanFrancisco, 1998.
22. Pythia Peay, "Dreams: A Bridge Between Worlds," *Common Boundary*, July/August, 1999.
23. Ibid.
24. Gayle Delaney, *All About Dreams: Everything You Need to Know About Why We Have Them, What They Mean, and How to Put Them to Work for You*, HarperSanFrancisco, 1998.
25. Ibid.

26. Fraser Boa and Marie-Louise von Franz, *The Way of the Dream: Conversations on Jungian Dream Interpretation with Marie-Louise von Franz*, Shambhala, 1992.

27. Jean Chevalier and Alain Gheerbrant trans., *The Penguin Dictionary of Symbols*, Penguin, 1994.

28. Ibid.

29. Hazrat Inayat Khan, *The Collected Works of Hazrat Inayat Khan*, Nature Meditations, Sufi Order Publications, 1980.

CHAPTER SIX: THE WAY OF THE SOUL SISTER

1. Christine Downing, *Psyche's Sisters: Reimagining the Meaning of Sisterhood*, Continuum, 1990.

2. "Soul Friends Share a Passion for the Spirit," column by Pythia Peay, *Religion News Service*, Feb. 14, 1998.

3. Carolyn Heilbrun, "Introduction," *Testament of Friendship*, by Vera Brittain, Wideview Books, 1981.

4. Ibid.

5. Christine Downing, *Psyche's Sisters: ReImagining the Meaning of Sisterhood*, Continuum, 1990.

6. Ibid.

7. Henri Corbin, *Creative Imagination in the Sufism of Ib'n Arabi*, Princeton University Press, 1969.

8. Ibid.

9. Ibid.

10. Pir Vilayat Inayat Khan, *Awakening: A Sufi Experience*, Tarcher/Putnam, 1999.

11. Ibid.

EPILOGUE: REFLECTIONS ON THE ULTIMATE QUALITY OF PEACE

1. Alfred North Whitehead, *Science and the Modern World*, Free Press, 1997.

INDEX

ABOUT THE AUTHOR

PYTHIA PEAY IS A NOTED JOURNALIST ON SPIRITUAL TOPICS who has written for *Utne Reader*, *Washingtonian*, *Common Boundary,* and other publications. As a former columnist and ongoing contributor to *Religion News Service,* her columns have appeared in newspapers around the country. She studied meditation with the Sufi teacher Pir Vilayat Inayat Khan, and collaborated with him on his book *Awakening*. She lives in the Washington, D.C., area.